# 卓有成效的管理者

中英文双语版

# THE EFFECTIVE EXECUTIVE

[美] 彼得·德鲁克 著
许是祥 译
那国毅 审校

机械工业出版社
China Machine Press

## 图书在版编目（CIP）数据

卓有成效的管理者（中英文双语版）/（美）彼得·德鲁克（Peter F. Drucker）著；许是祥译 . —北京：机械工业出版社，2020.1
书名原文：The Effective Executive

ISBN 978-7-111-63656-4

I. 卓… II. ①彼… ②许… III. 企业管理–汉、英 IV. F272

中国版本图书馆 CIP 数据核字（2019）第 262767 号

本书版权登记号：图字 01-2005-3663

Peter F. Drucker. The Effective Executive.

Copyright © 1993 by Peter F. Drucker.

Chinese (Bilingual English and Simplified Chinese Edition) Trade Paperback Copyright © 2020 by China Machine Press.

This edition arranged with The Peter F. Drucker Literary Trust (D)/Drucker 1996 Literary Works Trust through BIG APPLE AGENCY. This edition is authorized for sale in the People's Republic of China only, excluding Hong Kong, Macao SAR and Taiwan.

No part of this book may be reproduced or transmitted in any form or by any means, electronic or mechanical, including photocopying, recording or any information storage and retrieval system, without permission, in writing, from the publisher.

All rights reserved.

本书中英文双语版由 The Peter F. Drucker Literary Trust (D)/Drucker 1996 Literary Works Trust 通过 BIG APPLE AGENCY 授权机械工业出版社在中华人民共和国境内（不包括香港、澳门特别行政区和台湾地区）独家出版发行。未经出版者书面许可，不得以任何方式抄袭、复制或节录本书中的任何部分。

## 卓有成效的管理者（中英文双语版）

出版发行：机械工业出版社（北京市西城区百万庄大街 22 号　邮政编码：100037）

责任编辑：林晨星　　　　　　　　　　　　　责任校对：殷　虹

印　　刷：北京文昌阁彩色印刷有限责任公司　版　　次：2020 年 1 月第 1 版第 1 次印刷

开　　本：170mm×230mm　1/16　　　　　　印　　张：24

书　　号：ISBN 978-7-111-63656-4　　　　　定　　价：99.00 元

客服电话：(010) 88361066　88379833　68326294　　投稿热线：(010) 88379007
华章网站：www.hzbook.com　　　　　　　　　　　　读者信箱：hzjg@hzbook.com

版权所有·侵权必究
封底无防伪标均为盗版
本书法律顾问：北京大成律师事务所　韩光 / 邹晓东

如果您喜欢彼得·德鲁克（Peter F. Drucker）或者他的书籍，那么请您尊重德鲁克。不要购买盗版图书，以及以德鲁克名义编纂的伪书。

# 目录

推荐序一（张瑞敏）

推荐序二（赵曙明）

推荐序三（彼得·德鲁克管理学院）

| 前言 | Preface |
|---|---|
| 第1章<br>1 / 卓有成效是可以学会的 | Chapter 1<br>Effectiveness Can Be Learned / 169 |
| 第2章<br>23 / 掌握自己的时间 | Chapter 2<br>Know Thy Time / 195 |
| 第3章<br>49 / 我能贡献什么 | Chapter 3<br>What Can I Contribute? / 227 |
| 第4章<br>67 / 如何发挥人的长处 | Chapter 4<br>Making Strength Productive / 249 |

| | |
|---|---|
| 第 5 章<br>94 / 要事优先 | Chapter 5<br>First Things First / 282 |
| 第 6 章<br>107 / 决策的要素 | Chapter 6<br>The Elements of Decision-making / 297 |
| 第 7 章<br>134 / 有效的决策 | Chapter 7<br>Effective Decisions / 330 |
| 第 8 章<br>155 / 结论：管理者必须卓有成效 | Chapter 8<br>Conclusion: Effectiveness Must Be Learned / 356 |

| 推荐序一 |

《卓有成效的管理者》对从事企业管理工作的读者来说是一本非常有效的书。对此我深有体会，并且是源自20年前海尔创业初期。那时管理类书籍少之又少，不记得是从什么地方找到的这本书。开始我想，一个外国人既不熟悉中国文化，又不了解中国企业，他所念的管理经能有多大用处？但出乎意料的是我很快就被这本书深深地吸引住了。因为书中没有晦涩深奥难懂的理论，有的只是来自现实生活中的案例，诠释的却是鲜活的思想。德鲁克先生就像是你的一位同事，虽然与你面对相同的事实，却从不同的视角说出了你不曾想、更不曾想到的新理念。

由此我也成了德鲁克迷，到处搜集他的著作。读他的书是一种享受，因为常常使人有茅塞顿开之感。而这本《卓有成效的管理者》我更是爱不释手，不知读了多少遍，常读常新。尤其是面对变幻莫测的市场和全球化竞争的困惑时，总能从书中得到新的启示。以下是我的切身体会：

首先，企业的管理必须有效，否则企业无法生存。

记得第一次读德鲁克的书时，给我冲击最大的一句话就是"管理得好的工厂，总是单调乏味，没有任何激动人心的事件发生"。对这句话当时很费解，因为那时好工厂的标志就是要轰轰烈烈，要激动人心。但细细琢磨才体会出道理所在：那些"心中无数决心大"的誓师大会表面上是轰轰烈烈，但从本质上看对提高管理的有效性却没有任何帮助；那些在突发事件中表现英勇的人和事的确激动人心，但我们需要的不是停留在对这些英雄人物大张旗鼓的表彰上，而是要扎扎实实建立避免发生这类突发事件的机制。

这使我们认识到有效管理的重要性，有效就要防患于未然，将例外管理变成例行管理。当时我们根据企业的实际，创造了"日清"工作法，即"日事日毕，日清日高"，将每项工作的目标落实到每人、每天，形成"事事有人管，人人都管事"的氛围，大到一台设备，小到一块玻璃，都有人负责。每天下班前要根据目标对工作完成的情况"日清"，而日清的结果又与其本人的奖罚激励挂钩，这样便形成了目标、日清、激励三者间的闭环优化和良性循环。

通过"日清"工作法的推行，一个濒临倒闭、开不出工资的集体小厂不仅迅速扭转了亏损局面，而且提高了整体管理素质，解决了当时在管理上普遍存在的无效无序的问题，这也使我们于1988年在行业中以劣势小厂的地位战胜许多优势大厂，摘取了中国冰箱史上的第一枚金牌。这枚金牌要归功于"日清"工作法，更要归功于德鲁克先生。

其次，没有组织和个人在管理上相辅相成的有效性，就难以应对信息化时代的挑战。

信息化时代管理的有效性体现在速度上，因为是流通制约制造，速度至上，谁赢得了用户，谁就赢得了一切。依靠原有的组织体系已难以适应这一变化，必须要靠组织和个人以速度为前提，共同推进管理的有效性。正如德鲁克所言，"在组织而言，需要个人提供其贡献，在个人而言，需要组织作为达到个人目的的工具"，即每个人对组织的贡献，是体现在如何能以最快速度去创造和满足用户的需求；而组织为个人所提供的工具，就是要支持其实现这一速度。

在信息化时代为实现这种管理的有效性，我们在1998年开始了市场链流程再造，在组织再造上，就是变直线职能金字塔式的组织结构为扁平化的结构，减少管理层次，以努力实现企业与市场之间的零距离。而在人员的再造上，则是将管理人员变成SBU（策略事业单位），即每个管理者都是一个独立作战的经营体，每个人都有自己的目标市场和市场目标，自主制定自己的市场策略，以最快的速度去创造新的市场、新的需求。正如德鲁克所言，"总有人单独作战，无一部属，然而仍不失为管理者"。

目前市场链再造的探索引起世界许多商学院的兴趣，有的将其作为案例进行研究，究其原因就是目前企业都面临着信息化时代如何提高管理有效性的问题。当然在这方面我们仍面临许多难题，但方向应该是对的，因为我们要做的就是改变过去那种组织与市场的割裂，个人只听命于内部上司，而不去面对外部用户的问题。现在要将组织与个人融为一体，组织要成为一个平台，而个人在这个平台上在为用户创造价值的同时，体现其自身价值。这就是德鲁克说的"在组织内部不会有成果出现，一切成果都是发生在组织外部"。

最后一点，管理者都应该学会有效性，这是成为一名有效的管理者的必经之路。

企业需要有效的管理者，那么管理者如何能具备有效性呢？"有效性虽然人人可学，但却无人可教"，德鲁克的这句话告诉我们有效性是可以学会，但不可以教会的。有效性的学习是一种挑战、一种实践，你既不挑战自己的目标，又不去应对市场的挑战，就不会有学习有效性的动力和压力。你想学习有效性，但又不肯在实践中去思考问题背后的问题是什么，不去探索创新的路径，企图找一个捷径，等待别人教给你一个现成的理论或模式，那你一定与有效性无缘。如同禅宗里的一句话，"借来的火，点不亮自己的心灵"。

在学习有效性上我的体会是，创新—求是—创新，在学习提高有效性的目的下去创新，再将创新的成果以求是的态度去探索其中规律性的东西，并在这个规律的指导下，向更高层次的创新冲刺，以求在不断学习有效性的过程中成为一名卓有成效的管理者。

张瑞敏

海尔集团

| 推荐序二 |

德鲁克教授是当代著名的思想家，一代管理学宗师，《经济学人》称他为"大师中的大师"。德鲁克教授于1909年出生于前奥匈帝国首都维也纳的一个贵族家庭，在维也纳度过其童年生涯后，即到德国和英国边工作边学习。1937年，因不习惯欧洲的"怀旧"政治气氛，他离欧赴美，终身以教学、著书和咨询为业。在美国，他曾任美国通用汽车公司、克莱斯勒公司、IBM公司等大企业的顾问，美国佛蒙特州本宁顿学院的政治和哲学教授，纽约大学商学院管理学教授，加利福尼亚州克莱蒙特研究生大学的社会科学克拉克讲座教授。德鲁克于1945年创办了德鲁克管理咨询公司，自任董事长。他著述颇丰，主要著作有《公司的概念》（1946年）、《管理的实践》（1954年）、《管理：使命、责任、实践》（1973年）、《后资本主义社会》（1993年）等。他特殊的家庭背景、传奇式的经历、渊博的学识及睿智的才思，使其在政治、法律、社会、管理、历史等多个学科领域都留下了精辟的见解和耐人寻味的启示。管理学更是他一生耕耘的主要园地。在此领域，他成就卓著。他是推动管理学发展成为一门严肃科学的先驱，是现代"管理丛林"中经验主义管理思想流派的创立者和代表人物。他的论著被译成二十多种文字，在世界各

国广为传播，成为全世界管理者、学者奉为圭臬的经典。

德鲁克教授所著的《卓有成效的管理者》一书于1966年由哈珀罗出版公司（Harper & Row Publishers）出版，一出版即获得了一致好评，赢得了广大读者的喜爱。至今，该书已成为领导学领域的奠基之作。在本书中，德鲁克认为现代组织中知识工作者数量日益增多，并且知识工作者的成果通常要与其他人的成果结合起来才能够产生效益，因而管理者的作用日益凸现。但是判断管理者的标准并不是下属的多少，而是其成果对公司的影响。德鲁克将"那些促进机构有效运转，负有行动和决策责任的知识工作者"都称为管理者。由于知识工作者难以监督，因而组织效率将取决于组织成员能够对自身进行有效的管理。在以后的几十年中，德鲁克先生进一步阐述和发展这一思想，提出了现代组织管理的核心在于"自我管理"的思想。时至今日，这些思想依然在领导学研究中处于前沿。例如，最近有学者提出内部企业家理论，认为真正有创造力的企业要使组织内部每个员工都具有企业家精神。殊不知，这些最新思想在德鲁克先生几十年前的著作中早已体现。

本书的独到之处不仅仅是对管理者的概念进行了重新界定，而且奠定了从行为角度研究管理者的现代领导学的学科基础。在20世纪60年代，大多数领导学方面的研究还认为有效的管理者是天生的，并试图从管理者的素质角度出发，寻找有效管理者所具有的不同于常人的个人和特质。德鲁克先生从自己的研究和咨询经历出发，认为没有一个有效管理者是天生的，他们之所以有效只是由于在实践中学会了一些有效的管理习惯。德鲁克认为："组织中的管理者通常会遇到四种情况，而他自己基本无法控制。每种情况都会向他施加压力，将工作推向无效，使机构运作不灵：（1）管理者的时间往往只属于别人，而不属于自己；（2）管理者往往被迫按照老一套方法开展工作；（3）只有当别人使用管理者的贡献时，管理者才具有有效性;(4)管理者身处组织之内,但如果他要有效工作,还必须努力认识组织以外的情况。"为应对这些情况,德鲁克认为:"作为一个有效的管理者,必须在思想上养成如下的习惯:(1)知道如何利用自己的时间;(2)注意使自己的努力产生必要的成果,而不是工作本身,重视对外界的贡献;(3)把工作建立在优势上——他们自己的优势,善于利用自己的长处,上级、同事和下级的长处;(4)精力集中于少数主要领域;(5)善于做出有效的决策。"如今,德鲁克对管理者在工作中面临的现实问题的描述和相关建议,已成为经典,被到处引用。

德鲁克先生自称为"旁观者"。他从社会、历史的高度,分析组织及组织管理的变迁。这一独特的视角使其避免了一叶蔽目的狭隘,从纷繁复杂的社会现象中,准确把握和预测组织发展和管理的变化。德鲁克先生的渊博知识、深刻思想不仅影响了学术界,也影响了企业界,可以说没有一个著名学者和成功的商界领袖不从他那里汲取养分。这是其他任何一个管理学家都难以企及的。

作为聆听德鲁克先生教诲的学生,我回国以后一直致力于传播德鲁克先生的学术思想。约20年前,我为机械工业出版社华章公司出版《现代管理宗师德鲁克文选》一书牵线搭桥,并即兴作序《德鲁克管理学说引进中国》。今天,德鲁克的著作在国内多次再版,我感到异常欣慰。但愿机械工业出版社这次系统地引进德鲁克著作,能够让国内更多读者欣赏到大师的真知灼见。

赵曙明博士

南京大学商学院院长、教授、博导

| 推荐序三 |

 

    虽然《卓有成效的管理者》于1966年首次出版以来，已经被翻译成了二十多种语言，但是2002年哈珀·柯林斯出版社在出版《哈珀企业管理经典丛书》的时候，还是毫不犹豫地把它收了进来。这不仅说明了对这本书的需求依然旺盛，更说明了德鲁克在书中提出的管理理念经得起时间和实践的考验。本书已经成了世界上众多企业管理者的必读书籍。德鲁克在书中提出的观点，近四十年来一直是管理实践中指导管理者如何做到卓有成效的指南。

    管理的书籍基本上都是讲如何管理别人，但本书讲的却是如何让管理者管理自己，使管理者本身变得更加卓有成效。正如德鲁克在本书的前言中指出的："管理者能否管理好别人从来就没有被真正验证过，但管理者却完全可以管理好自己。"这本书是关于管理者如何管理自己的书。

    本书一共分为七章。前五章主要讲管理者如何管理自己，最后两章讲管理者如何做决策。

    谁是管理者？是不是只有管理别人的人才称得上是管理者？德鲁克在本书中对管理者的定义远远超出了我们一般理解的范畴。在当今的知识社会中，一个知识工作者也许并没有处于一个大企业或者一个大机构的最高管理层，但是他却影响着一个组织的绩效和结果。这样的知识工作者在我们的社会中正起着越来越大的作用。在《卓有成效的管理者》这本书中，德鲁克也称这些知识工作者为管理者。

德鲁克在本书的一开头就开宗明义地指出，不管一个管理者是在企业工作，还是在医院、在大学，或者是在部队工作，他必须首先要去"做正确的事"。做到卓有成效是知识工作者在一个组织中的一种特殊技能。管理者能否做到卓有成效不是天生的，卓有成效的管理者更不是什么天才。只要管理者遵循一定的实践，卓有成效是完全可以做到的。管理者不仅可以做到卓有成效，而且也必须做到卓有成效。在我们这个越来越多样化的社会里，不仅企业的管理者必须做到卓有成效，其他各种组织的管理者也必须要卓有成效。因为我们社会中的每一个组织，不论它在社会中的作用如何，这个组织的成功都依赖于组织的管理者的卓有成效。

管理者最缺乏的是时间。因此，如何管理时间是管理者必须要解决的一个问题。按照德鲁克在第2章中提出的管理时间的原则和方法，只要坚持做下来，就一定能够收到惊人的效果。

管理者要做到卓有成效，必须明白自己的长处和短处；管理者应该使自己的长处得到发挥，而使自己的短处变得与工作无关；要集中时间和精力做最必须做的事情；做事情要有优先顺序等关于如何做到卓有成效的具体方法和实践，一定会让你受益匪浅。

本书的最后两章是关于决策的。

决策的正确与否是关系到管理者能否做到卓有成效的关键。决策有哪些要素？决策过程是不是有一个可以遵循的规律？是不是每个问题都需要决策？什么样的问题需要决策，什么样的问题是因为我们的"系统"或者规定出了问题，需要有一个根本的解决方法？人事决策有什么样的规则可循？集体决策和个人决策各有什么利弊？计算机能够代替决策吗？在最后两章中，德鲁克用大量的实际例子回答了所有这些问题，而且是比这多得多的关于决策的问题。比如说，人事决策，为什么有的决策非常成功，有的决策却是失败的；人事决策要注意哪几条原则。相信德鲁克在本书中根据成功的经验和失败的教训总结出来的原则，不仅对管理者，而且对所有渴望提高管理水平和决策水平的管理者和知识工作者都有莫大启示。

德鲁克的管理理念都着重于最后的结果，卓有成效的管理者也不例外。管理者要做到卓有成效，必须最后体现在工作的结果上。这个结果，必须对组织有贡献，同时也要使个人能够得到发展。

德鲁克的管理理念，都必须落实到"实践"上来，因为管理是实践。管理者必须把学到的理念诉诸实践。因为，管理不在于"知"，而在于"行"。

机械工业出版社曾经在1999年出版英文版的《现代管理宗师德鲁克文选》。这本书曾使不少中国读者受益匪浅。现在，机械工业出版社又要翻译出版中文版的德鲁克系列著作，相信这些著作一定会给中国的广大读者和管理者带来更大的实实在在的价值。我们期待着这本书的出版，也期待着机械工业出版社出版更多的德鲁克著作。

*彼得·德鲁克管理学院*

| 前　言 |

　　关于管理方面的著作通常都是谈如何管理别人的，而本书的主题却是关于如何才能使自己成为卓有成效的管理者。管理者能否管理好别人从来就没有被真正验证过，但管理者却完全可以管理好自己。实际上，让自身成效不高的管理者管好他们的同事与下属，那几乎是不可能的事。管理工作在很大程度上是要身体力行的，如果管理者不懂得如何在自己的工作中做到卓有成效，就会给其他人树立错误的榜样。

　　要做到卓有成效，仅靠天资聪明、工作努力或知识渊博是不够的。要使你的工作卓有成效，还必须要有其他的一些因素。但是要做到卓有成效，并不需要特殊的天赋、出众的才能或者专门的培训。要成为卓有成效的管理者，就要做到某些事情。这些事情实际上相当简单，那就是亲自实践。它们包括本书中提到并加以讨论的一些实际做法，不过这些做法并不是"与生俱来"的。在我45年的咨询生涯中，我与大大小小各种各样的组织中的众多管理者打过交道，有企业界、政府机构、工会、医院、大学及社区服务机构的管理者，有美国、日本，以及欧洲和拉丁美洲国家的管理者，但是，我从来没有遇见过一个"天生"的卓有成效的管理者。他们都是通过不断的实践，最终将追求成效变成一种习惯。所有那些想努力让自己成为卓有成效的管理者的人都成功地做到了这一点。卓有成效是可以学会的，也是必须学会的。

　　卓有成效是管理者的职责所在，无论他们是负责他人和自己绩效的管理者，还是仅仅对自己绩效负责的专业工作者。如果做不到卓有成效，就谈不上"绩效"，不管你在工作中投入了多少才智和知识，花了多少时间和心血。然而，我们习以为常的是，至今为止我们对卓有成效的管理者重视不够。组织机构——不管是工商企业、政府机构、工会、大医院还是大学，毕竟都是全新的。一个世纪前，除了偶尔去当地的邮局寄一封信，几乎没有人与这类组织接触过。管理者的工作是否有效那只是企业内部的事。直到最近，人们才开始关注管理者的成效，或者说对众多管理者缺乏成效感到忧虑。但是，现在的大部分人，特别是那些受过相当程度的教育的人，可能都会在某个组织中工作一辈子。在所有发达国家，社会已经成为一个由各种组织构成的社会。个人的成效越来越取决于其在组织中的工作是否能取得成效，是否能成为卓有成效的管理者。现代社会及其运转的成效，也许还包括其生存的能力，也越来越取决于各类组织中管理者的成效。卓有成效的管理者正在迅速成为社会的一项关键资源，而能够成为卓有成效的管理者已成为个人获得成功的主要标志，对于刚刚开始工作的年轻人和处于事业发展过程中的人们都是如此。

彼得·德鲁克<br>1985年元旦于加利福尼亚州克莱蒙特

# 第1章 | CHAPTER 1
# 卓有成效是可以学会的

　　管理者的工作必须要卓有成效。推敲起来,"使某项工作产生效益"(to effect)和"完成某项工作"(to execute),可视为同义词。身为管理者,不管是企业主管、医院主管、政府机构主管、工会主管、学校主管,还是军事机构主管,首先必须要按时做完该做的事情。换言之,管理者做事必须有效。

　　然而,值得注意的是,在担任管理职位的人中,真正卓有成效者,殊不多见。一般来说,管理者普遍才智较高、想象力丰富,并具有很高的知识水准。但是一个人的有效性,与他的智力、想象力或知识之间,几乎没有太大的关联。有才能的人往往最为无效,因为他们没有认识到才能本身并不是成果。他们也不知道,一个人的才能,只有通过有条理、有系统的工作,才有可能产生效益。相反,在每一个机构中,总会有一些极为有效的勤勉人士,当别人忙得晕头转向的时候(许多聪明人常误以为这是有创造力的表现),那些有效的勤勉人士却像龟兔赛跑中的乌龟,脚踏实地,一步一个脚印,率先到达目的地。

智力、想象力及知识，都是我们重要的资源。但是，资源本身仅是限制性因素，只有通过管理者卓有成效的工作，才能将这些资源转化为成果。

## 为什么需要卓有成效的管理者

上文所述，听起来都是理所当然的。在当今这个时代，有关管理者任务的专著和论文已是汗牛充栋，却很少有人关注管理者的有效性问题，这是为什么呢？

原因之一，就是"有效性"只是"知识工作者"（knowledge worker）的一种特殊技能，而知识工作者直到最近才逐渐增多。

对"体力工作"而言，我们所重视的只是"效率"。所谓效率，可以说是"把事情做对"（to do things right）的能力，而不是"做对的事情"（to get the right things done）的能力。体力工作的成果，通常可以用数量和质量来衡量，例如制成了多少双鞋子及其质量如何。近百年来，对如何衡量体力工作的效率和质量，我们已有相当的研究，现在我们已经能够运用测定体力工作效率的方法，来促使工作者的产出大为增加。

在过去，一个机构的组成多以体力工作者为主体，例如操作机器的工人，或前线打仗的士兵，所以，关于有效性的需要不太迫切，问题也没有今天严重。位居高职的管理者只不过是下达命令，要求下属执行而已，而且管理者的人数，也只占全部工作人数中一个极小的比例。所以，不管是否站得住脚，我们暂且假定他们都是卓有成效的。在那样的情形下，我们不妨完全信任管理者的天赋，认为他们已具备了一般人所不容易具备的能力。

这种情况不仅仅存在于企业和军队中。100年前，美国南北战争时期的"政府"只由极少数人组成，这对今天的人来说简直是难以理解的。林肯时代的战争部⊖只有不到50个文职官员，其中绝大多数人既不是"管理者"，也不是决策者，仅是通信报务人员。20世纪初西奥多·罗斯福总统时期的美国联邦政府，其全部机构人员，可以在今天国会大厦前的任何一座办公楼之内享有宽敞的办公空间。

医院也是一样。从前的医院，并没有所谓X光及化验技术员、营养师、治疗专家以及社会工作者等。而今天美国的医院，平均每100位病人，就需要各类医务人员250人。从前的医院，除了几位护士，只需雇用几名清洁工、厨师和杂工即可。那个时候，只有医生才是医院中的知识工作者，而护士是他们的助手。

总而言之，在从前的机构中，主要的问题就是如何提高听命于人的体力工作者的效率。知识工作者在从前的机构中并不占多数。

实际上，早期的知识工作者中只有极少一部分人在机构里工作，大部分人都是自行开业，最多雇用一位助手。因此，他们的工作是否有效，只会对他们自己产生影响。

而今天，由知识工作者构成的组织比比皆是，而且都颇有规模。现代的社会，是一个由组织化的机构形成的社会。其中的每一个机构，包括军事机构，都在把重心转向知识工作者，他们在工作中需要使用更多的智慧，而不是发达的肌肉或灵巧的双手。那些受过教育，懂得使用知识、理论和概念的人渐渐取代仅有体力技能的人，成为组织里的主力，他们只有对组织真正做出贡献，才能算是有效。

今天我们已经不能再想当然地假定，凡是管理者都一定是有效的。有效性的课题已不容忽视。

---

⊖ Secretary of War，战争部，现在该部门已不存在，其职能由国防部接管。——编者注

关于体力工作，我们已有一套完整的衡量方法和制度，从工程设计到质量控制，但是这种衡量方法和制度，并不能适用于知识工作。如果所设计的是一项错误的产品，则尽管工程部门能迅速绘制出精美的蓝图，其结果也是极其可悲的。唯有从事"对"的工作，才能使工作有效，而这一点，却是无法用衡量体力工作的方法来衡量的。

我们无法对知识工作者进行严密和细致的督导，我们只能协助他们。知识工作者本人必须自己管理自己，自觉地完成任务，自觉地做出贡献，自觉地追求工作效益。

《纽约客》(The New Yorker)杂志某期曾刊载一幅漫画。画中一间办公室玻璃门上写着"爱洁肥皂公司销售总经理史密斯"。办公室内墙壁上只有一块一个词的标语："思考。"画中的经理大人，双脚高搁在办公桌上，面孔朝天，正向着天花板吐烟圈。门外刚好有两位较年长的人走过，一人问另一人："天知道史密斯是不是在思考我们的肥皂问题！"

的确，谁也不知道一位知识工作者在想些什么。然而，思考却正是他的本分，他既然是在思考，他就是在工作。

知识工作者的工作动力，取决于他是否具有有效性及他在工作中能否有所成就。㊀如果他的工作缺少有效性，那么他对做好工作和做出贡献的热情很快就会消退，他将成为朝九晚五在办公室消磨时间的人。

知识工作者并不生产本身具有效用的产品。他不生产有形的产品，例如

---

㊀ 这一点已被许多研究所证实，特别是以下3本根据实践经验写成的书：弗雷德里克·赫茨伯格的《工作的动力》；戴维·C.麦克莱伦的《不断取得成就的社会》；弗雷德里克·赫茨伯格的《工作与人性》。

挖一条水沟、制造一双鞋或一个机械零件。他生产的是知识、创意和信息。这样的产品本身并无用途，只有通过另一位知识工作者，把他的产品当作投入，并转化为另一种产出，它们才具有实际的意义。再伟大的智慧，如果不能应用在行动上，也将只是毫无意义的资料。因此，知识工作者必须做到一些体力工作者不需要做的事，他必须具有有效性。他不能指望他的产出像一双制作精美的鞋子那样，本身具有直观的用途。

知识工作者是一项特殊的"生产要素"，通过这项生产要素，当今一些高度发达的社会和经济实体，如美国、日本和西欧国家，才能获得及保持强大的竞争力。

> 美国是这方面的典型，美国今天占优势的资源首推教育。美国的教育虽然仍有很多有待改进的地方，但它的投入确实是其他较贫穷的国家望尘莫及的。美国在教育方面投资之庞大，可以说是史无前例的。培养一位自然科学方面的博士，需10万～20万美元的社会投资。即使是培养一位没什么特殊职业技能的大学毕业生，也得花费5万美元以上。这种投资，只有非常富足的社会才能负担。
>
> 所以，在美国这个富足的社会中，教育就是它所拥有的一项真正的优势。当然这一优势能否得到充分发挥，还取决于知识工作者的工作是否卓有成效。而所谓知识工作者的生产力，就是"做好该做的事情"的能力，也就是有效性。

## 谁是管理者

在一个现代的组织里，如果一位知识工作者能够凭借其职位和知识，对该组织负有贡献的责任，因而能对该组织的经营能力及达成的成果产生实质性的影响,那么他就是一位管理者。经营能力对企业机构而言,也许是推出一项新产品,或扩大在某一特定市场的占有率。对医院而言,也许是为病人提供更妥善的医疗服务。这样一位管理者,不能仅以执行命令为满足,他必须能做决策,并承担起做出贡献的责任。他既然学识渊博,就应该比其他人更能做出正确的决策。他的决定可能会被取消,他也可能被降职,甚至可能丢掉饭碗。但是,只要他有一天身为管理者,他就不能忘记他的标准、目标和贡献。

绝大多数的经理人都是管理者(当然并非全部)。在现代社会中,许多非主管人员也正渐渐成为管理者。在一个知识型组织中,固然需要经理人,同样也需要能做出贡献的"专业人才",来担任需要负责、决策,并拥有一定职权的职位。

美国报纸曾刊登一篇对于越南战场上一位青年步兵上尉的采访,最能清楚地说明这一点。

> 记者问:"在战场混乱的情况下,你如何指挥你的下属?"那位青年步兵上尉回答说:"在那里,我是唯一的负责人。当我的下属在丛林中遭遇敌人却不知道该怎么行动时,我也因为距离太远无法告诉他们。我的任务,只是确保他们知道在这种情形下应该如何行动。至于实际上该怎么做,应由他们根据情况加以判断。责任虽然在我,但行动的决策却由战场上的每个人自己决定。"

在游击战中,每一个人都是"管理者"。

在主管人员中,也有许多人并不是管理者。换言之,许多人只不过是别人的上司,甚至是许多人的上司,但他们的行为,并不能对组织的经营能力产生重大的影响。制造业的工厂领班大多属于此类,他们只是"监工"而已。由于他们管理别人的工作，所以他们确实是主管人员，但对其下属的工作方向、工作内容、工作质量及工作方法，他们既无责任，也无职权。所以他们的工作，大部分还可以用效率和质量来衡量与考核，而且我们用来衡量与考核体力工作者的尺度对他们仍然适用。

与此相反，一位知识工作者是不是一位管理者，我们不能以他有没有下属而定。例如在一家企业机构里，一位市场研究员也许有200位下属，而另一家竞争企业里的市场研究员也许只有一个秘书。然而就这两位市场研究员做出的贡献来说，却无太大差别，即使有所差别，也只是行政工作上一些细节的不同。有200位下属，当然远比只有一个秘书能够多做许多事，却并不表示他的产出和贡献一定更大。

知识工作不能用数量来衡量，也不能用成本来衡量。衡量知识工作主要应看其结果，而不是看机构的规模有多大或管理工作有多繁杂。

当然，市场研究部门人数众多，可以集思广益，增强企业成长和发展的潜力。果真如此，那雇用200人也算便宜。可是，200人在一起工作必然会产生各种问题，如果他们把问题带到工作中来，主管人员就会被这些问题搞得焦头烂额，太忙于"管"而无暇顾及真正的市场研究和基本决策了。他也许会成天忙于审核数字，根本没有时间考虑"我们的市场"到底情况如何。甚至于当市场发生了重大变化，足以影响公司的存亡时，恐怕他也会疏于察觉。

当然，单枪匹马的市场研究员，可能会非常能干，也可能能力很低。他可能成为公司发展的知识和愿景的源泉，也可能将他的时间耗于细枝末节（一般人以为这就是研究），以至于对其他事情视而不见、听而不闻，更别提思考研究了。

在每一个知识型组织中，总有人单独作战，虽然他们没有下属，但他们仍然算是管理者。当然，像上面所举的越南战争的例子，每一个人都必须随时做出影响整体存亡的决策，这样的实例毕竟不多。但是实验室里的化学家，当他决定采取甲研究路线而放弃乙研究路线时，他也许是做了极可能大大影响公司前程的重要决策。这样的一位化学家，可能是实验室的主任，也可能是一位根本没有主管职责的研究员，甚至可能是一位初级研究员。同样地，从财务角度对某种产品进行决策，可能是公司资深副总裁的职责㊀，也可能是由一位普通职员来决定的。这种情况在今天的大型组织中，可以说是屡见不鲜的。

在本书中，"管理者"一词，将泛指知识工作者、经理人员和专业人员，由于其职位和知识，他们必须在工作中做出影响整体绩效和成果的决策。（但这并不意味着大部分知识工作者都是管理者，因为知识工作也像任何其他工作一样，有些是属于日常事务性的、不需要什么技能的工作。）在这样的管理者的定义下，知识工作者中管理者的人数，往往比任何一张组织结构图中所公布的人数多得多。

这是我们应该明了的起点——我们已看到有关这方面的种种努力，对经理人员和做出贡献的专业人员的嘉奖与报酬，建立了平行的晋升通道。㊁但是到目前为止，对下面这一问题心中有数的人还不是太多：在今天最普通的机构中，不论是企业机构、政府机构、研究机构还是医疗机构中，到底有多少人必须做出具有重大意义且具有决定性影响的决策？要知道所谓的知识权威，实际上与职位权威同样都是合法的。基于知识权威所做的决策，与高级管理层所做的决策具有相同的性质（这正是凯培尔发言的主要论点之一）。

我们现在已经知道，大部分的一般经理人员，其工作性质跟企业机构的董事长或政府机构的行政领导其实是相同的，那就是计划、组织、整合、激

---

㊀ 关于这一点，请见我写的《为成果而管理》(*Managing for Results*) 一书，特别是该书的第 2 章。

㊁ 关于这一点最好的说明，是美国电话电报公司总裁凯培尔在 1963 年 9 月纽约召开的第 13 届国际管理大会上发表的演讲，凯培尔的主要论点引用了《为成果而管理》的第 14 章。

励和考核。他的管辖范围也许相当有限，但在他所管辖的范围内，他是一位管理者。

同样地，任何一位做决策的人，其工作也跟董事长和行政领导相同。即使他的管辖范围有限，甚至于他的职能或他的大名并不见于组织系统中，办公室连专用电话也没有，但他确实也是一位管理者。

不论职位的高低，只要你是一位管理者，就必须力求卓有成效。

本书引用的许多实例，都来自政府、军队、医院、企业等机构的高级主管的工作与经验，这主要是因为我所接触的人士以高级主管为多，而且因为高级主管常为人所共见。同时，也是因为大事总要比小事更容易分析，也更容易说明问题。

但是，本书讨论的并不是高级主管要做些什么或应该做些什么。本书是为每一位对促进机构有效运转负有行动与决策责任的知识工作者而写的。换言之，是专门为那些我称之为"管理者"的人而写的。

## 管理者必须面对的现实

每一位管理者都要面对的现实是，一方面要求他们具有有效性，一方面却又使他们很难达成有效性。诚然，一位管理者如果不能致力于使工作卓有成效，现实必将迫使他一事无成。

让我们先来看一下组织以外的知识工作者所处的实际环境，看看他们的问题所在。一位自行开业的医生，基本上不会有有效性的问题。病人前来求诊，将一切事情都带了进来，使医生的医学知识能够得到有效发挥。医生面对病人，通常可以专心诊断，不会有其他事情来打扰。医生应该有什么贡献是一目了然的，他的一切努力，都在于减轻病人的痛苦。什么是重要的，什么又是不重要的，都视病人的痛苦而定。病人的主诉决定医生工作的优先顺序。其目的和目标也是既定的，那就是要恢复病人的健康，至少是减轻病人的痛苦。因此，医生并不需要有什么组织能力，但他们在有效性上，并没有太大的问题。

而一个机构里的管理者面对的现实问题就大不相同了，他必须面对四类非其本人所能控制的现实难题。每一类难题，都是由机构内在因素造成的，与他的日常工作也是分不开的。出于无奈，他不得不与这些不可避免的难题打交道。每一项现实难题都在向他施加压力，使他的工作难以取得成果和绩效。

（1）管理者的时间往往只属于别人，不属于自己。如果我们从工作的情形来替管理者下一个定义，我们简直可以说他是组织的囚徒。每一个人都可以随时来找他，而事实上每一个人也正是这么做的。看起来任何一位管理者都几乎不可能解决这个难题。他不能像医生一样，告诉门外的护士小姐："半小时内不要让人打扰我。"因为很可能正在这个时候，电话铃响了，来电话的，也许是公司最大的客户，也许是市政府的一位要员，也许是他的上司，他不能不接电话。于是，接下来的半小时就这样过去了。㊀

（2）管理者往往被迫忙于"日常运作"，除非他们敢于采取行动来改变周围的一切。

在美国，管理者的这种抱怨非常普遍。公司的总经理或其他高级职员负责的是整个企业，按理说他应该将时间花在这一方面，但他仍免不了要兼管市场营销或者工厂事务。为什么会出现这种现象？有人说是因为美国的管理者通常是从某一专业部门提升上来的。因此他们虽然升上了高层职位，却未

---

㊀ 这一情况在苏内·卡尔松于1951年出版的《管理者行为》一书中有详细的描述。该书专门研究大公司高层管理人员的时间使用问题。在卡尔松教授的研究中，即使是最讲效率的管理者也发现自己的时间绝大部分都被别人占用，而且往往并不产生任何效益。实际上，管理者或许可以被定义成通常没有自己时间的人，因为他们的时间总被别人的一些重要事情占用了。

能改变一辈子养成的工作习惯。但是在人事晋升渠道大不相同的其他国家，也有同样的抱怨。比如在一些欧洲国家，升任高层管理的人士，大多是具有通才经验的核心秘书处的精英。但是德国、瑞典、荷兰等国公司的高层管理人士也和美国的同行一样，因只抓具体业务不抓总体管理而受到批评。而且，这种现象还不仅局限在高层中，组织内的每一位管理者，几乎都有同样的困扰。如此看来，产生这种现象除了管理者的晋升渠道和个人的习惯偏好之外，一定还有其他原因。

问题的症结，还是在于管理者周围的现实因素。除非他能够毅然决定改变周围的一切，否则他的面前将出现一连串要干的事，让他忙得无暇他顾。

对医生来说，干好摆在面前的一连串事情是很正常的。病人来了，医生问："你什么地方不舒服？"医生期望病人能告诉他有关的事实。病人说："我睡不好，失眠已经3周了。"病人的这句话，正是告诉了医生什么是"优先"。即使经过进一步检查，医生发现病人的失眠不过是一项次要症状，病人还另有更严重的病情，他也会让病人先有几晚安稳的睡眠。

而管理者所面临的一连串工作却很少告诉他任何情况，更不可能向他提示真正的问题所在。对医生来说，病人的主诉便是重心，因为那是病人认为的重心。而一位管理者需要关注的，却是更复杂的世界：哪些事情是重要的，是管理者必须去做的，哪些事情只会分散他的注意力，这并不是一目了然的，也不能像病人叙述症状、为医生提供线索那样帮助管理者做出有效的决策。

如果管理者被迎面而来的一连串事务所左右，根据事情先后顺序来决定做什么、研究什么、重点对待哪项工作，那他不久就只能穷于应付了。也许他具有了不起的才干，足以应付得了，但实际上他却是在浪费自己的知识和能力，把原本可能达成的成效撇开了。管理者需要的是一套判断标准，使他能够针对真正重要的事项去工作。但是在日常事务中，常常找不到他所需的标准。

（3）使管理者缺乏有效性的第三项现实因素，是管理者本身处于一个"组织"之中。只有当别人能够利用管理者的贡献时，管理者才算有效。组织是能使个人才干得以增值的一种工具。个人的知识一旦被组织吸收，就可以成为其他知识工作者做好工作的动力和资源。然而，知识工作者彼此之间最难协调，其原因正是由于他们都是知识工作者。每一位知识工作者都有各自的专长、各自的志趣。有人热衷于税务会计，有人热衷于细菌学，也有人热衷于培训市政人员，而就在隔壁办公的另外一个人也许只对成本会计中的一些细节感兴趣，或只注意医院的经营情况，要不就是只关注市政的法律问题。他们每个人都需要使用别人的成果。

对管理者的有效性而言，最重要的人物，往往并不是管理者直接控制的下属，而是其他部门的人，即所谓"旁系人士"，或是管理者本人的上司。一位管理者如果不能与这些人主动接触，不能使这些人有效利用他的贡献，他本身就没有有效性可言。

（4）最后，管理者身处一个组织的"内部"，受到组织的局限。

每一位管理者，不论他的组织是企业机构、研究机构、政府机构、大学还是军队，通常他总以为组织内部的事才是与他最密切相关的现实。即使他要认识外部世界，也是像戴上了一副变形的眼镜。他不能亲身体验外部事物的变迁，只能通过资料和报告来了解外部世界，而这些内容都事先经过了组织的过滤。换言之，他看到的外部世界，是已经经过主观加工的、高度抽象的外部世界，是已将组织的相关标准强加给外部的客观现实。

但组织本身就是一种抽象的存在。用数学术语来说，组织只是一个点——没有大小，也没有延伸。与其所处的现实环境比较，即使是规模最大的组织，也显得难以捉摸。

具体地说，在组织的内部，根本不会有成果出现，一切成果都存在于组织之外。举例来说，企业机构的成果，是通过顾客产生的，企业付出的成本和努力，必须通过顾客购买其产品或服务，才能转变为收入和利润。也就是说，做决定的人在企业之外，不在企业之内。

同样的道理，医院的成果肯定表现在病人身上。但病人并不是医院组织中的一分子。对病人而言，只有当其患病时医院才"存在"。病人最大的愿望，却是尽快离开，回到他的非医院的世界里去。

在组织内部所发生的，只有人工和成本。我们说企业内部的"利润中心"，其实是客气的称呼而已，实质上应该是"人工中心"。一个组织要产生一项既定成果，其所需工作量越少，表示其成绩越好。如果要用10万人来生产市场上需要的汽车或钢铁，那就是一项工业技术的失败。人数越少，规模越小，内部的工作越轻，组织就越接近于完美，就越有存在的理由。而组织存在的唯一理由，就是服务于外部环境。

这种外部环境是真正的现实，而这个现实却不能从组织内部有效控制，充其量也必须内外两方面共同作用才能产生成果。例如一场战争，成果是由敌我双方的行动和决策所决定的。当然，一个企业可以付出种种努力，通过促销和广告来塑造顾客的喜好和价值。不过，除非是在一种极端缺乏的情况下（例如战时经济），否则顾客仍然握有最后的决定权和有效的否决权。但是，管理者能看得清清楚楚的只是组织的内部，组织内部才是他最密切接触的。内部的种种关系和联系、内部的种种问题和挑战以及种种错综的情况和意见，不停地由各个方向向他袭来。除非他能付出特殊的努力，使自己与外界保持直接的联系，否则他必将日益局限于组织内部。他在组织中的地位越高，他的注意力就越容易为内部的问题和挑战所困，而看不到外部的情况。

组织是存在于社会之中的一种人为产物，与生物有机体完全不同。但是组织也要受支配自然生物结构、体型生长的同样定律的制约：面积与半径的平方成正比，质量则与半径的立方成正比。一个生物成长得越大，它所消耗的资源也就越多。

阿米巴虫（变形虫）身体的每一部分，都能随时与环境直接接触。因此，阿米巴虫无须特殊的器官来感知外界，或支撑其身体。但是一种庞大而复杂的生物，例如人类，就需要一组骨骼来支撑其躯体，也需要各种系统和器官来摄取食物和消化、呼吸和排泄、输送氧气、生殖。而且，人类还需要大脑和复杂的神经系统。再说阿米巴虫，其大部分机体都是与生存和繁殖直接相关的。而较高等动物的大部分机体，如资源储备、食物供给、能量供应以及体内组织等，都是为克服及抵消其本身结构的复杂性，以及与外界的隔离性而服务的。

一个组织绝不能像生物一样，以自身的生存为目的，仅仅把能够延续后代视作成功。组织是社会的一种器官，只有能为外部环境做出自己的贡献，才能算有所成就。但是，当组织的规模日益扩大，并且看来日益成功时，其内部的种种事务也将变得更多，这些事务将占据管理者更多的兴趣、精力和能力，使其难以顾及自己的真正任务，无法为外界提供有效的服务。

这一危机自电脑和信息技术问世之后，已演变得更加严重了。电脑可以说是一种"机械白痴"，它只能处理可被量化的资料。当然，它能处理得快速、准确和精密。自从有了电脑，从前无法获得的大量计量资料，现在可以通过它提供了。然而，通常只有组织内部的资料，才是可以量化的，例如成本和生产数据、医院病人的统计数据、培训报告等。至于外部的情况，则大多难以量化，即使能够量化，得到的也只能是滞后的信息。

但这并不是说，我们对外部信息的搜集能力，落后于电脑的技术能力。如果这一点使我们担心的话，只要改进统计工作即可，而且电脑也能帮忙克服这一局限性。真正的问题是,外部情况往往是质的性质,难以量化,它们还不能被称为事实。所谓事实,应该是已经认定,已做分类,并且已确知其关联性。在我们对事实进行量化之前,必须先掌握一个概念,那就是:必须先从无数现象中抽象出某一具体的特性,并对其命名,然后才能进行计算。

医药上的沙利度胺(thalidomide)造成畸形婴儿的悲剧,正是一个实例。等到欧洲大陆的医生面对充分的统计数字,发现畸形婴儿的数量已大大超过正常数字的时候,他们才觉得其中一定有什么特殊的新原因,但这时才意识到问题的严重性已太晚了,损害已经发生了。而在美国,这种损害幸得避免,原因是美国一位公共卫生医师早察觉到一种质的变化——用此药后会出现一种轻微的皮肤刺痛感,并将这一现象与早先发生的事件联系起来,于是在该药被广泛使用之前向大家敲响了警钟。

福特公司的一款名为 Edsel 的汽车,也是一个类似的例子。在推出这种车型之前,福特公司搜集了一切能够得到的数据,证明这款新车必能畅销。没想到美国的汽车消费者发生了质的变化,从"收入决定购买"转变到"兴趣决定购买"了。而这种质的变化,却无法用统计数字来显示。等到后来这种质的变化可以用充分的数据来说明的时候,为时已晚,公司的新车已经推出,结果导致了失败。

对于外部的情况,真正重要的不是趋势,而是趋势的转变。趋势的转变才是决定一个机构及其努力的成败关键。对这种转变,必须要有所觉察,转变是无法计量、无法界定、无法分类的。虽然有时候分类也能产生预期数字，例如福特 Edsel 型车的例子，但这样获得的数字已经不能反映真实的购买行为了。

电脑是一种逻辑的机器，这是它的优点，同时也是它的限制。外部世界的重要情况，不能转化为可以用电脑（或任何其他逻辑系统）处理的资料形式。而人的逻辑性虽然不是特别强，但是人能够觉察，这正是人的优点所在。

令人担忧的是，有了电脑，管理者对不能转化成电脑逻辑与语言的资料和刺激，恐怕就会不屑一顾了。管理者可能会因此失去觉察力（对情况的觉察），而仅仅重视事实（即情况发生之后的数字）了。这样一来，大量的电脑信息反而会使管理者与外界的实际隔离。

电脑是潜在的、最有用的管理工具，最终它将使管理者意识到这种隔离，并帮助他们从内部事务中解脱出来，有更多的时间来应对外界。然而在短时期内，仍难免存在着"迷恋"电脑的危险，这是一个严重的问题。

电脑只能反映已经存在的情况。而身为管理者，必须生存及工作于企业之内。所以，一位管理者，如果不能有意识地努力去觉察外部世界，则组织内部的事务必将蒙蔽他，使他看不见真正的现实。

上面所说的 4 项现实问题，是管理者无力改变的，也是管理者之所以存在的必要条件。因此他必须明了：如果他不致力于学习以提高自己的有效性，就不可能成为卓有成效的管理者。

## 对有效性的认识

要想提高管理者的绩效和成就，使工作达到令人满意的程度，唯一可行的办法，就是提高有效性。

我们当然可以在各方面任用能力特别强的人，知识特别丰富的人。但是我认为这两类人才毕竟难以找到。过不多久我们就会发现，我们正在勉强做那些根本不可能办到的事，或原本就无利可图的事。我们不可能为此专门培养一批新的超人，而只能运用现有的人才来经营我们的组织。

在许多讨论管理发展的书籍中，常将"未来的经理人"描写得无所不能。这类书籍说：一位高级管理者应该具有非凡的分析能力与决策能力；他应善于与他人共事，也应了解组织与权力关系；他擅长数学，又应有艺术的修养，还得是创造的天才。看起来我们需要的人，简直是文武全才，样样精通。而这样的人才，实在少之又少。事实上根据我们人类以往的经验，容易找到的人肯定不会是全才。所以，我们任用的人才，充其量也只能在某一项能力方面比较优秀。而若人才的某一项能力较强，自然在其他能力方面就不免平平了。

我们必须学会这么一种建立组织的方式：若某人在某一重要领域具有一技之长，就要让他充分发挥这一特长。这一点我们将在本书的第4章中详细讨论。我们不能一味拔高能力的标准来期望管理者的绩效，更不能期望万能的天才来达成绩效。我们只有通过改进工作的手段来充分发挥人的能力，而不应该寄望于人的能力突然提高。

上述原则大抵也适用于知识方面。不管我们多么急需具有广博知识的人才，在知识改进上所花费的努力，往往都大于我们可能获得的回报。

例如在15年前，当"运筹学"刚开始流行的时候，有人开出了从事运筹学研究的学者应具备的条件。他提出的要求是，一位运筹学者应该是一位"万能博士"。他应该懂得一切，而且对人类各方面的知识都能做最佳的应用。甚至有人说，运筹学者必须具有62门自然科学和人文科学的知识。如果真能找到这样一位"万能博士"，让他来研究库存水平或生产规划问题，那岂不是绝大的浪费！

至于所谓经理人发展计划，当然不像培养运筹学者那样雄心勃勃，但它也要求经理人拥有各方面的技能，诸如会计、人事、营销、定价和经济分析，还有诸如心理学之类的行为科学，以及诸如物理学、生物学、地质学等的自然科学。而且，我们确实还希望他们懂得现代的技术发展，了解现代的国际经济和政治。

上述的每个方面都是很大的知识领域。其中任何一项，有些人即使钻研一辈子也会嫌时间不够。要知道学术研究一向有越分越细的趋势，学者们只能选择很小的范围研究，谁也不敢说自己对该领域的知识比一位新闻记者懂得更多。

当然我说这些，并不表示一个人连各领域的一些基础知识都不需要掌握了。

今天有许多年轻的受过高等教育的人士，不论是在企业机构、医院还是政府，他们的缺点之一，是往往以自己精通了某一狭窄领域的专门学问而自满，不屑于其他。一位会计当然不一定需要钻研人际关系，一位工程师当然也不一定需要钻研如何促销新产品；可是，他们至少应该知道那些是什么样的领域，为什么要设立那些领域，那些领域到底做些什么。泌尿科专家当然不一定要精通精神病学，但至少该知道精神病学是一门什么学问。农业部的专家当然不一定要精通国际法，但至少该具备足够的国际政治的常识，以免由于褊狭的农业政策损害国际关系。

但是，这种精而后博的人与所谓通才不同。通才也和天才一样，可遇而不可求。我们应该努力的是，学会善用那些专精于某一领域的人。也就是说，我们必须提高有效性。我们既然不能增加资源的供应量，就应该设法增加资源的产出量。所谓有效性，就是使能力和知识资源能够产生更多、更好成果的一种手段。

考虑到组织的需要，有效性应该受到优先的重视。同时，有效性也是管理者达成目标和绩效的必要手段，因此更应该受到高度优先的重视。

## 卓有成效可以学会吗

假如有效性是人类的一种天赋，就像音乐天赋和绘画天赋一样，那事情可就糟了，因为天才总是少之又少。于是我们不得不及早发掘潜在的有效人士，培养他们，让他们发挥自己的才干。但即使这样，我们恐怕也很难发掘到足够的人才，以满足现代社会的需要。说实话，如果有效性只是人类的天赋，那么我们今天的文明即使尚能维持，也肯定是不堪一击的。今天的大型组织的文明，所依赖的是大批具有一定有效性而且可以担任管理者的人。

如果说卓有成效是可以学会的，那么问题便是：卓有成效应该包括哪些方面？我们应该学些什么？该用怎样的方式学习？卓有成效是一种可以系统学习的知识吗？还是要像学徒那样学习才能掌握的技能？还是要通过反复实践来养成的习惯？

近几年来，我一直在不断思索这些问题。我是一位管理顾问，常常与许多组织的管理者接触。因此，卓有成效对我来说起码有两方面的意义。第一，当管理顾问其实就是做智囊，别无任何权力。管理顾问必须有效，否则将会一事无成。第二，最有效的管理顾问也得仰仗委托机构的内部人士来合作完成工作。因此，管理顾问是否能有所贡献，是否能达成成果，或者是否会变成一个光花钱而不起作用的"成本中心"，或者顶多只是变成被利用的小丑，这一切的一切，都视委托机构内部人士的有效性如何而定。

但是我终于明白了世上并无所谓的"有效的个性"○。我认识许多有效的管理者，他们脾气不同、能力也不同；他们所做的事不同，做事的方法也不同；他们的个性、知识和志趣，也各不相同。事实上，他们几乎在每一方面都各自不同，却有一项共同点：人人都具有做好该做的事情的能力。

在我认识和共事过的许多有效的管理者中，有性格外向的，也有令人敬而远之的。有超然世外，卓尔不群的，也有遇人羞答答的。有的固执独断，有的因循附和。有的很胖，有的很瘦。有的生性爽朗，有的总是心怀忧虑。有的能豪饮，有的却滴酒不沾。有的待人亲切如家人，有的却严峻而冷若冰霜。有的少数人生就一副令人一望而知其为"领导者"的体型；有的其貌不扬，显得毫无吸引力。有的具有学者风度，有的却像是目不识丁。有的具有广泛的兴趣；有的除了自身的狭窄圈子外，其他一概不懂。还有些人虽不是自私，却始终以自我为中心；而有的却落落大方，心智开放。有人专心致力于他的本职工作，心无旁骛；也有人其志趣全在事业以外，做社会工作、跑教堂、研究中国诗词、演唱流行歌曲。在我认识的那些有效的管理者中，有人能够运用逻辑和分析，有人却主要是靠他们本身的经验和直觉。有人能轻而易举地决策；有人却每次都一再苦思，饱受痛苦。

换言之，有效的管理者，他们之间的差别，就像医生、教师和小提琴家一样各有不同类型。至于不称职的管理者，也同样各有各的不同类型。因此，有效的管理者与不称职的管理者，在类型、性格及才智方面，很难加以区别。

---

○ 耶鲁大学克里斯·阿吉里斯教授在哥伦比亚大学商学院研究生班讲课时曾提到该词，此讲话未公开发表（未注日期）。根据阿吉里斯教授的说法，"成功的"管理者有十大特点，其中包括"有很强的挫折忍受能力"，对"商战规律"有透彻的理解，能"与不同的集团进行沟通"。如果这些果真是我们希望管理者必须具备的共同特点的话，那我们就遭殃了。因为有这类个性的人实在是太难找了。幸好我认识不少卓有成效、颇为成功的管理者，不过他们大多都不具备阿吉里斯所提到的那些个性。我的确也认识一些人，他们虽然符合阿吉里斯的条件，但他们却是工作效率极低的人。

卓有成效的管理者有一个共同点，那就是他们在实践中都要经历一段训练，这一训练使他们工作起来能卓有成效。不管他们是在企业机构内、政府机构内、医院内，还是学校内，不管他们是干什么的，这些训练的内容都是一样的。

反之，我也发现，一个人如果没有经过这些训练，则无论他有多大的智慧、多大的努力、多大的想象力和多丰富的知识，也必然是一位缺乏有效性的管理者。

换句话说，有效性是一种后天的习惯，是一种实践的综合。既然是一种习惯，便是可以学会的。从表面上看，习惯是很单纯的，一个七岁的小孩也懂得什么是习惯。不过要把习惯建立得很好，却是不容易的。习惯必须靠学习才能养成，就像我们学习乘法口诀一样。我们每天没完没了地读乘法表，"练到吐"，直到我们熟练得不加思考随口可以说出"六六三十六"，那就成为我们固定的习惯了。学习习惯就非得反复地实践不可。

记得小时候我的钢琴老师告诉我："你弹莫扎特的曲子时，也许不可能像钢琴家施纳贝尔演奏得那样好，但是并没有理由说，你不必像施纳贝尔那样练习音阶。"回想起来，我的钢琴老师显然少说了一句话：最伟大的钢琴家，如果不肯辛勤演练，也一定无法演奏莫扎特的曲子。

也就是说，没有任何理由不让普通人通过练习来获得胜任某项工作的能力。当然，若要把什么东西演练到炉火纯青的地步是很不容易的，那也许需要有特殊的天赋。但卓有成效所要求的只是能够胜任，只是能演奏出音阶来。

下列5项是要成为一个卓有成效的管理者，必须在思想上养成的习惯。

（1）有效的管理者知道应该将他们的时间用在什么地方。他们所能控制的时间非常有限，他们会有系统地工作，善用这有限的时间。

（2）有效的管理者重视对外界的贡献。他们并非为工作而工作，而是为成果而工作。他们不会一接到工作就一头钻进去,更不会一开头就探究工作的技术和手段,他们会首先自问:"别人期望我做出什么成果?"

(3)有效的管理者善于利用长处,包括自己的长处、上司的长处、同事的长处和下属的长处。他们还善于抓住有利形势,做他们能做的事。他们不会把工作建立在自己的短处上,也绝不会去做自己做不了的事。

(4)有效的管理者集中精力于少数重要的领域,在这少数重要的领域中,如果能有优秀的绩效就可以产生卓越的成果。他们会按照工作的轻重缓急设定优先次序,而且坚守优先次序。他们别无选择,只能要事第一。重要的事先做,不重要的事放一放,甚至不做,两种事都做,反倒会一事无成。

(5)最后,有效的管理者必须善于做有效的决策。他们知道有效的决策事关处事的条理和秩序问题,也就是如何按正确的次序采取正确的步骤。他们知道一项有效的决策,总是在"不同意见讨论"的基础上做出的判断,它绝不会是"一致意见"的产物。他们知道快速的决策多为错误的决策,真正不可或缺的决策数量并不多,但一定是根本性的决策。他们需要的是正确的战略,而不是令人眼花缭乱的战术。

以上这些就是管理者卓有成效的要素,也是本书的主题。

第2章 | CHAPTER 2

# 掌握自己的时间

关于管理者任务的讨论，一般都从如何做计划说起。这样看来很合乎逻辑。可惜的是管理者的工作计划，很少真正发生作用。计划通常只是纸上谈兵，或只是良好的意愿，很少能够真正实现。

根据我的观察，有效的管理者并不是一开始就着手工作，他们往往会从时间安排上着手。他们并不以计划为起点，认识清楚自己的时间用在什么地方才是起点。然后他们管理自己的时间，减少非生产性工作所占用的时间。最后，再将"可自由运用的时间"，由零星而集中成大块连续性的时段。这三个步骤，是管理者有效性的基础：

- 记录时间；
- 管理时间；
- 统一安排时间。

有效的管理者知道，时间是一项限制因素。任何生产程序的产出量，都会受到最稀有资源的制约。而在我们称之为"工作成就"的生产程序里，最稀有的资源，就是时间。

时间也是最特殊的一项资源。在其他各项主要资源中，资金一项实际上是相当充裕的。我们很久以前就已经了解到，制约经济增长与经济活动的，并不是资金的供给不足，而是对资金的需求不大。此外另一个限制因素是人力，尽管要雇用到足够的优秀人才并不容易，但总还是可以雇到人才。只有时间，是我们租不到、雇不到，也买不到，更不能以其他手段来获得的。

时间的供给，丝毫没有弹性。不管时间的需求有多大，供给绝不可能增加。时间的供需没有价格可资调节，也无法绘制边际效用曲线。而且，时间稍纵即逝，根本无法贮存。昨天的时间过去了，永远不再回来。所以，时间永远是最短缺的。

时间也完全没有替代品。在一定范围内，某一资源缺少，可以另觅一种资源替代。例如铝少了，可以改用铜；劳动力可以用资金来替代。我们可以增加知识，也可以增加人力，但没有任何东西可以替代已失去的时间。

做任何事情都少不了时间，时间是必须具备的一个条件。任何工作都是在时间中进行的，都需要耗用时间。但是对这项最特殊的、无可替代的和不可或缺的资源，绝大多数人却都以为可以取用不竭。有效的管理者与其他人最大的区别，就是他们非常珍惜自己的时间。

但是人却往往最不善于管理自己的时间。

人类像其他生物一样，生理上有自己的"生物钟"——任何人如果有乘飞机越洋飞行的经验，应该都能了解。但是心理学实验却证明，人的时间感觉是最不可靠的。把人关在黑房间里，很快他就会丧失对时间的感觉。即使在黑暗中，绝大多数人也能保持空间的感觉。但是禁闭室内的人，即使有灯光，也无法估计时间的长短。他们有时对时间估计过长，有时又估计过短。

所以，如果完全靠记忆，我们恐怕说不清楚自己的时间是怎样打发的。

有些管理者常自诩其记忆力很强，我有时请他们把自己使用时间的过程凭记忆做一下估计，并且写下来。然后，我把他们这份东西暂时保存起来。与此同时，我又请他们随时记录他们实际耗用的时间。几个星期或几个月之后，我把他们原来的估计拿出来，跟他们实际的记录相对照，却发现两者之间相去甚远。

某公司的董事长，十分肯定地对我说他的时间大致分成三个部分：1/3 用于与公司高级管理人员研讨业务；1/3 用于接待重要客户；其余 1/3 则用于参加各种社会活动。但是，等实际记录了 6 个星期之后，跟他原来的估计比较，结果发现在上述三个方面，他几乎没花什么时间。原来，他所说的三类工作，只不过是他认为"应该"花时间的工作而已，因此他的记忆告诉他已将时间用在这三个方面了。6 个星期的实际记录，显示他的时间大部分都花在调度工作上了，例如处理他自己认识的顾客的订单，打电话给工厂催货。事实上，顾客的订单，本来可以顺利处理的，由于他的干预，反而弄得不能准时交货。这份时间记录是由他的秘书记下来的，当秘书把记录送给他看时，他简直一点儿都不能相信。后来他的秘书又仔细地做了几次记录，他才相信，关于时间的使用情况，记录要比记忆可靠多了。

所以，有效的管理者知道，如果要管理好自己的时间，首先应该了解自己的时间实际上是怎么耗用的。

## 时间对管理者的压力

管理者经常受到种种压力，迫使他不得不花费一些时间在非生产性的和浪费时间的事务上。身为管理者，不管他是不是经理人，总有许多时间耗在毫无贡献的工作上。大量时间都不可避免地浪费了。而且管理者在组织中的地位越高，组织对他的时间要求往往越大。

有一家大公司的负责人告诉我，他在担任公司总经理的两年中，除了圣诞节和新年元旦两天，每天晚上都有应酬。凡是宴会，都是"公事"，每一次都得花几个小时，而他又非参加不可。不管是欢送服务满50年的老同事退休，还是宴请与公司有往来的政府官员，他都需要出席，因为参加这种会见是他的一项任务。这位负责人对这类应酬并不抱幻想，他知道这种饭局对公司的发展没什么好处，他本人对此既没有兴趣，也不认为这有助于自我发展，但他仍然必须出席，仍然需要高兴地参加宴会。

诸如此类的时间浪费，实在不胜枚举。比如，公司一位重要客户打来电话，销售经理绝不敢说："等一下，我太忙了。"也许这位大客户，谈的只是上星期六的一场桥牌，或是他的千金考上了理想的大学，但销售经理不能不洗耳恭听。医院院长得出席每一次医务会议，要不然所有的医生护士和职员都会认为院长瞧不起他们。政府官员也同样得忙于应付议员们的来访和了解某些情况，而那些情况也许只要随手一翻电话簿或是《世界年鉴》，就马上可以得到。这样的事，每天都在不断地发生。

非经理人员也不见得好到哪里去。他们也同样会受到各种占用时间的要求的轰炸，这对他们的生产力一点作用也没有，但他们却不能不应付。

每一位管理者的时间，都有很大部分是被浪费掉的。表面上看起来，每件事似乎都非办不可，实际上却毫无贡献或贡献太少。

但是，即使是只想获得最低程度的有效性，管理者在绝大部分任务上也需要相当多的整块时间。如果每一次所花的时间少于这个极限，事情就做不好，所花的时间就是浪费，再做就得从头开始。

举例来说，一份报告大概得花6～8小时才能完成初稿。如果说每次花15分钟，每天2次，一共花上2星期，虽然总时间也达到7小时，恐怕结果还是一张白卷，不过是在上面胡乱涂写了一些东西而已。但是如果能够关起门来，切断电话，连续做上五六个小时，一份相当不错的草稿就应该差不多了。有了这份草稿，管理者才能做零星的补充，才能逐句逐段地润色、修改和整理。

科学实验工作也与此相似。起码需要5～12小时的整块时间，才能把仪器调整妥当，做成一次实验。如果中间被打断，恐怕就得重新开始。

每一位知识工作者，尤其是每一位管理者，要想有效就必须能将时间做整块的运用。如果将时间分割开来零星使用，纵然总时间相同，结果时间也肯定不够。

尤其是与他人一起工作时，这一点更为重要。与他人一起工作，正是管理者的中心工作之一。人都是时间消费者，而大多数人也是时间浪费者。

与他人只接触三两分钟，是绝不会产生什么结果的。要想与他人做有效的沟通，总得花上足够的时间。一位经理人员如果以为他与下属讨论一项计划、一项方针或是一项工作表现，只需15分钟就够了，那他一定是自欺欺人。如果你真想影响别人，那至少需要一小时以上。如果你想和别人建立良好的人际关系，就需要更多的时间。

与其他的知识工作者建立关系尤其费时。不管出于什么原因，不管在知识工作者中有没有等级与权力的隔阂，不管他们是不是把自己看得过分重要，知识工作者对其上级主管及同事所要求的时间，往往比体力工作者多得多。而且，由于知识工作不能用衡量体力工作的方法来衡量，因此我们实在没法用三言两语说明知识工作者是否在做该做的工作，是否做得出色。对一位体力工作者，我们可以说："标准是每小时完成50件，而你只做了42件。"但是对一位知识工作者，我们却需要坐下来与他共同讨论应该做些什么，为什么该做，然后才能弄清楚他的工作做得怎样。这就很费时间了。

知识工作者只能自己制定工作方向，所以他必须了解别人期望他做出的贡献是什么，原因是什么，对必须使用其知识成果的人的工作情况，他也要有足够的了解。因此，知识工作者需要信息，需要讨论，还需要指导他人，这都是极为费时的。而且，他不但需要占用他上级的时间，也同样需要占用他周围同事的时间。

知识工作者要想取得成果和绩效，就必须着眼于整个组织的成果和绩效。换句话说，他还得匀出时间来，将目光由自己的工作转到成果上；由他的专业转到外部世界，因为只有外部世界才有绩效可言。

在大型组织中，如果知识工作者的绩效表现不错，往往是因为该组织的高级主管能定期抽出时间来与他们进行交流，甚至与一些资历较浅的知识工作者交流："你认为我们组织的领导，对你的工作应该了解些什么？你对我们这个组织有什么看法？你觉得我们还有哪些尚未开拓的机会？你觉得我们有哪些尚未察觉的危机？还有，你希望从我这里知道些什么？"

这样的轻松交流，不管是在政府、企业、研究机构，还是在军事单位，都同样很有必要。如果没有这样的交流，知识工作者就容易丧失热情，成为得过且过的人，或者是只关注自己的专业领域，看不到整个组织的需要和机会。不过，进行这样的交流是很费时间的，特别是这种交流必须在不慌不忙、轻松自在的气氛下进行。只有这样，大家才会觉得"我们有足够的时间"，可以从容不迫地交流看法。这实际上意味着管理者要快速地做许多事，同时也意味着他必须腾出整块的时间来，而且中间不能有太多的中断和打扰。

人际关系和工作关系的协调确实很费时间。太匆忙了，恐怕反而会造成摩擦。然而任何组织都少不了这种协调。人数越多，协调相互关系所需的时间就越长，而真正用于创造成就、取得成果的工作时间便相对地减少了。

管理理论中早就有所谓"管理幅度"之说。所谓管理幅度，是指一个管理者能有效地管理多少个工作上互有关联的人（例如会计、销售经理和生产经理三个人，彼此必须互相关联，才能产生成果）。但从另一方面来说，同一公司分设各地的连锁商店，各分店经理的工作不一定必须互相关联。所以一位副总经理即使同时管理数十位分店经理，也并不违背管理幅度的原则。这种管理幅度原则是否合理，我们暂且不论，但毫无疑问的是：一起工作的人数越多，工作者用于彼此协调关系的时间肯定越多，而真正用于工作的时间就越少了。因此大型组织只有在大量耗用其管理者的时间之后，才能变得强大有力。

所以，组织规模越大，管理者实际可掌握的时间越少。身为管理者，因此更应该知道自己的时间应该用在什么地方，并且更应该妥善运用那剩下来可自由支配的少量时间。

同时，组织的人数越多，有关人事的决策也肯定越多。对人事的问题决定得太快，很容易铸成错误。人事决策往往需要大量的时间，因为决策所涉及的一些问题，只有在反复考虑多次之后才能看清楚。

在我认识的许多卓有成效的管理者中，有人做决策很快，也有人比较慢。但是，不管他们决策速度的快慢，只要是遇到人事问题，他们总是决定得很慢，而且常常需要经过多次考虑，才能最后定案。

据说通用汽车公司前任总裁斯隆先生（Alfred P. Sloan, Jr.）对于人事问题，从来不在问题第一次提出时就做决定。他通常是先做一个初步判断，而初步判断往往也得花费好几个小时。然后，他将问题搁置一旁，隔几天甚至几星期之后，再拿出来重新考虑，而且不会受第一次判断的影响。只有当同一个提名连续出现2～3次的时候，他才愿意继续向前推进。斯隆先生一向以知人善任而闻名。有人问他用人的秘诀是什么，据说他的回答是："我没有秘诀。我只是有这样的感觉，我第一念就想到的人选，往往不会是最适当的人选。因此，我总要对整个思考和分析过程做好几次回顾之后，才做最后决定。"斯隆用人如此谨慎，然而我们也知道，其实在别的方面他并不是一个很有耐心的人。

实际上，需要做如此重要的人事决策的人不是太多。可是据我所知，凡是有效的管理者，都知道他们如果想在人事方面做出最佳的决策，总得花费几个小时进行不间断的考虑。

一家研究所的所长想要解聘一位高级主管时，也遇到了同样的问题。那位高级主管已经50多岁了,一辈子供职于这个机构。可是在多年的优良表现之后,他忽然不行了,不能再胜任现职。虽然按照人事规定,研究所可以将他解职,但这样的人不能就这样被辞退。当然也可以降级使用,但又恐怕会打击他。所长觉得他过去多年对研究所曾有过许多贡献,总不能太亏待他。然而现在,他却不宜续任了,他的缺陷太明显,如果继续留任管理职位,恐怕整个研究所都将受到影响。

这位所长跟他的副所长讨论了好多次,始终找不到适当的办法。直到有一天,他们两人利用了一个晚上,整整花了三四个小时研究,不让任何别的事情来打扰,他们才忽然发现解决办法原来那么"明显"。说来其实简单极了,但是谁也弄不懂为什么过去那么久都没有想出来。办法是将那位主管由目前不合适的职位,调到另一个重要的新职位,而这个新职位并不需要他担当他能力所不及的行政责任。

实际上许许多多类似的人事问题,都需要较长的、连续性的和不受打扰的时间才能决定。例如,为某项特殊任务成立一个专案小组,该派些什么人?对于接管新组织经理人员,或对于在组织中新上任的经理人员,应赋予他们什么职责?某一职员对营销很有研究,却没有受过技术培训,能不能提升他?还是该提升另一位不懂营销但技术一流的人?

人事决策都是费时的决策。原因很简单:上帝创造人时并没有想到让他们成为组织的"资源"。任何人都很难完全合乎组织要求的条件,而人又不是可以随意"修整",随意"更改"的。最多,人不过是"大致符合要求",而我们开展工作又必须用人(没有别的资源可以代替人)。所以在人事决策上,就需要较长时间的思考和判断了。

东欧斯拉夫人有句谚语:"用脚走不通的路,用头可以走得通。"这句谚语，我们不妨把它视为"能量守恒定律"的一种颇为新奇的解释，但它也有"时间守恒定律"的意味，意思就是说：一件工作，用"脚"的时间越少（体力劳动），则需用"头"的时间肯定越多（脑力劳动）。我们为了使一般工人、机械操作员以及一般职员的工作变得更容易，就必须要求知识工作者承担更多工作。我们的工作是脱离不开脑力劳动的，必须把脑力劳动放回到工作中去，而且必须让脑力劳动占更大的分量。

对知识工作者的时间要求也不会下降。机械操作员现在每周只工作40小时了，将来还有可能减少到35小时，而且不论他们工作时间的长短，其生活必将日益改善。其实机械操作员相对轻闲的工作完全是知识工作者超时工作的结果。当今工业化国家里的那些管理者也想过安逸悠闲的日子，但事与愿违，他们的工作时间越来越长，把一件事做到满意所需的时间也越来越多。这种趋势还将加剧。

为什么会有这种趋势？原因之一，是今天生活水准的提高是以不断创新和变革的经济为前提的。创新和变革，形成了对管理者时间的过度需求。如果时间短促，一个人就只能考虑他已经熟悉的事，只能做他曾经做过的事。

近几年常有人研究为什么英国在第二次世界大战后的经济会如此落后。大家觉得其中的原因之一，是英国老一辈的企业家都想跟他们的工人看齐，要过得舒服，要缩短工作时间。其实，除非英国的工商业甘愿墨守成规，规避创新和变革，否则企业家们不可能跟他们的工人看齐，企求安逸。

上述种种原因，组织本身的需要、处理人事问题的需要以及创新和变革的需要，都使得管理者不能不讲求时间的管理了。但是管理者如果不了解自己是如何使用时间的，就别想管理好时间。

## 如何诊断自己的时间

要了解时间是怎样耗用的，从而据以管理时间，我们必须先记录时间。这个道理其实我们几十年前就已经明白了。早在20世纪初期的科学管理时代，我们就已经知道了记录工作时间，不过那是以体力工作为对象。时至今日，几乎所有国家在工业管理上都学会这套方法了。

但是我们却一直将这套方法应用在时间因素并不太重要的工作上。在那些工作中，时间的利用和浪费，充其量只会对效率和成本稍有影响。而在某些越来越重要的工作领域，我们却没有应用这套方法，尤其是那些时间因素特别重要的知识工作，特别是管理者的工作。须知只有在这些方面，时间的运用和浪费才是直接与有效性和成果密切相关。

所以，要提高管理者的有效性，第一步就是记录其时间耗用的实际情形。

> 时间记录的具体方法，我们在此不必赘述。事实上许多管理者都备有一本小册子，自己记录，也有人请秘书小姐代为记录。重要的是，必须在处理某一工作的"当时"立即加以记录，而不能事后凭记忆补记。

许多有效的管理者都经常保持这样的一份时间记录，每月定期拿出来检讨。至少，有效的管理者往往以连续三四个星期为一个时段，每天记录，一年内记录两三个时段。有了时间耗用的记录样本，他们便能自行检讨了。半年之后，他们都会发现自己的时间耗用得很乱，浪费在种种无谓的小事上。经过练习，他们在时间的利用上必有进步。但是管理时间必须持之以恒，才能避免再回到浪费的状态上去。

因此，第二个步骤就是要做有系统的时间管理。我们先要将非生产性的和浪费时间的活动找出来，尽可能将这类活动从时间表上排除出去。要做到这一步，可以试问自己以下几个问题。

（1）首先要找出什么事根本不必做，这些事做了也完全是浪费时间，于最终的成果无助。将时间记录拿出来，逐项逐项地问："这件事如果不做，会有什么后果？"如果认为"不会有任何影响"，那么这件事便该立刻取消。

然而许多大忙人，天天在做一些他们觉得难以割舍的事，比如应邀讲演、参加宴会、担任委员和列席指导之类，这些活动不知占去了他们多少时间。而这些工作，他们本身既不感兴趣，做得也根本不够精彩。然而他们得承受这些负担，一年又一年，就像从天而降的灾难一样躲也躲不了。其实，对付这类事情，只要审度一下对于组织有无贡献，对于他本人有无贡献，或是对于对方的组织有无贡献。如果都没有，简单谢绝就可以了。

前文说起的那位天天有应酬的总经理，在经过一番检讨后，发现其中至少1/3的宴请根本没有参加的必要。有时他甚至有点哭笑不得，因为主人并不真心希望他出席。主人发来邀请，只不过是一番礼貌。其实主人倒真希望他在请帖回执上写个"敬谢"，而他每次敬陪，主人反而不知如何为他安排席次。

（2）第二个该问的问题是："时间记录上的哪些活动可以由别人代为参加而又不影响效果？"

前述总经理还发现，在他参加的宴会中，事实上有1/3只要有公司的高级管理人员到场即可，并非每次都要他亲自参加。主办单位只不过希望把该公司列在请客名单上而已。

多年来管理学者一直在研究授权问题。任何一个组织——企业、政府、学校和军事机关，几乎每一位主管人员都接到过上级有关做好授权的指示，而且他们本人也曾屡屡对其下属阐明授权的重要。但是这样的谆谆告诫是否产生了预期效果，实在令人怀疑。原因非常简单：没有完全明了授权的意义。如果认为所谓授权，意思是说："我的"工作应由别人来做，那就错了；因为你既然拿了薪水，就该做你自己的工作。又有人认为：充分授权之后，最闲散的经理人便应该是最好的经理人。这样的看法不但荒唐，而且也是不道德的。

但是我却从来没见过一位管理者，在检讨过自己的时间记录后，还不改变自己的习惯，将不必亲自处理的事交给别人。只要翻阅一下时间记录，他就能立刻发现他的时间全用在不必要的事上了，而对于确属重要的事、他自己希望做的事和他已经承诺过的事，他却没有时间来处理。其实他如果真想有所作为，只要将可由别人做的事交给别人就得了。

公务旅行就是个例子。帕金森教授（C. Northcote Parkinson）在他诙谐的讽刺作品《帕金森定律》一书中指出：要想尽快摆脱不胜任的上级主管，最好的办法就是让他不断出差旅行。把飞机当作管理工具来用，这实在是过高地估计了飞机的作用。当然出差是必要的，但是派一位资历较浅的人员同样可以完成任务。资历较浅的人员通常喜欢出差，同时年轻人在旅馆中也容易睡好。年轻人总更能耐劳，因此往往比经验丰富但易于疲劳的高级人员，更能胜任外出工作。

参加会议也是问题。虽然会议上本来并没有什么别人处理不了的大事，但管理者总得出席。在文件的初稿出来之前，管理者往往要花上好几个小时参与讨论。研究所为了发布研究成果的新闻，得由主持该项研究的高级研究员来撰写新闻稿。研究所里有很多人都知道该项研究的经过，新闻稿如果由别人写，写出来一定文笔流畅、通俗易懂，而高级研究员却只能写出一些高深莫测的数学公式。总而言之，管理者所做的工作，确实有许许多多可由别人去做，而且也应该由别人去做。

"授权"这个名词，通常都被人误解，甚至是曲解了。这个名词的意义，应该是把可由别人做的事情交付给别人，这样才能做真正应由自己做的事——这才是有效性的一大改进。

（3）还有一项时间浪费的因素，是管理者自己可以控制并且可以消除的，这项因素是：管理者在浪费别人的时间。

这种现象并不明显，但有一个简单方法可以诊断出来：去问问你的下属。有效的管理者懂得有系统及诚恳地问他的下属："请你想想看，我常做哪些浪费你的时间而又不产生效果的事情？"问这样的问题，而且问得对方敢说真心话，才是有效管理者的特色。

即使管理者处理的都是颇有成效的工作，其处理方式仍可能造成别人时间的浪费。

某一大企业机构的财务经理，深感会议浪费了太多时间。通常不管讨论的是什么，他都通知财务部各单位主管全体前来开会，其结果是会议每次都拖得很长。出席会议的每一位主管，为了表示自己对问题的关切，都得提出自己的意见，而这些意见却大多与问题无关，会议时间自然拖长了。

直到有一次这位财务经理诚恳地问了大家，才知道大家也都认为会议太浪费时间了。可是，他又想道：每一个人在组织中都至为重要，都应该了解情况，开会时如果少请几个人，他又担心会使未被邀请的人觉得他们被忽视。

后来这位财务经理终于找到一个两全其美的办法了。开会前，他先分发一份开会通知："兹订于星期三下午3时，于四楼会议室，邀请赵钱孙李四君开会讨论下年度资本预算问题。如哪位需了解这个问题或愿参与讨论，亦请届时出席。如果无法出席，我们将于会后立刻呈送记录，供各位参考并希望提供宝贵意见。"

过去每次会议都要12人参加，花费整个下午，而现在只要4人出席，一小时就可以结束了，并且没有一个人有被忽视的感觉。

许多管理者都意识到了哪些事情会浪费他们的时间，然而他们却不敢面对这个问题。他们怕因小失大，造成错误。殊不知即使有了错误，也能很快弥补。能够大量削减不必要的和非生产性的工作，则工作就进行得快多了。

美国总统四年一任，每一位新当选的总统起初总会接到各式各样的邀请。经过一段时间，他才会发现要做的事太多，而接受邀请也大多对他的有效性并无帮助。于是，他开始谢绝各种邀请，结果又被认为没有人情味了。于是他就会进行必要的调整，在被人剥夺工作的有效性与利用公开场合开展工作之间寻求一种比较合适的折中方法。

事实上，一位管理者大刀阔斧地减少不必要的工作，绝不会有太大的风险。人常常会有高估自己地位的重要性的倾向，认为许多事非躬亲不可。纵然是最有效的管理者，仍然免不了有许多不必要的和非生产性的工作。

大胆减少自己的工作，真会出问题吗？只要看有些管理者虽然身患重病，甚至于身有残疾，仍能干得有声有色，就可以知道这种顾虑是多余的。

第二次世界大战期间，罗斯福总统的机要顾问霍普金斯先生就是一个实例。霍普金斯当年已体衰力竭，举步维艰，每隔一天才能办公几个小时。因此，他不能不把一切事务都撇开，仅处理真正重要的工作。但这丝毫无损于他的有效性。丘吉尔还对他钦佩备至，赞美他是一位"盖世奇才"。他完成的任务，在当年的美国政府中无人能出其右。

当然，霍普金斯只是一个特例。但他的故事，告诉了我们大胆减少无谓的工作，绝对无损于有效性。

## 消除浪费时间的活动

上面介绍的三项诊断的问题，是关于非生产性的和浪费时间的活动的处理。每一位知识工作者和每一位管理者都该自问那些问题。但时间浪费有时也是由于管理不善和机构有缺陷，身为主管者也应予以同等的重视。管理不善不仅会浪费大家的时间，更重要的是会浪费主管自己的时间。

（1）首先要做的是，找出由于缺乏制度或远见而产生时间浪费的因素。应注意的现象，是机构中一而再，再而三出现同样的"危机"。同样的危机如果出现了第二次，就绝不应该再让它出现第三次。

工厂中每年发生的库存危机问题，就属于这一类。这种问题今天固然可以用电脑来解决，解决得比从前更为彻底，但也比从前更加费钱了。这样的解决方法很难说是了不起的进步。

一项重复出现的危机应该是可以预见的。因此，这类危机可以预先防止，或可以设计成一种例行工作，使每个人都能处理。所谓例行工作，是将本来要靠专家才能处理的事，设计成无须研究判断，人人均可处理的工作。例行的工作，可以说是专家们从过去的危机中，学会的一套有系统、有步骤的处理方式。

重复出现的危机,并不仅限于组织的较低层次。组织中每一部门都深受其害。

某一大型企业,多年来每到 12 月初,就会发生这样一个危机:该公司业务的季节性很强,每年第 4 季度为淡季,销售和利润均不易预测。按照公司规定,管理当局要在第 2 季度结束时提出的中期报告中,预估全年的盈余。3 个月后第 4 季度开始时,整个公司各部门都立刻紧张起来,为达成管理当局预估的目标而忙碌。在年底前的三五个星期之内,管理层没法做任何其他事情。然而这项危机,其实只要动一动笔便能解决:预估数字不必过于确定,只要列出一个上下范围来就行了。这项措施,事实上完全符合公司董事会、股东和金融界的要求。自从推广新措施,过去每年 12 月份的危机,现在已不复存在,甚至几乎没有人知道了。而且因为管理者不必再浪费时间来配合预估成果,每年第 4 季度的业务绩效反而比过去好了。

另一个例子,是麦克纳马拉出任美国国防部长之前,国防部内也是每年一度发生定期性的危机。那是在 6 月 30 日会计年度结束前,国防部上上下下都为了要消化当年度的预算而忙碌。如果国会核定的预算不能消化,就得将剩余部分缴还国库。但在麦克纳马拉接任后,很快看出了这根本不是一项问题。原来美国法律一向规定,对于必需的预算尚未用完的部分,可以转入一个临时账户。

同一个危机如果重复出现,往往是疏忽和懒散造成的。

多年以前我初次做管理顾问时,常常无法准确区分一个企业机构管理的好坏——但并不是说我没有生产方面的知识。后来我才发现：一个平静无波的工厂，必是管理上了轨道。如果一个工厂高潮迭现，在参观者看来大家忙得不可开交，就必是管理不善。管理好的工厂，总是单调无味，没有任何刺激动人的事件。那是因为凡是可能发生的危机都早已预见，且已将解决办法变成例行工作了。

同理，一个管理上了轨道的组织，常常是一个令人觉得兴味索然的组织。在这样的组织里，所谓"引人注目"的事情大概就是为未来做决策，而不是轰轰烈烈地处理过去的问题。

（2）人员过多，也常造成时间的浪费。

记得我初学算术时，曾有这样的问题："某工作2人在2天内可以完成，4人一起做，需几天完成？"这样的问题，对小学生来说答案应该是1天。但是在一个组织里，正确答案将可能是4天，甚至于是永远无法完成。

当然，人员太少，力量不够也不行，否则工作纵然完成了，也肯定不理想。但这却不是一成不变的定律。常见的现象是人员太多，以至于没有有效性。因为大家的时间，可能没有花在工作上，而是用来协调人员之间的关系了。

判断人数是否过多，有一个靠得住的标准。如果一个高级管理人员，尤其是经理，不得不将他工作时间的 1/10 花在处理所谓"人际关系问题"上，花在处理纠纷和摩擦上，花在处理争执和合作等问题上，那么这个单位人数就过多了。人数过多，难免彼此侵犯，也难免成为绩效的阻碍。在精干的组织里，人的活动空间较大，不至于互相冲突，工作时也不用每次都向别人说明。

多用几个人，总是以"有此需要"为借口。"我们实在少不了一位热力学专家，少不了一位专利法律顾问，少不了一位学经济的人才。"但在增加了一位专家后，实在不大用得上，也许根本用不上。然而任用理由很多，例如："养兵千日，用在一时呀！""他总得熟悉我们的业务呀！""总得一开始和我们共处呀！"用一个人，应该是每天的工作都需要他。偶尔才有需要的专家，必要时才需向他请教的专家，就不该正式聘用。要知道在有问题时花顾问费向专家请教，远比正式聘用便宜得多。何况把这样的专家留在组织里，对整个团体的有效性肯定有不良的影响，用了他反而将成为组织的祸害。

（3）另一个常见的浪费时间的原因，是组织不健全。其表现就是会议太多。

所谓会议，顾名思义，是靠集会来商议，是组织缺陷的一种补救措施。我们开会时就不能工作，工作时就不能开会，谁也不能同时又开会又工作。一个结构设计臻于理想的组织，应该没有任何会议（在今天动态的世界中，这样的组织当然只是理想而已）。每个人应该都能了解他工作所必须了解的事，也应该都能随时获得他工作所必需的资源。我们之所以要开会，只是因为各有各的工作，要靠彼此合作才能完成某一特定任务。我们之所以要开会，只是因为某一情况所需的知识和经验，不能全部装在一个人的头脑里，需要集思广益。

但问题在于会议太多。一个组织如果经常要以会议方式来共同工作，那么行为科学家们出于善意而为合作所研创的各种机会，就将是多余的了。一位管理者花费在会议上的时间如果过多，便是组织不健全的表现。

每一次会议都会衍生出许多别的会议，有的是正式的，有的是非正式的，但每次会议总要花好几个小时。所以，要开会，就得有一定的计划，否则不但令人讨厌，而且是一种危险。会议应该是不得已的例外，不能视为常规。一个人人都随时开会的组织，必是一个谁都不能做事的组织。试着看看我们的时间记录，如果发现开会太多——例如参加会议的时间占总时间1/4以上，那一定是一个浪费时间的不健全组织。

当然也有例外。有些特别的组织，设立的目的就是开会，例如杜邦公司和新泽西标准石油公司的董事会，它是最高的审议机构，但不执行任何运营工作。这两个公司很久以前就规定董事们不得兼任任何职务。同样地，法院的法官也不准许业余担任律师。

原则上，一位管理者的时间，绝不能让开会占用太多。会议太多，表示职位结构不当，也表示单位设置不当。会议太多，表示本应由一个职位或一个单位做的工作，分散到几个职位或几个单位去了。同时表示职责混乱以及未能将信息传送给需要的人员。

某大企业机构的会议像传染病似的越来越多。究其原因，是由于该公司的机构已经老化。1900年以前，该公司的传统产品是蒸汽涡轮机，当时公司设有一个蒸汽涡轮机部门，该部门有自己的管理层和幕僚。到第二次世界大战期间，这家公司踏入了航空发动机的领域，于是，又新成立了一个专门负责飞机和军品的部门。后来，该公司又增设了原子能部门。该部门是由公司研究所分出而设的，因此原子能部门在组织上，仍与研究所保持着密切的关系。

到今天，蒸汽涡轮机、航空发动机和原子能，虽然各有不同的市场，但这三种电力资源已不再是各占一片市场，互不相关了。这三种产品在利用上也渐渐地可以互相代替、互相辅助。其中任何一种，在某些情况下都是最经济和最有利的发电设施。由此看来，三者可以说是互相竞争的。可是，如果能将其中两种合并使用，则得到的效果，可能远比单独使用任何一种都好。

所以，该公司最需要的，是一项能源战略。他们需要的是一项决策：究竟该三个部门并重，让它们去互相竞争，还是该以某一部门为主要业务，而以另两个部门为辅助？或者该在三中选二——选择两项以发展一项最佳的"能源组合"？再者，该公司也需要决定，如何将资金分配给三个部门。尤其重要的是，该公司既然是从事能源事业，就需要一种组织，能配合事实上只有一个能源市场的现实，为同样的顾客供应同样的最终产品——电力。然而，该公司却分设了三个部门，各自为政，各不相属，各有各的办法和制度。更有甚者，各部门自信能在今后十年内独享全部能源市场的75%。

这样的结果是，多年来三个部门都忙于永无止境的会议。而且，因为管辖这三个部门高层管理的并非同一人，所以他们的会议也侵入了公司的整个高层。到现在，情况总算已有好转。三个部门在组织上已改变了过去的形式，归并为一个组织单位，由一位经理人管辖。虽然问题仍未完全解决，内部还有不断的冲突，有许多大策略尚待决定，但至少大家都能了解这类大决策究竟是什么了，至少公司的最高当局，可以不必老是在会议中担任裁判员。会议的时间自然也比以前大为减少。

（4）最后一项浪费时间的因素，是信息功能不健全。

某一医院的院长，多年来一直为应付院内医生们的电话而苦恼。医生们打电话给他，要求他为病人安排一个床位。住院部都说是没有床位了，但这位院长几乎每次都可以找到空床位。原因是在病人出院时，住院部不能立刻接到通知。当然，有没有床位，各病房的护士长随时都很清楚，主办出院结账手续的出纳台也能随时知道。住院部的人，是在每天清早5点办理"床位调查"工作，而通常病人大多是在上午医生查房之后才办出院手续。其实像这样的问题，只要各病房护士长在填写出院通知单给出纳台时，多填一份副本送住院部就解决了。

另一种同样常见的现象，是信息的表达方式不当，其后果有时更为严重。

制造部门常遭遇的一项困扰，是生产数字无法直接供生产作业部门使用。例如产量，报表中往往只列出会计部门所需的"平均产量"。可是直接作业人员需要的却不是平均数字，而是范围和大小，包括产品的组合、产量的变动和每批生产的时间等。所以，他们需要这类资料时，不是每天都得花费几小时来推算，就是在本单位内设置一个自己的秘密统计组。当然这种资料在会计部门一定都有的，可是通常谁也不想去告诉会计部门，说自己需要的是怎样的信息。

以上所说的种种时间浪费的缺点，例如人数过多、组织不健全或信息系统失灵等，有时是轻而易举就可以改善的，但有时也要花费许多时间和耐心才能改善。不过，只要你肯付出努力，这种改善的效果是很大的，特别是可以帮你省出许多时间来。

## 统一安排可以自由支配的时间

管理者在做过了自己的时间记录和分析后，当然了解究竟有多少时间可用于重要事务了。换句话说，有多少时间可以自由支配，又有多少时间可以用在确有贡献的大事上。

但是，对于可以自由支配的时间，也别存太大奢望。一位管理者无论怎样无情地删掉了浪费的部分，其自由时间仍不会太多。

曾有两年的时间，我在某银行担任顾问工作，研究该行高层管理的结构。这家银行的总裁，应该是我认识的主管中最善于管理时间的了。两年间，我每月与他会谈一次，每次他都只给我一个半小时。而且每次会谈，他都先有充分的准备，因此我也不能不事先准备。我们谈话的内容，每次仅以一个主题为限。在我们谈到1小时20分时，这位总裁开始催我了："德鲁克先生，我看我们该做个结论了，也该决定下一次谈什么主题了。"一个半小时的时间一到，他就站起来跟我握手再见。过了大约1年，我终于忍不住问他："总裁先生，为什么我们谈话时，每次你都以一个半小时为限？"他回答说："原因很简单，我的注意力只能维持一个半小时。不管研究什么问题，超过了这个限度，我的谈话就没有任何新意了。而且，我还知道，如果时间太短，不够一个半小时，我恐怕会掌握不住问题的重心。"

每次会谈，我发现从来没有电话打进来，他的秘书也从来没有推门进来说什么大人物等着见他。有一天我问起这一点，他说："我的秘书知道，在我思考问题时，绝不许任何人来打扰。只有两个人例外：美国总统和我夫人。但是，美国总统很少来电话，而我夫人也深知我的脾气。所以，任何大事，秘书都要等我们谈完后才来告诉我。然后，我再花半小时接听电话，接待访客。当然，你知道，我这样安排也是一种冒险，说不定在我们谈话时，真会有什么天大的事等不及一个半小时呢。"

不用说，这位银行总裁，在我们每月一次会谈中办成的事，远比任何一位同样能干却天天开会的管理者多得多。

然而，即使像他这样一位自律极严的管理者，也常常得至少花费一半时间，来处理许多次要且不一定有意义的事，以及许多身不由己的事，例如接待"顺道来访"的重要客户，参加不一定非他参加不可的会议，批阅不必由他批阅的公文之类。

每次我听到高级主管告诉我，说他至少可以控制自己的一半时间，而且真能自己认为该做什么就做什么。我听了，实在深感有足够的理由来怀疑他根本不知道自己时间耗用的情形。高级主管真能自由运用的时间，大概只有1/4。就是说他只有1/4的时间能用在重大事务上，能用在有所贡献的事务上，能用在他应该做的事务上。这种估计一点不假，任何组织都肯定如此。要有例外的话，也许是政府机构的高级官员——他们非生产性的工作时间，往往要比其他组织的高级主管更多。

一位管理者的职位越高，其不能自行支配的时间也一定越多。组织的规模越大，其用于维系组织运行，而非用于发挥组织功能及生产的时间也一定越多。

因此，有效的管理者知道他必须集中他的自由时间。他知道他需要集中整块时间，时间分割成许多段，等于没有时间。时间如果能集中，即使只有一个工作日的1/4，也足可办理几件大事。反之，零零碎碎的时间，纵然总数有3/4个工作日，也是毫无用处。

所以，时间管理的最后一步，应该是将可由管理者自行支配的零碎时间集中起来。

至于如何集中，则各人有各人的办法。有些高层人员，在一星期内，留有一天在家工作。许多杂志主编和主持研究的科学家，就常采用此法。

还有人将会议、审核、问题分析等例行工作，规定排在一星期内的某两天中办理，而将其他日子的整个上午保留下来，用于处理真正重大的事务。

上个例子中的某银行总裁，正是这样管理时间的。召开业务会议、约请高级职员讨论和接待重要客户之类的工作,都排在星期一和星期五。星期二、三、四的下午,则不排固定的工作,用来处理其他事务,例如研究突发的人事问题、约见回国的国外分行经理、接待重要客户或前往华盛顿出差之类。但是在这三天的上午,他会事先排定时间来处理重要事项,并以90分钟为一个单元。

另一个常见的办法,是每天下午都排定一段时间,在家里办公。

卡尔森教授在他的研究报告中,曾提到一位最有效的管理者。这位管理者每天上午上班前,总有90分钟时间留在家里,不接电话,专门从事研究工作。如果还要准时上班,那么早上在家里自然就得早早开始工作了。不过这种做法,总比每天下班后把重要事务带回家去,晚饭后再花3小时处理的方式好得多。因为那样不免过度劳累了,中年以上的人最好是早睡早起。但现在喜欢把工作带回家来开夜车的人越来越多,这往往会造成一种不好的情况:人们以为可以晚上加班,因此反倒没有抓紧白天的工作时间。

不过,话又得说回来:集中自己的时间,集中的"方法"倒在其次,重要的是时间如何使用。许多人把次要的工作集中起来办理,因而匀出一段整块时间来。但这样的方法并无太大的作用。因为这样的方法,使人在心理或时间上,仍然放不下那些次要的事情,放不下那些很少贡献而又认为不能不做的事情。结果终究还会产生新的时间压力,来占用他的自由时间,牺牲他应该做的事。几天或几星期后,他已经"集中"的自由时间,又会被那些所谓"新的问题、新的紧急事件、新的麻烦"瓜分得无影无踪了。

有效的管理者,第一步应先估计究竟有多少"自由时间"真正是他自己的时间，然后保留出相当分量的一段连续性的整块时间来。一旦发现还有别的事情在"蚕食"他保留的时间，便立刻再仔细分析他的时间记录，再将其中比较次要的工作重新过滤一次。他们已知道这层道理，因此不至于过分删减。

一切卓有成效的管理者都懂得：对时间的控制与管理不能一劳永逸。他们要持续不断地做时间记录，定期对这些记录进行分析，还必须根据自己可以支配的时间的多少，给一些重要的活动定下必须完成的期限。

> 有一位极有效的主管，身边经常带着两张这样的完成期限表。一张是有关紧急事件的，一张是做起来自己并无兴趣但却非做不可的。每次在发现完成时间比预定期限落后时，他就警觉到可支配时间已有溜走的迹象了。

总而言之，时间是最稀有的资源。若不将时间管理好，要想管理好其他事情就只是空谈。而分析自己的时间，也是系统地分析自己的工作，鉴别工作重要性的一种方法。

"认识你自己"这句充满智慧的哲言，对我们一般人来说，真是太难理解了。可是，"认识你的时间"却是任何人只要肯做就能做到的，这是通向贡献和有效性之路。

第3章 | CHAPTER 3

# 我能贡献什么

有效的管理者一定注重贡献,并懂得将自己的工作与长远目标结合起来。他常自问:"对我服务的机构,在绩效和成果上,我能有什么贡献?"他强调的是责任。

重视贡献是有效性的关键。所谓有效性,表现在以下三个方面:①自己的工作,包括工作内容、工作水准、工作标准及其影响;②自己与他人的关系,包括对上司、同事和下属;③各项管理手段的运用,例如会议或报告等。

可是大多数管理者的视线都集中在下方。他们重视勤奋,但忽略成果。他们耿耿于怀的是:所服务的组织和上司是否亏待了他们,是否该为他们做些什么。他们最在意的是"应有"的权威,结果是做事没有成效。

管理顾问公司向委托机构提供服务,总是先花几天时间与委托机构的高级主管交谈。在谈完咨询项目、弄清楚委托机构的组织和历史情况后,管理顾问会问(当然,他不会直接用这里的语句):"你做什么,才匹配得上公司付给你的薪酬?"通常对方的回答总不外是："我主持本公司的会计业务。""我负责销售部门。"也不乏这样的回答："呵！我要管850人的工作！"但是很少有人这样回答："我的任务，是向我们的经理提供他所需的资料，使他能做出正确的决策。""我负责研究本公司的顾客将来需要些什么产品。""我必须深入思考，为我们的总经理即将面临的一些决策问题准备相关资料。"

一个人如果只知道埋头苦干，如果老是强调自己的职权，那不论其职位有多高，也只能算是别人的"下属"。反过来说，一个重视贡献的人，一个注意对成果负责的人，即使他位卑职小，也应该算是"高层管理人员"，因为他能对整个机构的经营绩效负责。

## 管理者的承诺

重视贡献，才能使管理者的注意力不为其本身的专长所限，不为其本身的技术所限，不为其本身所属的部门所限，才能看到整体的绩效，同时也才能使他更加重视外部世界。只有外部世界才是产生成果的地方。因此，他会考虑自己的技能、专长、作用以及所属的部门与整个组织及组织目标的关系。只有这样，他才会凡事都想到顾客、服务对象和病人。事实上一个组织之所以存在，不论其产品是商品、政府的服务，还是健康医疗服务，最终目的总是为了顾客、为了服务对象或为了病人。因此，重视贡献的人，其所作所为可能会与其他人卓然不同。

美国某一颇具规模的公立科学研究所，几年前发生了这样一件事。该研究所的出版部主任退休了。这位主任，早在20世纪30年代该所成立时即服务于出版部。但他本身既不是科学家，也不擅长笔墨。因此,他主持出版的各种书刊常受到批评,说是缺乏学术水准。后来其职位改由一位科学家来继任。当然,从此该所出版的书刊面貌为之一新,具有高度学术水准了。然而,出人意料的是,一向阅读该所书刊的科学团体却从此停止订阅了。一位与该研究所关系甚为密切的大学教授发现了原因。这位教授说:"你们的前任出版部主任,出版的书刊都是'为我们'而写的,而现在的新主任,却把我们当成了写的对象。"

前任主任常自问:"我能为本所贡献些什么?"他认为:"我应该引发外界年轻科学家对本所研究工作的兴趣,吸引他们来参加本所的工作。"因此,他特别强调研究所内的重大事件、重大决策甚至于内部的争执。他这样的做法,曾经屡次引起所长的不满,而且造成了正面冲突。然而他始终坚持这一原则。他说:"我们的出版品是否成功,不在于'我们'爱不爱看,而在于有多少年轻而素质良好的科学家,因读过我们的书刊而愿意前来应征工作。"

提出"我能做出什么贡献"的问题,是为了挖掘工作中尚未发挥的潜力。事实上许多工作看起来成绩辉煌,但是与潜在的贡献比起来,实在是微不足道。

美国某一商业银行设有"代理部",其工作非常单调,却是个盈利部门,专门代理各大公司办理股票债券的登记及交易业务。代理部保存有各发行公司的全部股东名册,要定期填送通知及发放股息,还要做其他各项类似的索然无味的工作。这些工作都需要高度的效率,而且数字绝不能有误。不过,这种工作不需要太多的想象力。

代理部一向这样进行他们的工作,直到有一天,一位新经理上任了。这位新经理提出这样的问题:"我们代理部究竟能做出什么贡献?"他终于发现,代理部经常与各大公司的高级财务主管来往,这些人常握有各公司的存款、贷款、投资和拨存退休金等的决定权。当然,以代理部本身来说,其本职工作必须先做好。但新任经理却从这里发现了一项最大的潜力:该部门可以成为银行其他部门的"推销员"。从此以后,本来只是一个文件处理性质的部门,一下子变成了该银行最成功的营销部门。

管理者如果不自问"我可以做出什么贡献",他在工作中就不会有远大的目标,甚至可能把目标搞错而且特别容易对"贡献"一词只有狭义的理解。

从上面的两个例子不难看出,"贡献"一词在不同的场合有不同的含义。一般机构对成效的要求往往表现在以下三个方面:直接成果;树立新的价值观及对这些价值观的重新确认;培养与开发明天所需要的人才。如果在成效中缺少这三方面中的任何一个方面,机构就会衰败甚至垮台。因此,管理者若想做点贡献,就必须在这三方面下功夫。不过在这三者之中,哪个最重要,哪个其次,就要看管理者本人的情况以及他所处的地位及机构本身的需要了。

以第一方面的绩效而言,直接成果通常最显而易见:在企业机构,销售和利润就是直接成果;在医院,直接成果是对病人的护理和治疗。但是,有时候直接成果也不一定是十分明确的。例如前例中某银行代理部的新任经理,发现该部可成为银行的"推销员"。但不管怎样,如果连管理者自己都弄不清楚应有什么直接成果,那就别想有任何成果了。

以英国的国营航空公司为例来说明。政府将这些航空公司作为企业来管理,同时又认为它们是执行国家政策和维护英联邦团结的工具。

然而，它们实际上又一直是英国航空工业生存与发展的资金来源。三种不同的直接成果混淆在一起，结果是哪一种成果都没有得到。

当然，直接成果应该是最重要的。组织的生存需要直接成果，犹如人需要营养食物一样。但是除了直接成果，一个组织还必须有价值观的承诺与实现，这就像人体除了食物外还少不了维生素和矿物质。一个组织必须有自己的主张和想法，否则就难免解体、混乱和瘫痪。以一个企业机构来说，其价值观的承诺也许是指建立一种技术权威，也许是指为社会大众寻求最好的商品和服务，并以最低的价格和最高的质量来供应。

对价值观的承诺，也像直接成果一样，有时是难以捉摸的。

美国农业部多年来曾为两种根本相异的价值观承诺而痛苦不堪：是为了发展农业生产力，还是为了扶植家庭农场，使之成为美国农业的支柱？为了农业生产力，美国已经朝着农业工业化、高度机械化、大规模商业化的方向发展了。为了扶植家庭农场，则必须设法保持生产力的普通农村形态。美国的农业政策，在这两个极端的价值承诺之间，曾经左摇右摆，真不知花掉了多少经费。

最后我们谈到未来的发展。人都免不了一死，纵然他有再大的贡献，其贡献也因此有一定的限度。而一个组织，大体言之，正是克服这种限度的工具。组织如果不能持续存在，就是失败。所以，一个组织必须今天准备明天的接班人，其人力资源必须更新，必须经常提高水准。下一代的人，应能以这一代辛苦经营的成果为起点。因此，下一代的人是站在他们前辈的肩头，再开创新的高峰，并在此基础上为他们的下一代准备更高的基准线。

一个组织如果仅能维持今天的视野、今天的优点和今天的成就，它就一定会丧失适应力。世事沧桑，一切都在变。所以，只满足于今天的企业，在变幻无常的明天就会感到难以生存下去。

一位管理者能重视贡献，是人才发展最大的动力，因为人可以随外加的要求调整自己。重视贡献的管理者还可以帮助那些与他共事的人将眼光放得更远，这样也就提高了他们的工作水准。

某医院新任院长在召开第一次院务会议时，以为一件棘手的事情经过讨论，已经获得可以使大家都满意的解决办法了。但这时忽然有人提出："这办法能使白莉安护士满意吗？"这个问题一经提出，会议中马上又掀起了热烈的辩论，正反两方都各不相让，直到另一个更为积极的解决办法研究出来。

这位新任院长当时颇为愕然。后来他才知道，白莉安过去曾是该院的一位资深护士。她本人并没有什么特殊才能，连护士长都没当过。但是，每次院中有关病人护理的事情要做出决定时，白莉安小姐都要问："我们对病人是否已尽了最大努力？"凡是白莉安小姐主管的病房中的病人，都痊愈得特别快。因此，多年以来，这家医院人人都知道了所谓"白莉安原则"，那就是，凡事都必须先自问："为贯彻本院的宗旨，我们真是做出了最大的贡献吗？"

虽然当时白莉安小姐早已在十年前退休了，但她所制定的标准，却一直流传至今，为医院同仁所信守。

对贡献的承诺，就是对有效性的承诺。没有这项承诺，管理者就等于没有尽到自己的责任，这必将有损于其服务的组织，也必将有损于与其共事的同事。

管理者的失败，原因有很多。常见的原因，应该是他本人在出任一项新职位时，不能或不愿为适应新职位的需要而改变自身。自以为过去做得成功了，因此满足于老一套的工作方法，结果必然遭到失败。职务有了改变，管理者所要贡献的成果也一定会有所改变，而且新职位所要求的上述三种绩效之间的相对比重也会改变。管理者如果不明白这层道理，仍然墨守他过去的处事方式，即使他过去是以对的方法做对的事情，现在也必将是"以错的方法做错的事情"。

第二次世界大战中，美国政府网罗了许多极具才干的人出任管理者，结果却不尽如人意，其主要原因就在于此。当时有人认为那些人之所以失败，是因为他们不懂"政治"，是因为他们原本独当一面，而到政府后才发现他们只不过是"巨型机器上的小齿轮"。这种说法固然不无道理，但最多只是次要的理由。因为我们同时也看到了许多原来不懂政治的人，许多从来没有领导过下属的人，进入政府后却干得有声有色。例如，当时受征召出任国防情报局长的舍伍德先生（Robert E. Sherwood），原本只是一位剧作家。如果说他曾经主持过什么组织，那也不过是一张书桌和一部打字机而已。然而他却是当年美国政府最有效的一位行政长官。

在战时美国政府有所作为的人，都是重视贡献的人。他们之所以成功，是因为他们能适应新职位而变，能适应不同的价值观承诺而变。而那些工作得很辛苦，却终因为他们不肯向自己提出新的挑战，不能看到改变努力方向的需要的人最终都失败了。

让我们再举一个成功的案例。这是一位年届60出任一家遍布全美的连锁商店总经理的人，之前他一直是该公司第二号人物，达

20多年之久。他的上司（原总经理）比他年轻几岁，是一位外向而积极的主管，但是因为意外去世了。而这位第二号人物之前从来没有想到自己会有机会接任公司的总经理。

这位新总经理，学财务出身，对数字特别在行。凡是公司的成本制度、采购、存货、新设分店的财务调度以及货品运输等，他都能掌握准确的数字。但在他的脑子里，人只是一个模糊的抽象概念。现在，他升任为公司总经理了。他开始自问："我能做哪些别人没有做过的事，如果做得好，能使本公司有所改变呢？"经过一番思索，他得到了结论：如果能替本公司造就明日的经理人才，那就是最有意义的贡献。本来，该公司多年来已有一套发展主管人才的政策。"可是，"这位新任总经理说，"仅有发展人才的政策是没有用的。认真执行这项政策，才是我应有的贡献。"

于是从这时起，每星期三次，在吃过午饭回到办公室时，这位新总经理都顺道前往人事部门，随机抽取八九份年轻干部的人事资料。到了办公室，他打开第一份资料，大致过目一番，然后打一通长途电话到某一分店去："罗经理吗？我是总经理。你们分店中有一位姓钟的小伙子，我知道你半年前曾说过要把他调职，好让他增加一些推销经验。有这回事吗？怎么，还没有调？为什么不给他调呢？"

接着他再打开第二份资料，又挂一通电话到另一家分店："史经理，我是总经理。你那儿有一位陆某某，年纪很轻，你过去建议要调他到会计部磨炼磨炼，是吗？我从人事资料中发现你已经把他调到会计部了。史经理，你是真正在为本公司培植年轻人，我很高兴！"

这位先生担任总经理的时间不长，没有几年就退休了。这段故事，发生在十多年前。但是直到今天，该公司上下每一位主管，都把公司今天的发展归功于他当年对青年经理的培养。

麦克纳马拉在担任美国国防部长期间，有许多了不起的成就。究其原因，大部分是由于麦克纳马拉常检讨"我能有什么贡献"这个问题。他原在福特汽车公司服务，但他完全没有料到1960年秋天，肯尼迪总统会征召他来接任那个内阁中最为棘手的职务。

麦克纳马拉在福特公司时期，是一位地道的"内向型"的人。出任国防部长初期，他完全不懂政治，所以常将国防部和国会之间的联系工作交给部下去处理。几星期之后，他才明白国防部的业务少不了国会的了解和支持。所以，一向不喜欢在公共场所出现的麦克纳马拉，至此也不得不亲自来处理这类他感觉既痛苦又乏味的事了：他要改善与国会的关系，要结识国防委员会中有影响力的议员，要了解协调国会的艺术。当然，麦克纳马拉在这方面的表现并未臻于理想，可是比起任何一位前任部长来，他做得毫不逊色。

麦克纳马拉的故事，说明了一位管理者的职位越高，他在对外方面所需的贡献也越大。因为在一个组织里，通常只有职位最高的管理者，才能在对外方面自由把握尺度。

美国的大学校长有一种通病，过于重视内部的行政管理和筹措经费之类的事务。以大学来说，学生就是学校的"顾客"，但是大学校长以及其他行政主管们，几乎从来没跟他们的顾客建立过关系。1965年加州大学伯克利分校所闹的一次学潮，便表现出大学生的不满与不安，其主要原因就是由于学校行政当局平时跟学生比较疏远。

## 如何使专业人员的工作卓有成效

对知识工作者来说，尤其应该重视贡献。唯有如此，才能够使他的工作真正有所贡献。

知识工作者并不生产"实物"，他生产的是构想、信息和观念。知识工作者通常是一位专业人员。原则上，只有当他掌握了某种专门知识后，他的工作才能卓有成效。也就是说，他必须有所专长。但是，所谓专长，本身就是片面的、孤立的。一个专业人员的产出必须与其他人的产出结合在一起，才能产生成果。

但这意思并不是说专业人员应变成"通才"，而是说专业人员必须使他本人有效，必须使他的专才有效。他必须考虑到他的产出供什么人使用，也必须了解用户应该知道些什么才能有效使用他的产出，从而产生成果。

今天有一种普遍的论调，说我们的社会可以分为"科学家"和"门外汉"两类，因此希望门外汉都应该多少具备一点科学家的常识，了解些科学术语及科学工具。殊不知我们的社会即使真能这样截然划分为两类人，那也是一个世纪以前的社会。事实上，在一个现代组织中，可以说每一个人都是专业人员，各有其专精的知识、工具、观念和术语。而现在科学的门类也越分越细，同是物理学家，可能你不懂我的工作内容，我也不懂你的工作内容。

生物化学家固然是"科学家"，成本会计师又何尝不是。每个人都各有其专业领域、专业知识，各有其假设、关注事项、专业语言。同样地，市场研究人员、计算机编程人员，甚至政府机构的预算人员、医院的精神科医师，也都是科学家。这些人要想使自己的工作卓有成效，就必须先让别人能了解自己。

这意思是说，知识分子有责任让别人了解自己。有些专业人员认为，普通人应该并且可以做出努力来理解他们，甚至认为他们只要能够和同行的少数专业人员沟通就够了，这真是傲慢的自大。即使是在大学或研究所，这样的态度也会使专业人员的工作变成无用，使专业人员的知识学问变成卖弄玄虚的手段（可叹的是，目前这样的态度仍然普遍）。一个人如果想成为管理者，换句话说，如果愿以贡献为目标，就必须使自己的"产品"——即他的知识能为别人所用。

卓有成效的管理者都懂得这一点，因为他们都有想把工作干得更好的心理动力，总想了解别人需要什么、发现了什么以及能理解些什么。他们会向机构内部人员（包括他们的上司、下属，特别是其他部门的同事）提出这样的问题："为便于你为机构做出贡献，你需要我做些什么贡献？需要我在什么时候，以哪种形式，用什么方式来提供这些贡献？"

如果一位成本会计人员能提出这样的问题，就会发现对他来说一目了然的数据，对需要这些数字的经理人来说却是完全陌生的东西。他也会发现，有些数字在他看来很重要，然而经营部门却用不上。他还可能发现，有不少资料是别人每天都需要的，但是他的报表中却没有。

如果制药工厂的生物化学家提出了这样的问题，也会发现他的研究报告应该采用临床医师熟悉的语言，而不能采用生物化学的语言。生物化学家的研究能否发展成为一种新药，是要经过临床试验才能决定的。

政府机构的科学家如果能重视贡献，也会懂得必须将科学发展的趋势及其可能的影响向政策决定人说明。他应打破科学家们的一般禁忌，即猜测一项科学调查的结果。

所谓"通才",应该也是一位专家,是一位能将其所专的一个小领域与其他广大知识领域联系的专家。有少数人也许可以精通几门知识,但这并不意味着他们便是通才,他们不过是精通几门知识的专家而已。仅通一门的专家固然可能偏执,精通几门的专家同样有可能偏执。但是一位专家只要能肩负贡献的责任,就一定能使他所专精的知识配合整体。他尽管不一定能将几门知识整合为一,但他一定知道应该了解别人的需要、别人的方向、别人的限度和别人的理解,以使别人能够应用他的成果。纵然他不能领略广大知识领域的丰富和趣味,至少可以使他不至于沾染傲慢自大的习气。这种习气会毁灭知识,会损害知识的完美和效用。

## 正确的人际关系

在一个组织中,管理者拥有良好的人际关系,绝不是因为他们有"与人交往的天赋",而是因为他们在自己的工作和人际关系上都注重贡献,他们的工作也因此而富有成效,这也许是所谓"良好的人际关系"的真义所在。在以工作或任务为主的环境下,如果我们不能有所成就,那就算我们能与人和谐相处,愉快交谈,又有什么意义呢?这种"和谐相处,愉快交谈"恰恰是恶劣态度的伪装。反过来说,如果能在工作上取得成绩,即使偶尔疾言厉色,也不至于影响人际关系的。

在个人的经验中,最具有良好人际关系的人士,我可以列举三个人:一位是第二次世界大战时美国的陆军参谋长马歇尔将军,一位是曾任通用汽车公司总裁达30余年的斯隆先生,还有一位是斯隆先生的高级主管之一杜瑞斯特。其中杜瑞斯特曾在美国经济萧条时期,替通用公司成功地开发了凯迪拉克牌汽车,此人不幸在第二次世界大战结束后不久去世，要不然很可能出任通用公司总裁。

这三位先生个性各不相同。马歇尔是职业军人，严肃忠诚，但不乏热情。斯隆生就一副"领导"模样，拘谨得体，有令人凛然不可侵犯之感。而杜瑞斯特则是一位具有德国"老海德堡"工匠气质的人，温暖而热情。但这三个人有一项共同点：他们都能极大地激发人们的工作热情，令人乐于亲近。他们三人待人的方式虽各有不同，但都把人际关系建立在"贡献"的基础上。他们能与人密切合作，凡事都设身处地替别人着想。当然，他们也要面临许多严峻的人事决策，但是从来没有受到所谓人际关系的困扰。他们所做的人事决策，人人都视为理所当然。

有效的人际关系，有下列4项基本要求，而着眼于贡献，正可满足这些条件：

- 互相沟通；
- 团队合作；
- 自我发展；
- 培养他人。

（1）互相沟通是多年最引人重视的一项管理课题。无论是在企业界、公共行政机构，还是在军事机关、医院里，这个课题都受到极大的关注。

但结果收效甚微。虽然早在20年前，我们就已知道现代组织需要沟通，也缺乏沟通，可是今天的沟通工作仍然未见有多大改进。不过，至少我们已经开始了解沟通不易收效的原因了。

原来是我们一直把沟通当成是上对下的事，是主管对下属的事。仅靠上对下的单向关系，沟通永远不可能成功。这是我们从实际经验和沟通理论上得到的结论。上级对下属说得越严厉，下属就越听不进去。下属要听的是自己想听的，而不是对方所说的。

一位在工作中以贡献为重的管理者，通常期望其下属也能以贡献为重。因此，他肯定常常问他的下属："我们的组织和我，应该期望你有怎样的贡献呢？我们该期望你做些什么？如何才能使你的知识和能力得到最大的发挥？"有了这样的检讨，才有沟通的可能性，也才容易成功。

下属经过思考提出他认为可以做出的贡献之后，主管才有权利和责任对他所提出的建议是否可行做出判断。

> 我们都有这样的经验：由下属自己设定的目标，往往会在主管的意料之外。换言之，主管和下属看问题的角度往往极不相同。下属越是能干，就越愿意自己承担责任，他们的所见所闻，所看到的客观现实、机会和需要，也就与他们的主管越不相同。此时下属的结论和主管的期望往往是明显对立的。

出现这种分歧时，主管和下属双方究竟谁对，通常并不值得重视，因为上下双方已经建立了有效的沟通。

（2）强调贡献有助于横向的沟通，因此能够促成团队合作。

"谁需要我的产出，并使它产生效益？"这个问题能帮助我们看到与管理者责任范围无关的一些人（既不是他的上级或下级，也不是授权给他或他授权的人）的重要性。这种认识，正是一个知识型组织的现实：在一个知识型组织中，主要有赖于拥有不同的知识和技术的专业人员组成的团队，工作才能有效。各路英雄的合作，贵在自动自发，贵在能依循情势的逻辑和任务的需要，而非仅依赖正式的组织结构。

例如在一所医院中（医院也许是最复杂的一种现代知识型组织），所有的护士、营养师、X光医师、药剂师、病理医师以及其他各方面的专家，都必须共同合作。他们面对同一位病人，但是谁也不觉得受了谁的管理和指挥。然而，他们必须为一个共同目的而工作，而且必须符合总的行动计划，即主治医生的治疗处方。但是从组织结构的立场来说，他们各有各的上级主管。而在医疗工作上，他们各自尽其所长，以专家的身份各尽其责。同时，对一位病人的任何特殊情况及特殊需要，每一个人都必须相互告知。否则，他们的努力很可能只会适得其反。

在一个医院里，如果人人都已将重视贡献，养成了一种近乎天性的习惯，则他们的配合与协作肯定不会有困难。反之，如果没有这种精神，则纵然有最完善的制度、有各式各样的委员会、有会议、有通告、有说教，也仍然不可能有这样的横向沟通，自然也不可能形成一个以正确的任务为中心的工作团队。

今天的机构中所存在的组织问题，绝非传统的观念和理论所能解决。知识工作者必须专精于他的本行，必须对自己的能力和工作标准负责。从正式组织形态来看，他们"隶属"于某一专业职能部门——例如医院中的生物化学部、护理部等。从人事管理立场来看，他们的培训、档案、奖惩、升迁等，也是由专业部门来管理的。但是他们在实际工作的时候，却必须是团队中的一位负责任的成员。他们的团队由来自全然不同领域的知识工作者组成，以当时承担的特定任务为中心。

当然，强调贡献并不一定必能解决组织问题，但至少能够提高对任务和沟通的认识，而使一个尚未臻于理想的组织也能发挥实效。

电脑问世以来，知识工作者相互之间的沟通已变得更加重要。

如何在"信息"中实现"沟通",长期以来一直是一个难以解决的问题。在过去,一切信息都靠人来处理和传送,故往往易因沟通而失真。这就是说,信息在沟通过程中受到各人的看法、印象、意见、判断和偏见的影响。而现在有电脑了,忽然间所有的信息都不经人手了,因而在沟通过程中就不再会带上个人的见解。所有的信息,忽然间都变成纯信息了。在今天,我们的问题是如何建立最低限度的必要沟通,以使我们能相互了解,能认识彼此的需要、目标、感受和处事方式。而纯信息能告诉我们什么呢?唯有靠人与人之间的直接接触,通过语言或文字,才能达到沟通的目的。

信息处理自动化程度越高,我们越需要去创造机会进行有效的沟通。

(3)个人能否有所发展,在很大程度上要看你是否重视贡献。

如果我们自问:我对组织能有什么最大的贡献?这就等于是说:"我需要怎样的自我发展,我应该学习什么知识和技能,才有助于我对组织做出贡献?我应该将我的哪些优点用在我的工作上?我应为自己设定怎样的标准?"

(4)重视贡献的管理者必然会同时启发他人寻求自我发展。这样的管理者设定的标准,一定不是他个人认定的标准,而是以任务需求为基础的标准。而且,他设定的标准,一般来说要求很高,是高度的期望,是远大的目标,是具有重大冲击力的工作。

关于自我发展,我们所知的还很有限。但是我们可以断言:一般人都是根据自己设定的目标和要求成长起来的,知识工作者更是如此。他们自己认为应有怎样的成就,就会有怎样的成长。如果他们对自己的要求不严,就只能原地踏步,不会有任何发展。反之,如果对自己要求很高,他们就一定能成长为杰出的人物,而所费的工夫也不见得比那些没出息的人更多。

## 有效的会议

管理者总不免要参加讨论会、汇报会和简报会等各种会议。会议正是管理者每日使用的管理工具。当然，这些工作也占去了管理者的时间。即使最善于分析其时间和管理时间的人，仍不免花费大量时间于会议和报告上。

卓有成效的管理者知道他们能从会议中得到什么，也知道会议的目的是什么或应该是什么。他会自问："我们为什么要召开这次会议？是为了某项决策？是为了宣布什么？还是为了澄清我们应该做些什么？"他会在事前想清楚会议目的，想清楚要求什么报告以及想清楚简报的用意。他一定坚持开会必须依据之前的承诺，真正有所贡献。

  有效的管理者在会议开始时，会先说明会议的目的和要求达成的贡献。同时，他还要设法让会议紧紧围绕着主题。他绝不会使会议成为一次摆龙门阵的机会，任大家随便发言。当然，如果会议的目的是在激发大家的思想和创见，他也不会仅让某一个人滔滔不绝。他会刺激每一位与会人员的发言兴趣。但是在会议结束之前，他会回到开场所介绍的主题，使会议获得的结论与主题相符。

当然还有其他一些使会议开得有效的办法。（举例来说，简单但是最易被人忽视的一条规则是：你可以主持会议，听取重要的发言，也可以是与大家共同讨论。但你不能既主持会议，又高谈阔论。无论如何，最重要的在于从一开始就把焦点放在贡献上。）

重视贡献，足以消除管理者的一项基本问题：让你在一团乱麻似的事务中理出轻重缓急来。重视贡献是一项组织的原则，使管理者能掌握各项工作的关联性。

重视贡献，还可将管理者的先天弱点（过分依赖他人以及属于组织之内）转变为力量，进而创造出一个坚强的工作团队来。

最后要交代的是，我们常有一种倾向：为组织内部所惑，跳不出组织之外。重视贡献，才能使管理者的视线从"内部事务、内部工作和内部关系"转移到"外部世界"，转移到组织的成果。重视贡献，才能使管理者努力与外界进行直接接触，包括市场和顾客、社区的病人及政府机构以外的公众。

总之，重视贡献，就是重视有效性。

第4章 | CHAPTER 4

# 如何发挥人的长处

有效的管理者能使人发挥其长处。他知道只抓住缺点和短处是干不成任何事的,为实现目标,必须用人所长——用其同事之所长、用其上级之所长和用其本身之所长。利用好这些长处可以给你带来真正的机会。充分发挥人的长处,才是组织存在的唯一目的。要知道任何人都必定有很多缺点和短处,而缺点和短处几乎是不可能改变的,但是我们却可以设法使其不发生作用。管理者的任务,就是要充分运用每一个人的长处,共同完成任务。

## 要用人所长

管理者要运用人的长处,面临的第一关即在于择人。有效的管理者择人任事和升迁,都以一个人能做些什么为基础。所以,他的用人决策,不在于如何克服人的短处,而在于如何发挥人的长处。

美国南北战争时,林肯总统任命格兰特将军为北方军的总司令。当时有人告诉他格兰特嗜酒贪杯，难当大任。林肯却说："如果我知道他喜欢什么酒，我倒应该送他几桶，让大家共享。"林肯总统并不是不知道酗酒可能误事，但他更知道在北军诸将领中，只有格兰特能够运筹帷幄，决胜千里。后来的事实证明了格兰特将军的受命，正是南北战争的转折点。这是一个有效的任命，因为林肯以"取得战役胜利的能力"为标准来选择将军，而不求其没有缺点，是个完人。

当然，林肯最终懂得这种用人之道，也是经过了一番周折的。在这以前，他曾先后选用了三四位将领，选用标准都是他们必须无重大缺点。但结果是，虽然北军拥有人力物力的绝对优势，在1861～1864年间却没有取得任何进展。反之，南方的李将军手下，从杰克逊起，几乎没有一位将领不是满身都是大小缺点。但李将军经过深思熟虑，发现这些缺点无关紧要。他知道他所用的人，每一位都各有所长。而李将军正是善用他们的长处，使他们充分发挥。所以，在那段时期，林肯麾下每一位"无缺点"的将领，一个一个都被李将军手下拥有"一技之长"的将领击败了。

不管是谁，如果他在任用一个人时只想避免短处，那他所领导的组织最终必然是平平庸庸的。所谓"样样皆通"者，即只有长处没有短处的人（也可用其他词来描述这类人，如"完人""个性成熟""个性完美"或"通才"），实际上可能一无是处。才干越高的人，其缺点也往往越多。有高峰必有深谷，谁也不可能是十项全能。与人类现有博大的知识、经验、能力的汇集总和相比，任何伟大的天才都不及格。世界上实在没有真正全能的人，最多只是有在某方面特别有能力的人。

一位管理者如果仅能见人之短而不能识人之长，因而刻意避其所短，而非着眼于发挥其所长，则这位管理者本身就是一位弱者。他会觉得别人的才干可能构成对他本身的威胁。但是，世界上从来没有发生过下属的才干反而害了主管的事。美国的钢铁工业之父卡内基的墓志铭说得最为透彻："这里躺着的人，知道选用比自己能力更强的人来为他工作。"当然，卡内基先生所用的人之所以能力都比他本人强，是因为卡内基能够看到他们的长处，在工作上运用他们的长处。他们只是在某方面有才干，而适于某项特定的工作。卡内基就是他们的卓有成效的管理者。

李将军有一段故事，可以说明使人发挥长处的意义。李将军手下有一位将领常不按照命令行事，往往使李将军预定的计划完全改变。李将军屡次都忍受了，但终于有一次他忍不住大发雷霆。当他平静下来时，一位幕僚问他："你为什么不将他革职呢？"据说当时李将军不禁一时愕然，无以为答，好一会儿他才说："多么荒唐的问题！把他撤了，谁还能打胜仗？"

有效的管理者知道他们之所以用人，是用人来做事，而不是用人来投主管之所好。剧团经理知道，如果女明星常发脾气而有助于票房，也许他之所以受聘为经理，就是为了承受她的脾气。以学校来说，第一流的优秀教师会不会奉承校长，肯不肯在教务会议上安静而不咆哮，那有什么关系呢？校长之所以应聘为校长，就是为了使第一流的教师或学者能够工作有效。所以，即使在其他方面不太愉快，也是值得的。

有效的管理者从来不问："他能跟我合得来吗？"他们问的是："他贡献了什么？"他们从来不问："他不能做什么？"他们问的是："他能把什么做好？"所以在用人时，他们用的都是在某一方面有所长的人，而不是在各方面都过得去的人。

识人之所长以及用人之所长，可以说是人的一种本能。所谓的"完美的人"或"成熟的个性"，这些说法其实都忽视了人最特殊的天赋：人本能地会将其一切资源都用于某项活动、某个领域，以期取得某个方面的成就。换言之，类似"完美的人"的说法是忽视了人的卓越性。因为卓越通常只能表现在某一个方面，最多也只能表现在个别的几个方面。

当然，世上确有多才多艺的人，这就是通常所谓的"全才"。但真正能在多方面都有杰出造诣的人，至今还没有出现。达·芬奇算是多才多艺了，但他最突出的成就只是在绘画上。歌德的诗如果没有流传下来，那即使他对光学和哲学有研究，也不见得能在百科全书上找到他的赫赫大名。几位世人皆知的伟人尚且如此，更何况我们这些凡人。因此，一位管理者如果不能发掘人的长处，并设法使其长处发挥作用，那么他只有受到人之弱点、人之短处、人之缺失的影响，结果是既完不成任务，又缺乏有效性。用人时老是坚持客观上不可能达到的标准，或过多地强调别人的弱点，那纵然算不上是对人力资源的滥用，起码也是误用。

重视一个人的长处，也就是要对他的工作绩效提出要求。如果管理者不在用人之前先问自己"他能做些什么"，那可以肯定他的下属绝难有贡献，这就等于他已经事先对下属的不称职采取了宽容的态度。这样的管理者成事不足，败事有余。真正"苛求的上司"（实际上懂得用人的上司大部分都是"苛求"的上司），总是先发掘一个人最擅长做些什么，再来"苛求"他做些什么。

过多考虑人的短处，会对组织成功实现自己的目标造成不利的影响。组织有一种特殊的手段，它既可以使人的长处得到发挥，又可以使人的短处所带来的不利影响减少到最低程度。能力特别强的人既不需要组织，也不想受组织的束缚，他们觉得自己一个人干最好。但我们绝大多数的人，只是具有若干长处，何况我们还有缺点。人际关系专家有一句俗语："你要雇用一个人的手，就得雇用他整个的人。"同样的道理，一个人不可能只有长处，他必然也有短处。

但是我们可以设置一个组织，使得身处其中的人的弱点不致影响到其工作和成就。换言之，我们可以把组织设置得有利于充分发挥员工的长处。一位优秀的税务会计师，自行执业时可能因拙于待人而遇到挫折。但是在一个组织中，他可以自设一间办公室，不与其他人直接接触。人的长处可在组织中产生实效，而人的短处可以使其不产生作用。同样的道理，一位小企业家精通财务，但可能因不懂产销而受困。而在较大规模的企业中，一位仅懂财务的人却可能极具生产性。

有效的管理者并不是不知道人有缺点。他了解他自己的任务在于如何使某人充分发挥其税务会计的才干，而不斤斤计较他不善于与人打交道。因此，他不会贸然指派这个人出任经理的职位。要与人打交道，完全可以找别人，而第一流的税务会计师则是不可多得的人才。所以，这个人能够做什么，才是组织器重他的原因。而他不能做什么，则是他的限制，仅此而已。

这层道理谁都清楚。可是，为什么做起来又是另一回事呢？为什么世间的管理者很多，而真能发挥他人长处者却不多？以林肯为例，为什么他要在三次关注缺点的任命之后，才能学会用人所长的道理？

原因很简单。主要是因为管理者往往以为他们首要的任务不在于因人设事，而在于因事用人。所以，通常是先有了某一个职位，再物色人选来出任该职位。这样的步骤，往往引人走入歧途，物色的对象，往往只是一位"最不至于出差错"的人选——也就是"仅合乎最低要求"的人选。其结果，自然难免都是平平庸庸的人选了。

要避免出现这一错误，最常见的解决办法是"因人设事"。然而这哪是什么解决办法，这也许比原有的错误还糟，除非是规模极小、事务极简的组织。要知道职位应该是根据客观需要而设定的，应由任务而定，而不应因人而定。

为什么"因人设事"不能解决问题，是因为组织中任何一个职位的变更，都会造成一连串的连锁反应。组织中的职位都是相互联系、相互依存的，牵一发而动全身。我们不能为了替某人安插一个职位，而使组织中的每一个人都受到牵连。"因人设事"几乎会导致一个必然的后果：造成职位的要求与现有人手之间更大的差距。因人设事的结果，是为了安插某一个人，一大群人都受到连累。

这种现象，并不仅仅出现在政府机构或大企业中。比如学校需要一位讲授生物化学概论的教授。这位教授当然应该是一位好老师，是一位专家。但是生物化学概论这门课程，不论教授个人的兴趣如何，都必须包括这门学科的基本原理。该讲授什么，应按学生的需要（这就是客观的需要）而定，无论由谁讲授，都应该讲授这些内容。交响乐团缺了一位大提琴手，乐团指挥绝不会选用一位不擅大提琴但双簧管吹得极好的人选来充数，即使此人吹双簧管的名气远比其他大提琴手响亮，指挥也不会这样做。当然，他更不会为了某一乐师而重写乐谱。剧团经理明知道他的卖座女明星爱耍脾气，也会承受她的脾气，但他却不会因为她发脾气而更改已经宣布的节目单。

我们要坚持因事用人而非因人设事，还有一个微妙的原因。因为只有这样，我们才能为组织提供所需的各种人才，也只有这样，我们才能容忍各色人等的脾气和个性。能容忍这些差异，内部关系也才能保持以任务为重心，而非以人为重心。衡量成就的高低，应该按照贡献和绩效的客观标准。只有在职位的设计和划分不以人为中心时，这种衡量才有可能。不然的话，我们就会只注意"谁好谁坏"，而忽略了"什么好什么坏"。用人的时候，我们也会仅考虑"我喜欢这个人吗"或"这个人能用吗",而不会考虑"这个人在这个职位上,是不是能干得非常出色"。

因人设事的结果,是必将产生恩怨派系,组织绝对不能出现这种情况。人事的决策,要凭公平和公正,否则就会赶走了好人,或破坏好人的干劲。同时,组织也需要各方面的人才,否则将缺乏改变的能力,也将难于得到做出正确的决策所需的不同意见(这一点将在第7章中讨论)。

> 我们常常可以听到这样的说法:能建立起第一流经营体制的管理者,通常不会与周围的同事及下属保持过分亲密的关系。不能根据个人的好恶来挑选人才,而应当看他们能干些什么,看他们的工作表现,绝不能看他们是否顺从自己。因此,为了确保能够选用适当的人选,管理者应该与直接的同事或下属保持适当的距离。
>
> 林肯起初也重视亲近的朋友,例如当时的国防部长斯坦顿。但是直到后来与僚属保持距离,林肯才成为一位有效的管理者。富兰克林·罗斯福总统也是如此:在他的内阁中,没有"亲信",即使他的国防部长摩根塞,也只在公事以外才是他的朋友。马歇尔将军和通用汽车公司的斯隆先生,也同样是可望而不可即的人物。其实这几位成功的人物也是很热情的,他们渴望有密切的人际关系,喜欢交朋友。但他们知道,"公事以外"才是朋友,他们知道不能受感情的影响。保持一定的距离,他们才能建立起人人各有所长的团队。

当然,凡事不可一概而论,有时确实有因人设事的必要。以斯隆先生为例,他一向不主张因人设事,但当他面对凯特林这位天才发明家时,忍不住为其设置了一个工程技术部门,这就是通用汽车公司早期的工程技术部。罗斯福总统当年任用体衰力竭的霍普金斯,为了借重此君的长才,也打破了各种常规。不过,这种例外总是极为罕见的,它只适用于有特殊的才能,从事非同一般的工作,并取得了杰出成就的人。

现在我们要问,卓有成效的管理者究竟该怎样用人,才能既发挥他人的长处,又不致陷入因人设事的陷阱呢?

大致来说,不外乎下面 4 个原则。

(1) 卓有成效的管理者不会认为职位是上天或上帝创造的。职位是由人设计,是人都可能犯错。因此,他们绝不会设计一个"不可能达成"的职位,换言之,不会设计一个"常人"不可能胜任的职位。

但是那样的职位却很常见。有些职位设定了,写在纸上,看起来非常合理,却永远找不到合适的人选。一个又一个颇有才能的人都尝试了这个职位,但是没有人成功,一年半载之后,所有的尝试者都失败了。

为什么会有这样的职位呢?通常是因为先前已有了一位非常人物,所以才按照这一人物的特殊天分和气质定下了职位条件。于是这一职位,便需要具有多方气质的人。可是天下哪里找这样的人?一个人也许能有多方面的知识,也许能有多方面的技能,但是谈到气质,谁也不能改变。如果一个职位,要有特殊气质的人才能胜任,这便注定了是不可能胜任的职位,是一个"坑人的职位"。

总之,这第 1 条原则非常简单:一个职位,如果先后由两人或三人担任都失败了,这就肯定是一个常人无法胜任的职位,这个职位就必须重新设计。

在营销学教科书中,常说销售管理应包括广告和促销,应隶属于同一位营销主管。可是,一些知名的消费品生产厂家的经验说明,设置一个总揽全部营销业务的职位,根本是行不通的。如果行得通,那么出任这一职位的人,一方面要有高度的第一线销售能力——如何有效推动"物";一方面又要有高度的广告和促销能力——如何有效推动"人"。这就要求做这项工作的人有各种不同的性格特点。这样的人，在世上是很难找的。

另一个例子：美国某一大学的校长，也是一个不可能胜任的职位。至少我们可以知道，曾经出任这所学校校长的人，先后不知有多少了，而能成功者，简直少之又少。历任的校长，过去在别的大学担任校长非常成功，而在这所学校却失败了。

还有一个例子：在今天的跨国大企业中，设置了专营国际业务的副总裁的职位。起初，这一职位也许还能找到理想人选，但是等到国外分公司的产销业务成长到相当程度，也许是成长到占总公司产销总额 1/5 以上时，就会将件件"非总公司"的事情推到副总裁身上，国际部副总裁便成为坑人的职位了。要解决这个问题，不是应按产品类别来调整组织（例如荷兰飞利浦公司所做的），便是应按市场的社会和经济背景来调整组织。例如：国际部副总裁不妨分设三位，一位管高度发达国家（美国、加拿大、日本和西欧国家）的业务，一位管发展中国家（澳大利亚、印度和拉丁美洲及近东的国家）的业务，另一位管其余不发达国家的业务。一些化学工业公司走的就是这条路。

今天一个大国的驻外使节，也要面临同样的情形。驻外的使馆，其业务之广、之难、之杂，实在叫身为大使者头痛至极。大使的能力尽管高强，但是在管理使馆业务之余，恐怕就没有时间，也没有心情去关心身为大使的首要工作了。例如，就没有时间去了解驻在国的国情，驻在国的政府、政策、人民以及如何使驻在国政府认识和信任他。再以美国的五角大楼来说，虽然麦克纳马拉有降龙伏虎的本领，堪当重任，但我还是觉得美国国防部长这个职位是很难做好的（然而我不能不承认，这一问题我也想不出解决的办法）。

所以，有效的管理者，第一项任务就是要将自己管辖下的职位都设置得合情合理。一旦发现某职位设计不当，他会立刻重新设计，而不会去设法寻找天才来担任，他知道组织的好坏不是由天才来验证的。只有"让平凡人都能做出不平凡的事"的组织，才是好的组织。

（2）用人所长的第2个原则是：职位的要求要严格，而涵盖要广。这是说，合理的职位，是对具有才干的人的挑战。同时因为职位的涵盖很广，所以人们可以把与任务有关的优势转化为切实的成果。

然而，许多大型组织的政策却与此背道而驰。它们的职位设计过于具体，看起来似乎非要经过"特殊设计"和"特殊加工"的人选，才能达成职位的要求，以便在某一特定时刻做出特定绩效。殊不知我们所能找出的人选，都是普通人。而且，职位的要求往往会随情况而变动，甚至变动得非常剧烈。于是，一位本来"绝对适合"的人选，可能忽然间完全不适合这一职位了。只有把职位设计得涵盖较广且要求较严，才能使人在情况有所变化时能适应新的需要。

对于初级的知识工作的职位，这一原则尤其适用。尽管一位新人的能力不高，但他出任一项职位后，应该使他能有充分展现其长处的机会。一位知识工作者在初任某一职位时，其职位的标准，应能作为他日后发展的引导，应能成为他衡量自己、评估贡献的依据。知识工作者在尚未担任一项成熟的职位之前，通常没有表现才能的机会。他在学校念书时，最多只能显示他将来的可能成就。而实际的成就，只有在实际工作中才能表现。研究所的工作，学校的教职，企业和政府机构的职位，莫不如此。对一位知识工作者，其同事及其上级主管最需要了解的，便是他实际上究竟能做些什么。

知识工作者职位的设计，还应该能够使人及早发现自己是否适合该职位，甚至是否适合此类工作。有关测试一个人是否适合某一职位，在体力工作方面我们已经有了相当可靠的方法了。例如，某人能否担任木工、某人能否担任车工，我们都可以事先测试出来。可是，在知识工作方面，我们还找不到一套事先测试的方法。这是因为对于知识工作，需要的并非这种技能或那种技能，对于其具体的工作要求最多只能大概描述出一个轮廓。因此，知识工作者是否适合某一职位，便只有靠实际的工作绩效才能印证了。

木工或车工的职位属于技能性质：这家工厂的木工或车工，与那家工厂的木工或车工，不会有太大的差异。可是知识工作者则大不相同：某人在某一组织能有什么贡献，他本身的知识和技能是一个因素，组织的价值观和目标也是同样重要的因素。一位年轻人在某一组织也许颇有贡献，而换到另一组织后，说不定完全不行了。而前后两个组织，表面上看来也许完全相同。因此，一位知识工作者出任某一职位时，该职位应使他能够衡量他自己，也应使他能够衡量他的组织。

这一原则，不但适用于性质不同的各种组织，例如政府机构、学校、企业机构，而且也适用于性质相同的各种组织。在我接触过的许多大企业中，几乎从来没有发现有两个组织的价值观完全相同，对贡献的重视完全相同。以学校来说，一位大学教授服务于某校，能够胜任愉快，贡献很大，但调到另一大学，很可能迷惘而不知所措。同样地，政府机构也是如此。虽然国会的内政委员会用了很大的力量，设法使政府机构都遵行同样的制度，都采取同样的尺度，可是不出三五年，一个机构必然会发展出其独特的性格来。每一个机构对其各级职员，尤其是对专业人员，必然各有不同的行为要求，以帮助他们做到卓有成效并有所贡献。

一个人在年轻时，要调动工作并不难。至少在西方国家，年轻人转换行业司空见惯。但是，如果某人在同一组织里干了十年以上，再想变动就难了,尤其是那些工作缺乏成效的人,就更为困难。所以,一位年轻的知识工作者,应该趁早做自我检讨:"就我的能力来看,我在这个组织中担任这个工作,是不是最适合?"

但是,如果他初任的职位涵盖太小,工作太简单,同时这职位又正是不需要经验、不能考验他能做什么的,那么他就无法做这样的自我检讨,当然也更无从回答了。

每次对年轻的知识工作者进行调查,例如军队里的医生、研究机构的化学家、工厂中的会计人员和工程师以及医院的护士等,几乎都得到同样的结论:凡是最能充分发挥其长处,而且最受到挑战的人,他的工作肯定最起劲,也肯定最能有所成就。而对工作不满的人,大都是异口同声地埋怨:"他们没有让我充分发挥所长!"

年轻的知识工作者的职位涵盖范围太窄,不足以向他的能力挑战,其结果不是他自请离职,便是很快变成"老油条"。我们常听到许多主管感慨地说:想不到满怀壮志的年轻人,会一个接一个消沉下去。其实这不怪别人,只能怪这些主管,是他们自己冻结了年轻人的热情,他们将职位设计得涵盖范围太窄了。

(3)第3个原则,是卓有成效的管理者在用人时,会先考虑某人能做些什么,而不是先考虑职位的要求是什么。换言之,有效的管理者早在决定将某人安置于某职位之前,会先仔细考虑这个人的条件,而且他考虑时绝不会只局限于这个职位。

这就是大家都广泛采用今天这种定期的评估程序来鉴别人才,特别是知识工作者的理由。其目的,就是帮助管理者在决定某人是否适宜担当重要职务前,先对其有个正确的评价。

尽管几乎每个大型组织都有一套评估考核人才的程序,但事实上这套程序很少被真正采用。管理者口口声声地说,他们每一年都按规定考评他们的下属,可据我所知,他们自己却从未被他们的上司考评过。情况通常是这样的:年年考评,年年归档,而在真要做某项人事决策时,谁也不会专门为此去翻阅档案,人人都将考评表视同无用的废纸。此外还有所谓面谈考评的制度:由主管与下属面对面地讨论。可是这种面谈考评,事实上也从来没有真正实行过。然而,面谈考评却正是整个考评制度的重心所在。为什么面谈考评没有人肯用呢?最近我看到一本管理新书的广告,道出了其中一个原因:原来所有的主管都认为面谈考评是一件最令上级感到难堪的工作。

今天大多数组织制定的考评办法,其实最初是由临床与变态心理学家出于自己的目的而设计的。医生的目的在于治病,医生重视的是病人的毛病,而不是病人的优点。凡是医生都有一种想法:健康的人是不会来找他的。所以,以临床心理学家或变态心理学家的立场来说,找毛病是诊断疾病的一个过程。

  我是在与日本管理界接触之后才开始意识到这个问题的。有一次在日本主持一个管理发展研讨会,参加者都是日本大企业的高层人员。我发现日本根本没有考评制度,当时我觉得万分奇怪。我问起他们,他们告诉我说:"你们的考评制度,目的只是发现一个人的错误和弱点。但在我们日本,由于不能因为某人有缺点而把他开除或降级,我们自然对考评制度不感兴趣了。反过来说,我们倒以为最好不要知道一个人的缺点。我们想知道的,是他有什么优点,他能做些什么。而你们的考评制度,根本不重视这一点。"日本人这一番话,西方心理学家听了,尤其是设计考评制度的人士听了,肯定会大不以为然。但事实上这正是每一位日本、美国或德国的主管,对传统考评制度的看法呢。

  西方人士似乎不能不对日本人的成就加以深思了。我们都知道,日本有一种"终身雇用"的制度。一个人进了一家公司,他就会逐年升迁,平均每15年薪水增加一倍。他不会随便辞职,公司也不能把他开除。除非年龄到了45岁,或者位置升到了顶点,才显出事业生涯的分歧:其中少数能力特别强的人,可以继续升到高级主管的位置。日本这套制度,与日本今天取得的巨大发展有什么关联呢?答案很简单:由于日本有这套制度,所以他们可以闭上眼睛,不看人的缺点。尤其是因为日本的管理者不能开除人,所以他们就只有从下属中去发掘能做事的人了。他们看人,只看人之所长。

其实,我也并不完全同意日本的办法,那毕竟不是一套理想的制度。在那种制度下,事实上只有很少数真有能力的人才能承担重任,而大多数的人都将成为公司的负担。但是,如果西方国家真正打算利用我们人事流动性的优点,看起来我们真该学学日本那套制度的精神:见人之所长和用人之所长。

如果一位主管专找下属的缺点——例如我们的考评制度,这必将破坏主管与下属之间的团结。许多管理者虽然实际上已把考评制度束之高阁,但是他们仍然有敏锐的直觉。他们认为面谈考评是找下属的错误和缺点,因此对这种制度索然寡味。这个看法的确情有可原。病人找医生,医生的责任当然是找出病人的毛病,这原是自古以来医生和病人之间天经地义的关系,这种关系是以专业性和享有特权为前提的。可是,将这层关系用到主管和下属之间,就有不伦不类之嫌,会造成双方无法合作。所以,管理者不肯运用考评制度是不足为奇的。考评制度的确是一种错误的工具,用错了地方,也弄错了目标。

但是考评制度及其指导思想,据说是可以发掘人的"潜能"的。然而,发掘潜能谈何容易。有经验的人都知道:事先发掘潜能,或根据一个人现在所做的工作去评估他做另一项工作的潜能,简直是不可能的事。所谓"潜能",只是"有希望"的一个代名词。即使"希望"存在,它也可能无法实现,而另一些人尽管从未显示出有什么希望(可能仅仅是因为不曾有这种机会),但他们实际上却做出了成绩。

我们所能评估的,只有绩效。我们所应该评估的,也只有绩效。这是必须将职位设计得涵盖较广且具有挑战性的另一个原因。这也是个人必须认真考虑,自己能为组织做出什么贡献的原因,因为一个人的绩效如何,只有在组织希望此人做出具体成绩的背景下,才能评估出来。

但是,一套适当的考评方式,毕竟是不可少的。否则,当一个职务需要某人来承担时,就没办法对他做出正确的评价。因此,有效的管理者,通常总有他自己的一套与众不同的考评方式。这套方式,第一步是列出对某人过去职务和现任职务所期望的贡献,再把某人的实际绩效记录与这项期望贡献相对照,然后检讨下面的 4 个问题。

①哪方面的工作他确实做得很好?
②因此,哪方面的工作他可能会做得更好?
③为了充分发挥他的长处,他还应该再学习或获得哪些知识?
④如果我有个儿子或女儿,我愿意让我的子女在他的指导下工作吗?
  a. 如果愿意,理由是什么?
  b. 如果不愿意,理由是什么?

这样的考评方式,显然与通常的做法不同,能更加客观地看待一个人。这套方式以当事人的长处为重心,以当事人能做些什么开始。而当事人的缺点,只是视为他发挥长处和力求成就与有效性的限制而已。

上面的问题,只有最后一题(如果我有个儿子或女儿,我愿意让我的子女在他的指导下工作吗)不是以当事人的长处为主。身为他人下属者,尤其是年轻、聪明和有志向的人,通常都会以一位有魄力的上司为楷模而塑造自己。所以,一个组织如果有一位具有魄力但很腐败的管理者,恐怕这是最糟的事了。像这样的人，如果他自己单干，也许还可以；如果是在一个组织里，但是不让他管辖别人，也许他还能得到容忍；可是如果在组织中叫他当权，那就成事不足、败事有余了。因此，在这方面，我们必须注意一个人的缺点所在，这是攸关组织成败的问题。

正直的品格本身并不一定能成就什么，但是一个人如果缺乏正直和诚实，则足以败事。所以人在这方面的缺点，不能仅视为绩效的限制。有这种缺点的人，没有资格做管理者。

（4）第4个原则是，卓有成效的管理者知道在用人之所长的同时，必须容忍人之所短。

> 古来许多军事名将，几乎没人不是以自我为中心、自高自傲的人物（但是反之却不尽然，自高自傲者未必能成为名将）。同样地，一个政治家如果不胸怀壮志，不立志成为总统或首相，那他就很难成为伟大的政治家，他最多只能成为一位优秀的人才。人要向上，必须有大志，自视甚高，以天下为己任（同样地，反之也未必尽然）。所以，如果需要的是一位确能履险如夷、担当重任的人物，我们就必须接受像迪斯雷利⊖或罗斯福那样的人物，而不必去介意他们的态度缺少谦恭。西方谚语说："仆从眼中无英雄。"与英雄接近的人，总能发现英雄的缺点。当然，令人发笑的一方肯定是仆从。仆从眼中所见英雄的缺点，无害其为英雄，更无害于他们在历史舞台上呼风唤雨。

所以，有效的管理者会问："这个人在某方面是否确有长处？他的长处，是否确为某一任务所需？这个人如果担当这项任务，是否确能表现得与众不

---

⊖ 迪斯雷利（Benjamin Disraeli），英国政治家，曾两度担任英国首相。——编者注

同？"如果答案为"是"，那就不必犹豫，而继续聘用此人。

俗语说："三个臭皮匠，顶个诸葛亮。"但是有效的管理者却不这样想。他知道，三个臭皮匠，往往还比不上一个臭皮匠，因为他们会各行其是。有效的管理者知道，要说人的能力，就必须具体到能不能完成任务。他们不喜欢笼统地说某人是个"能人"，而只会说某人在完成某项任务方面是个"能人"。这些管理者总是结合具体任务来寻找别人的长处，以达到用人之长的目的。

这也意味着这些管理者在用人时必须重视机会，而不能只抓存在的问题。

更重要的是，有效的管理者对一位得力的人才，绝不会说："我少不了他，少了他，我的事就办不成了。"通常我们说"少不了某人"，其原因不外三点：一是某人其实并不行，不过是管理者没有对他苛求而已，他本人也只能在这种保护下生存；二是管理者本人的能力太差，实际上是误用了某人的才干来勉强支持一个自己很难站得住脚的上司；三是本来就潜伏着某项严重问题，因为误用某人的才干而将该项问题掩盖住了。

在上述三种情形之下，所谓"少不了的某人"，无论如何都应该调职，越快越好。否则的话，某人的才干再高，也将被糟蹋掉。

本书第 3 章曾说到美国一家连锁商店新任总经理提拔年轻职员的故事。那位总经理还有一套手法：只要一位主管说起"少不了某人"，他便立刻将那位"少不了的某人"调职。他说："一位主管如果说少不了某人，那么不是主管不行，就肯定是那位少不了的某人不行，甚至于两人都不行。所以，我每次听到这句话，就会设法尽快找出答案来。"

总之，只有经得起绩效考验的人，才是可以提升的人。这应该是一条用人的铁律。不管别人以什么理由反对，说"少不了他"，说"调到别处怕别处不能接受"，说"他年纪太轻了"，或者说"他在第一线的经验不够，所以不宜调任"，都不必理会。要知道这并不仅仅是因为一个职位需要最适当的人选，也是要让有绩效之人能赢得机会。用人应着眼于机会，而非着眼于问题，这样做不但能开创一个有效的组织，也能够激发热情和忠诚。

反过来说，对一个没有突出表现的人，尤其是一个没有突出表现的主管，应该无情地调职，这是管理者的责任。任他留下来，必将影响全体人员，而且对于整个组织也是不公平的。对他的下属，则尤为不公平，因为主管无能，则不啻剥夺了下属发挥长处的机会。而且，对于他本身，也是一种残忍。不管是否承认，他肯定自知能力不够。结果此人不是饱受压力和痛苦的煎熬，就必是默默祈求早日脱离苦海。日本所谓的终身雇用和西方国家的文官制度，都不主张撤换已被证实不胜任的人，这的确是个严重的问题，我们没有必要再去犯这样的错误。

第二次世界大战时，马歇尔将军也曾说过：一位将军如果没有特优表现，就必须立即调职。马歇尔将军认为如果不调职，那是与军队和国家赋予军人的职责背道而驰的。但是常有人说："主管调职，我们找不出继任人选了。"而马歇尔将军并不理会这类意见。他说："我们重视的，只是这位主管不能胜任工作，至于如何去物色继任人选，那是另外一回事。"

但是马歇尔将军还认为，将一位不称职人员调职，与其说是反映了对这个人的看法，倒不如说是对任命他的人有看法。他说："某人不称职，只是不称'此'职，并不是说他也肯定不能胜任别的职务。所以，选派某人出任这个职务，是我的错误，我应该负责再给他找到适合的工作。"

马歇尔将军的故事，是如何用人所长的最佳说明。20世纪30年代中期，马歇尔将军出任要职之前，美国陆军几乎没有堪当重任的年轻将官（事实上马歇尔将军本人，1939年9月1日出任参谋总长时，是仅以4个月之差，躲开任职年龄的限制——他的60岁生日是该年12月31日）。第二次世界大战期间，经马歇尔将军提拔而后来升为将级军官的人选，在当时几乎都是籍籍无名的年轻将官，艾森豪威尔将军也是其中之一。在20世纪30年代，他只是个少校。到了1942年，由于马歇尔将军的用人得当，已替美国造就了一大批有史以来最能干的将领。经他提拔的将领，几乎无人失败，而且他们都是第一流的人才。

这真是美国军事教育史上最辉煌的一页。然而写下这一页的马歇尔将军，其本人"望之不似人君"，不像蒙哥马利、戴高乐和麦克阿瑟等人那样具有慑人的威仪和高度的自信，他坚持的是原则。他用人时常自问："此人能做些什么？"只要能做些什么，则这个人的不足之处就成为次要的了。

举例来说，马歇尔将军曾一再替巴顿将军辩护，说这位有雄心而自负的战时将领，不应因为他缺少做幕僚应有的气质，以及不能担任和平时期的军人，而否认他是一位优秀的将军。其实，马歇尔本人并不喜欢巴顿将军那种少爷型的军人性格。

但是马歇尔将军也并非完全不顾一个人的弱点。在弱点可能影响这个人充分发挥长处时，他就要考虑这个人的弱点了。但他所考虑的，是如何运用工作和职业机会来帮助这个人克服这些弱点。

例如艾森豪威尔将军在年轻时，马歇尔将军曾有意将他安插在作战计划部门，以帮助他获得系统的战略知识，而艾森豪威尔显然缺乏这方面的知识。当然，艾森豪威尔将军并没有因此成为战略家，却从此懂得了战略的重要性。正因为如此，不长于战略原为艾森豪威尔将军的弱点，但由于那段经历，使他更能发挥组织和策划方面的长处。

马歇尔将军任命一个人出任某个新职，从来不考虑此人在原单位"如何重要，如何缺少不了"。每次当他宣布某人调任新职时，总有人劝他考虑，说某人在原单位确实是"缺少不了的"，但他的答复是："调他出任新职，是工作的需要，是为了他本身，也是为了部队。"

只有一次例外：马歇尔将军本人在政府工作时，罗斯福总统曾说他"实在离不开马歇尔"。马歇尔因此毅然留在罗斯福身边，而将欧洲统帅之职交给了艾森豪威尔将军，放弃了实现毕生最伟大理想的机会。

后来马歇尔将军终于认识到（别人也可以从他的经历中学到这一点）：任何一项人事任命都是一个赌注。但是，只要能抓住某人的长处，这至少是合理的赌注。

主管对下属的工作负有责任，也掌握了下属前途发展的权力。用人所长，不仅是有效性的要素，也是主管对下属的道义责任，是主管对其职权和地位的责任。专注于人之所短，不仅是愚不可及，更是有愧职守。尽量发挥下属的长处，不但是管理者必须对机构承担的义务，更重要的是，这也是为人处世的道理：他应该协助下属得到应有的发展。组织必须为每一位成员服务，使每一位成员都能凭其才干达成成就，而不必顾念其所短。

这项原则在今天已日显重要，而且攸关成败。从前，知识工作的职位为数很少，知识工作的就业范围也很窄。以欧洲的德国和斯堪的那维亚半岛的几个国家来说，在那时候，政府公务人员只有获得法律学位的人才能担任。数学家根本用不上。再说，一位年轻人希望学有所用，只有三四条路可以选择。然而时至今天，知识工作的种类已大为扩展，知识分子可走的路也增加了很多。20世纪之初，知识工作的范围仍只是几项传统的自由职业——律师、医师、教师等。而今天，几乎每一门学问，都有广大的天地。尤其是企业机构和政府，都在招收学有专精的人才。

从一方面来说，今天的人才有可能找到最适合自己能力的工作领域，不必像过去一样要迁就工作的需要。但从另一方面来说，年轻人要选择适合自己的工作也显得越来越困难了，因为他不一定能得到有关自己和有关工作机会的各种信息。

这种情况下，个人更需要得到适当的指导，好帮助他们发挥长处；组织中的各级主管也更需要用人唯才，并致力于发挥人们的长处。

总结一句：用人所长是卓有成效的管理者必须具备的一种素质，是一个组织工作是否有效的关键，也是知识工作者和社会不可或缺的素质。

## 如何管理上司

卓有成效的管理者还要设法充分发挥上司的长处，这也是非常重要的。

但是，我却很少看见哪位管理者注意如何管理上司的课题。他们也许会说："管理下属，我没有什么困难。但是我如何能管理我的上司呢？"管理上司其实不难，但只有有效的管理者才能了解其中的奥妙，就在于运用上司的长处。

在具体做法上当然应该谨慎小心。实际上，如果上级主管的能力不够，下属通常是无法爬升上去的。上司如果没有升迁，下属只好永远屈居其下。如果有一天上司因成绩不佳调职了，继任者也往往都是来自别的部门，很少在本单位中选人提升。而且新上司到任时，也总是带来他自己的亲信。反之，凡是成功而升迁得快的主管，其下属也是最容易成功的。

暂且不谈谨慎小心，实际上，运用上司的长处，也是下属工作卓有成效的关键。只有如此，身为下属者才能将精力集中在自身的贡献上，完成自己想做的工作，取得希望取得的成就。

要使上司能发挥其所长，不能靠唯命是从，应该从正确的事情着手，并以上司能够接受的方式向其提出建议。

有效的管理者了解他的上司也是人（然而年轻的下属却不容易有此了解）。上司既然是人，所以肯定有其长处，也肯定有其短处。若能在上司的长处上下功夫，协助他做好能做的工作，便能使上司有效，下属也才能有效。反之，如果下属总强调上司的短处，那就像上司强调下属的短处一样，结果将一无所成。所以，有效的管理者常问："我的上司究竟能做好什么？他曾有过什么成就？要使他发挥他的长处，他还需要知道些什么？他需要我完成什么？"至于上司不能做些什么，那就不必细究了。

一般人常想到如何"改变"他的上司。以政府机构来说，能干的高级官员，常以老师的姿态对待新到任的领导，设法使他的领导克服其缺点。但是有效的管理者考虑的却是："这位新领导能做些什么？"如果说"他擅长应对，与国会的关系好，与白宫的关系好，与社会各界的关系也好"，那么下属就该设法使这位新领导充分发挥这方面的长处。因为即使有最好的行政，有最好的决策，如果没有好的政治技巧加以表达的话，那就等于零了。一旦这位新领导知道下属的官员支持他，他也会很快在政策及行政方面采纳官员们的意见。

有效的管理者知道他的上司是人，所以也知道他的上司一定自有一套有效的方式，他会设法探寻出上司的这套方式。所谓方式，也许只是某种态度和习惯，但这些态度和习惯却是客观存在的。

人大致可以分为两种类型："读者型"和"听者型"。（只有极少数的人是例外。例如有人靠与他人谈话来获取资料，从谈话中来观察对方的反应，好像装备了一个心理雷达。罗斯福总统和英国的丘吉尔都属于这一例外的类型。）此外也有读者型和听者型兼而有之的，也该算是例外——例如律师。我们面对"读者型"的人侃侃而谈，那是徒费口舌，因为他只能在读过之后才能"听"得进去。同样，我们面对听者型的人递送一册厚厚的报告书，那是徒费笔墨，因为他只能"听"了之后才能掌握要点。

有人只能阅读浓缩为一页的报告，例如艾森豪威尔总统。也有人需要了解整个理论推演的过程，所以他要的是厚厚的报告全文或是大串数字，虽长达 60 页也不在乎。有人喜欢及早了解情况，以便做最后的判断。也有人非等你研究成熟之后，才愿听你的报告。

正因为人有上述的各种类型，所以要了解上司的长处，并发挥其长处，需要一个过程。它所涉及的，与其说是"提什么建议"的问题，倒不如说是"如何提出这一建议"的问题。换言之，向上司提出建议时，应关注"建议"中的各相关方。与事情的轻重是非相比，陈述的先后顺序才是更应考虑的。如果说上司长于政治能力，而这项工作又有关政治，那么我们提出的报告就应以政治方面的问题居先，这样才能使上司易于掌握问题的重心，从而易于发挥其所长，使新政策得以成功。

俗语说："观人易，察己难。"观察别人，我们都是"专家"。因此，要使上司有效其实不难。问题只在于应了解上司的长处，知道上司能做些什么。只在于重视上司的长处，使其弱点不产生影响。协助上司发挥其所长，是促使管理者有效的最好方法。

## 充分发挥自己的长处

有效的管理者对于本身的工作，也同样要从长处出发，使自己的长处得以充分发挥。

在政府、医院和企业机构，我接触过许多管理者，大部分管理者能了解他们自己不能做什么。他们抱怨说：老板不同意他们做什么，公司政策不让他们做什么。因此，他们的时间和才干，都在无限委屈中浪费了。

当然，有效的管理者肯定关心自己所面临的局限性，但他们也应该了解自己能做的和该做的其实还有很多。尽管有人觉得委屈，不能做事，但有效的管理者却能勇往直前。由于他们能勇往直前，所以别人感到非常严重的限制，在他们面前都烟消云散了。

美国某一民营铁路公司的管理层人人都知道政府的限制很多，几乎不准许公司做任何计划。但当一位主管财务的新任副总裁到任之后，由于还没有顾虑政府的限制，所以不久就直趋华盛顿，拜访"州际商业委员会"，提出他构想中的几项革新方案要求核准。委员会告诉他说："你提出的方案，大多数与我们无关，至于其他的方案，你回去试行一下，如果可行，我们自会支持你。"

这样看来，所谓"别人不让我干"，恐怕是惰性和没有勇气的借口吧。

就算是客观条件真有限制（事实上任何人做任何事均免不了有限制），也一定仍然可以做出许多有意义的重要工作来。有效的管理者会发掘机会。他只要先问："我到底能做些什么？"他准能找出许许多多重大的工作，就只怕他的时间和资源不够。

进一步说，发挥自己的长处，对自己的能力和工作习惯，也有着同样重要的意义。

我们怎样达成成果通常不难明了。我们从小到大，总知道自己是在上午还是晚上最有精神。我们一定知道，当自己撰拟一份文稿时，是习惯于先写好草稿再来修改，还是习惯于一字一句推敲后完成全文。我们一定知道，要向大众发表演说时，要先准备好全文讲稿呢，还是只需准备一份纲要，或是根本无须准备便能讲得头头是道。我们也同样知道，自己是适宜参加一个工作小组呢，还是一个人单独做事更出色；或者说自己在小组中工作是否毫无成效。

有人做事，需要先有一个详细的计划，换言之，他们要先经过周密的通盘思考之后才能动手。但也有人一开始就做，最多只要先拟订几个粗枝大叶的要点。有人做事要靠人催逼，但也有人凡事都心急，没有到期就先交卷了。有人是属于"读者型"，也有人是"听者型"。自己的工作能力和习惯，自己最清楚，就像是自己习惯用左手还是右手一样，各人都一定有自知之明。

但是这些习惯都只是表面的，无所谓好，也无所谓坏，大都是反映一个人的个性，反映他对客观世界和对他自己的认识。不过，即使是表面的，这些工作习惯也事关有效性。而且这些习惯，大部分都可与任何种类的工作相适应。有效的管理者都能了解自己的类型，配合自己的习惯而行动。

重要的是，有效的管理者会顺应自己的个性特点，不会勉强自己。他注意的是自己的绩效、自己的成果，从而发展出自己的工作方式来。他会问：

"哪一类工作别人做起来要费九牛二虎之力,我做起来却是轻而易举?"举例来说,有人能够很快写出一份报告书,有人却觉得难之又难。有人觉得起草报告容易,但分析报告,并针对报告来做决策却十分困难。换言之,这样的人更适合担任幕僚,因为幕僚只需要把材料综合起来,把问题罗列出来,他不适合担任决策者。

有人适宜单独行动,从头到尾一手包办。也有人擅长谈判,特别是进行情绪激烈的谈判,例如劳资合约之类的谈判。在这方面,往往需要预测劳方的对策,有人料事如神,有人却常常判断错误。

在讨论一个人的长处和短处时,人们很少考虑到上述这些情况。他们想到的通常只是针对一门学问的知识,或一种艺术才能。但是,人的性情却往往是事情成败的关键。成年人一般都能了解自己的性情。我们要求有效,就要以了解自己能做些什么为基础,然后以最适合自己的方式做下去。

本章所讨论的如何用人之长,不仅有个态度问题,而且有一个敢不敢去实践的问题。用人之长,可以从实践中获得改进。我们只要注意认识我们的下属,观察我们的上司,多问"此人能做些什么",而不必问"此人不能做些什么",最后我们肯定能养成重视人之所长及善用人之所长的态度。久而久之,我们也能以同样的问题来问自己了。

在一个组织中,有效性的每一面,都是"机会的开发,问题的消失"。尤其是对人,这一点更是特别重要。有效的管理者,把每一个人都视为可以开发的机会,包括他本人在内。他知道唯有长处才能产生成果,而抓住弱点则只能造成令人头痛的问题。纵然没有弱点,也不能产生什么成果。

而且,有效的管理者也知道,任何一个团体,其行事标准都取决于领导人的表现。所以,有效的管理者决不允许把自己的表率作用建立在充分发挥所长以外的任何方面。

运动场上每出现一个新纪录，这个新纪录必成为全世界的运动员努力的新标准。多年来，谁也没有打破 4 分钟跑 1 英里⊖的纪录。但后来罗杰·班尼斯特打破了纪录。于是，世界上每个田径俱乐部里的一般运动员的成绩都接近了这个纪录，而新的领头羊则纷纷突破这个纪录。

领导人和一般人之间总有一段差距。领导人的绩效高了，一般人也竞相争高。有效的管理者一定明白这层道理：提高领导人的水平容易，但提高全体人员的水平很难。所以，他一定要找出有条件做出突出贡献，并能起带头作用的人才，赋予他们领导人的地位，把他们安置到能"制定标准"并能创造成绩的位置上。这就要求管理者能重视人的长处，而不介意其缺点。当然，如果缺点足以阻碍其长处的发挥，则另当别论。

总而言之，管理者的任务不是去改变人。管理者的任务，在于运用每一个人的才干。就像圣经中那段"塔兰特寓言"⊜所说的一样，管理者的任务就是要让各人的才智、健康以及抱负得到充分发挥，从而使组织的整体效益得到成倍的增长。

---

⊖ 1 英里 =1609.344 米。

⊜ 塔兰特（Talent）系古罗马的钱币。该寓言说的是一位主人在外出前分别给他的三个仆人几个塔兰特。其中两个仆人拿着钱就去做生意，各赚了几个塔兰特。而另一个仆人却将主人给的钱埋在地里，以防遗失。等主人回来时，前面两个仆人得到了奖赏，后一个仆人却受到了惩罚。——编者注

CHAPTER 5 | 第 5 章

# 要事优先

卓有成效如果有什么秘诀的话,那就是善于集中精力。卓有成效的管理者总是把重要的事情放在前面先做(first things first),而且一次只做好一件事(do one thing at a time)。

为什么需要集中精力?这不但是管理者工作性质的需要,也是由人的特点决定的。至少有几项因素是人尽皆知的。首先,我们要做的贡献太多,而时间有限。任何一项有关管理者贡献的分析,都显示出管理者的重要工作非常多。任何一项有关管理者时间的分析,都显示出管理者的时间实在少得可怜。不管一位管理者如何善于管理其时间,总有绝大部分时间非他本人所能控制。因此,无论如何时间总是不够。

管理者越是想做出重大的贡献,越是需要有更长的"整块时间"。管理者越是想将繁忙纷杂转化为成就,越是需要持续不断的努力,越是需要较长的连续性的时间。然而,即使只想"偷得浮生半日闲"来处理真正有生产性的工作,也要自律和具备非常大的决心对某些事说"不"。

同样地,一位管理者越想发挥长处,就越感到应在重大的机会上,集中一切可用的长处。这是获得成果的唯一办法。

进一步说，我们多数人即使在同一时间内专心致志地只做一件事，也不见得真能做好；如果想在同一时间内做两件事，那就更不必谈了。当然，人确实有处理各种事务的能力。可以说，人是一种"多功能工具"。但是，要有效地利用人类的才能，最好的办法，莫过于集中个人所有的才能于一件要务上。

杂技演员可以双手同时抛掷七八个球，但即使是最好的演员，恐怕也只能玩上 10 分钟。时间久了，他肯定难以继续，所有的球都得掉下来。

当然，这也不能一概而论。世上确实有人能在同一时间内交替地做两件事，因此两项工作有先后错落的变化。但这只是表示他们能够对两件事，交替分配一段"最低的整块时间"而已。要说一个人能同时处理三件事，恐怕就绝无仅有了。

作曲家莫扎特就是这样一位特殊人物，他能同时作曲数首，每首都是杰作。他真是一位不世出的天才。其他第一流的作曲家，巴赫、韩德尔、海顿、威尔第等人，都只能同一时间专心于一曲。他们得在完成一曲之后，再着手另一曲，要不也要将未完成的工作暂停搁置起来，才能去写另一首曲子。对一般的管理者而言，想像莫扎特一样，同时做好几件事是不太可能的。

正因为管理者面对的事务太多太杂，才特别需要专心。一次只做好一件工作，恰恰就是加快工作速度的最佳方法。越能集中我们的时间、努力和资源，我们所能完成的工作也就越多。

在我认识的许多企业负责人中，有一位制药公司的总裁，他在职期间所完成的工作恐怕谁也比不了。在他初上任时，这家公司规模极小，业务也仅限于国内。当他在职11年后退休时，该公司已成为世界性的大公司了。

这位先生最初几年集中力量于研究工作，推动研究计划，搜罗研究人才。该公司在研发方面一直没有优势，甚至追随也感到吃力。而他虽然不是科学家，却明确地意识到，公司绝不能再花5年时间去做别人5年前就已经在做的事了。他当机立断，决定了自己的方向。结果不到5年，该公司就已在两项新计划上高居领先地位了。

接着他又将这家公司发展成为国际性的大企业。在当时，瑞士的制药业一向执世界之牛耳。他仔细分析了全世界药品消耗的趋势，断然判定健康保险和大众医疗服务将来必是刺激药品用量的主要因素。因此，他配合了某一国家的健康保险的发展，大踏步地打入了新的国际市场，而且没有卷入竞争的漩涡，不需要从地位稳固的国际医药公司手里争夺市场。

他在职的最后5年，又集中力量制定了一项新策略，以配合现代医疗制度的战略。这种制度正在很快地把医疗变成一种"公用事业"。在这种制度下，病人看病，医生开处方，而费用则由政府、非营利性医院及社会福利机构（例如美国的蓝十字会）负担。他这项新的策略，制定于1965年他退休前不久。这项新策略是否真能成功，现在来看还为时尚早。但是在我看来，制药公司能着眼于战略、价格、市场和全球性行业关系的，恐怕只此一家。

作为总裁，要在任期内做成一件这样非比寻常的工作已非易事，而这位先生在职十多年，竟然做出了三项重大决策，同时还把公司发展成实力强大、人才济济的世界性企业。他之所以能取得如此成就，就是因为他能每次专心只做好一件事。

一个人如何能够完成这么多的大事，而且是这样艰巨的大事，"秘诀"尽在其中：每次只集中精力干好一件事。而结果是，他们所用的时间总比别人少得多。

有些人一事无成，而实际上他们却做得很吃力。第一，他们低估了完成一件任务所需的时间。他们总以为万事顺利，却总不免有出乎意料的情况发生。然而每个管理者都知道，没有任何事情会是一帆风顺。其实，所谓意料之外者，正应该在我们意料之中。而所谓意料之中，往往从来没有令人愉快的意外。所以，有效的管理者对时间需求的估计宁可有余，而不可不足。第二，一般的管理者（往往也是不大有效的管理者）总喜欢赶工——而赶工的结果，总不免使进度更加落后。有效的管理者不愿赛跑，他们按部就班，稳定前进。第三，一般的管理者喜欢同时着手几件要事，结果对每一件事，他们都无法获得足够的最少整块时间。只要任何一件事情受阻，全部事情也都会跟着受阻了。

有效的管理者知道他们必须要完成许多工作，并且要有效地完成。因此，他们在一段时间内只集中努力做好一件事——集中他们本人的时间和精力，以及整个组织的时间和精力。他们坚持把重要的事情放在前面先做，而且每次只做好一件事。

## 摆脱昨天

管理者专心一志,第一项原则是要摆脱已经不再有价值的过去。有效的管理者必须经常检讨他们和同事的工作计划,他们会问:"如果我们还没有进行这项工作,现在我们该不该开始这项工作?"如果不是非办不可,他们就会放弃这项工作,或者会将它搁置起来。至少他们不会再将资源投入不再产生价值的过去。而对于已经投入的最佳资源,尤其是非常匮乏的人力资源,他们会立即抽调出来,转而投入未来的新机会。

但是一位管理者往往不可能完全摆脱过去,这真是无可奈何的事。所谓今天,乃是昨天所做决策和所采取行动的结果。人终归是人,有谁能够预见未来?昨天的决策和行动,不论当时看起来如何勇敢、如何睿智,都有可能形成今天的困难和危机,甚至被证明是愚蠢的选择。不管是在政府、企业,还是在其他机构,管理者的一项具体任务就是要把今天的资源投入创造未来中去。换句话说,每一位管理者都必须不停地花费时间、精力和才智,来弥补或跳出昨天的行动和决策。不论昨天的行动和决策是他自己做的,还是前任做的,他都得弥补或跳出。事实上他在这方面所耗的时间,应该比其他任何任务所耗的时间都多。

但是我们至少可以把昨天遗留下来的、不能再产生成果的工作尽量减少。

人若遭遇了重大的失败,改正并不太难,他们能检讨自己。可是昨天的成功,却能留下无尽的影响,远超出成功的有效期。尤其危险的是,有些活动本应该产生良好的效果,但是由于一些原因却没能产生效果。过去的成功和活动,往往演变成"经营管理上的自我主义的资产",并且是神圣不可侵犯的㊀。但是,这些过去的成功和活动最需要无情的检讨,否则组织的血液都流失到这种自我之中了。而且这种"经营管理上的自我主义的资产",往往

---

㊀ 引自《为成果而管理》一书。

占用了组织中最能干的人才，却还说那是"值得的"。

所有的组织都很容易染上这种毛病，即不能正确地看待过去的成功和失败，在政府机构中这种情况更为常见。政府机构的计划和措施，如其他机构一样，过一段时间就会跟不上形势变化的需要。这些计划和措施不但被认为是永恒的原则，还会演变成法令规章，谁也动它不得，成为一部分人的既得利益，并且得到政府立法部门有关人员的支持。

在1914年之前，美国政府的组织规模不大，其对社会生活的影响也有限的时候，这种毛病还不致为害过甚。但是时至今日，政府机构已承受不了将精力和资源浪费到昨天的事情上了。然而，在我看来，今天的美国至少有半数的联邦政府机构，不是仍然拘泥于根本不必要的规章（例如"州际商业委员会"，其最初成立的目的本在于防止私营铁路的垄断，而铁路垄断的可能性，30年前就已经不存在了），就是把精力放到满足政治家的私愿上（绝大部分农业法案便属此类）。各项本应有成果的努力，实际上却注定永远不会有任何成果。

所以，以美国来说，当前最迫切需要的，莫过于一项强有力的新原则：政府的每一项法案、每一个机构、每一个计划，都要视为是"临时性质"的，经过一定年限后便该自动失效。否则的话，也必须客观地研究其存在价值、成果和贡献，再重新立法来延长其有效期。

约翰逊总统在1965～1966年间，曾对政府的每一个机构及其计划做过一项研究。约翰逊总统的这项研究，是仿效国防部长麦克纳马拉的"计划检讨"制度：删除过时的和无效的计划。约翰逊总统这一步走得很对，确实迫切需要。不过，如果我们仍旧抱着传统观念，认为一切计划如果无法证明其确属无效，就应继续存在，那么这项研究恐怕仍难产生结果。我们应有的观念是：任何计划如果无法证明其确属有效及需要，便该立即放弃。否则，现代的政府会用其种种法令规章不断地窒息整个社会，到最后政府本身也将因自己的臃肿而窒息。

政府机构容易受上述毛病的感染，其他组织也不能免疫。奉劝各大公司的企业家在抱怨政府官僚习气的同时，也检讨自己的公司是否充满了形形色色的"控制机制"，其实却什么也控制不了。自己的公司是否在进行种种研究，其实只是用来掩饰自己缺乏果断？自己的公司是否拥有各方面的人才，其实只是为了表示你们"有"各种研究和"有"各种关系？自己的公司是否沉湎于昨天的过时产品，浪费自己的主要智囊人物的时间，也扼杀了明天的产品？再奉劝各学术机构，也请别再谴责大型企业里惊人的浪费现象了，在会议上，你们同样会为将已过时的学科列入必修课而力争。

一位希望自己有效，也希望其组织有效的管理者，必然会自我检视一切的方案、活动和任务。他会问："这件事现在还有继续做的价值吗？"如果认为没有价值了，他便立即停手，而将时间精力转移到其他只要做得好，便能使自己更为有效的任务上，也能促使他的组织更为成功。

尤其重要的是：有效的管理者打算做一项新的业务时，一定要先删除一项原有的业务。这对控制组织的"膨胀"是非常必要的。"膨胀"如不加以控制，组织就会变得涣散、难以管理。社会组织恰如生物有机体，必须保持"瘦且有肌肉"的状态。

有效的管理者都知道创业维艰，新工作不易上手，总会遇到困难。一项新的工作在开始之前，便该有遭遇极大困难的时候予以克服的手段，否则便是在开始时种下失败的种子了。要准备克服重大困难的手段，唯一靠得住的办法只有靠最有才干的人来主持。但是最有才干的人，通常总是太忙了。如果不把他原有的负荷减轻，怎能期望他再承担新的工作？

当然，有人会想到另聘新人来负责新工作，但这太冒险了。我们增添新人，大部分是增添在已有成规可循的工作上。而对于新工作，我们应责成确能证明有能力的人来负责。老实说，做一项新工作，本身就是一场赌博即便其他人已经多次做过的工作也是如此；倘若再另聘新人来做，就更是赌上加赌了。我们都亲眼见过许多人在其他单位工作成绩非常卓越，而转换单位后，工作却一败涂地。这类教训实在应该记取。

当然，任何一个组织都必须时时输入新血。如果任何职位都只能在原有名单中找人提升，这组织必将萎缩。问题是新人不宜用于风险最大之处，例如高层职位，或主持某一新工作的职位。任用新人，可用在"比高层略低"的职位上，用在已有成规或目标明确的职位上。

要"出新"，必从"推陈"着手。任何一个组织，都不缺乏新的创意。所以，严格说来，我们的问题不是缺乏"创意"，所缺乏的只是创意的执行。人人都在为昨天的任务而忙碌。只要能定期审视当前的计划或活动，并抛弃那些不再有产出的事情，即使是最暮气沉沉的机构，也能获得生机。

杜邦公司（Du Pont）有一个好例子：某一产品或流程在"尚未"开始走下坡路之前，他们就毅然放弃。杜邦公司从来不将其有限的人力和资金，用来保卫昨天。但是大部分的公司，往往抱着另一种观点。他们总是说："只要我们努力，我们总会有市场！"他们总是说:"我们公司靠这项产品起家,我们有责任让这项产品在市场上维持下去。"

有趣的是,这样的公司,虽然常常选派他们的管理者参加各种有关创造力的研讨会,却偏偏找不出新的产品。而杜邦公司,却天天忙于生产和推出新的产品。

推陈才能出新,这是放诸四海皆准的原则。我们有理由相信:如果美国仍旧采用1825年的各项交通制度,可断言今天一定还有古董马车——当然一定是国营事业,一定有巨额的经费补助,也一定有"重新训练马匹"的狂热研究方案。

## 先后次序的考虑

在管理者面前,摆着许多值得去做的工作,但管理者的时间却非常有限。未来的机会也很多,但能抓得住机会的能人却太少。而且,管理者还难免会遇到不少问题和危机。

因此,这就涉及哪些事情需要优先处理,而哪些事情可以缓一缓再办的决策了。那么,到底根据什么来做这一决策呢?是由管理者来决定,还是由压力来决定?但是,不论如何决定,工作量总得配合我们可用时间的多寡;也只有在我们确有足够的人力去做时,才能为我们带来机会。

如果按压力来决定优先次序,结果必将牺牲许多重大的要务。这样的话,我们肯定没有时间来完成一件任务中最耗时间的部分——将决策转化为行动的过程。除非我们能将一件任务转化为组织的行为,否则任何任务都无法完成。也就是说,除非组织中人人都能以某一任务为己任,除非人人都能以新方式来处理其原有的工作,除非人人都确认有承担新工作的必要,也除非人人都能将主管的新计划化为他们的日常工作，否则任何任务都肯定无法完成。如果因为没有时间而忽略了这些准备，必将一事无成。而一事无成，正是身为管理者未能集中主要精力，未能抓住首要任务的结果。

按压力来决定优先次序，还会产生另一种后果：组织中的高层，完全无法完成其职责。一般来说一件新任务肯定不是为了解决昨天的困难，而是为了一个新的明天，所以总是可以缓办的。而说到压力，往往总是为了昨天。特别是既然高层让压力来决定优先，那么他们会忽略掉没有其他人能做的最核心的管理职责。高层必然会疏于注意组织之"外"，必将与组织的外界现实脱节。而只有外部世界，才可能产生成果。因为所谓压力，总是偏爱机构内部的事务，偏爱已经发生的事情而忽视未来，总是喜欢危机而忽视机遇，总是倾向于急功近利而对真正的现实世界视而不见，总是看重紧急事务而对关系重大的事务反应木然。

我们要做的事情并不只是弄清楚哪些事情必须优先去做，那是很容易做到的，每个人都可以做得到。很多管理者不能做到集中精力于某项工作，其主要困难在于他们确定不了哪些事情可以缓一缓，就是说要能确定哪些事情可以暂时不去做，并且能把这一决定坚持到底。

许多管理者都知道，所谓"暂行缓办"，实际就是"永远不办"。许多管理者都知道，一个计划如果该办时不办，日后再恢复办理，恐怕就不一定适当了。进行一件计划，时机的掌握何等重要。本来5年前就该开始的工作，延后5年几乎必然是最大的失策。

19世纪末英国维多利亚女王时代的小说中，有一篇描写一对相恋的青年男女，21岁时没有结婚，直到他们38岁，男已鳏、女已寡，两人复遇而结合。但此时他们已不再有当年年轻的欢乐了。如果21岁时成就良缘，他们也许能共同生活、共同成长。可是17

年后，虽复相遇，两人都已在不同的环境中成长，性格也产生了很大的差异。

一个人在年轻时有志学医，但因种种原因走上了经商之路。后来到了50岁，虽然已经商有成，但是如果再想回头学医，恐怕难以如愿，至少也很难成为名医了。他将深感年老学医之难，而以学医为一大苦事。

以机构的合并为例：两个企业如果在六七年前合并，至今应该已有相当发展了。只因为当时某一企业的总经理不愿在合并后屈居他人之下，而未能成为事实。六七年之后，那位当初不愿屈居的总经理已告退休，这两个企业的合并是否值得旧事重提？时过境迁，合并恐怕不见得合适了。

由于被搁置实际上等于被取消，所以管理者都不敢轻易地延缓任何工作。他们明白，被延缓的工作虽不是他们最优先要做的事情，不过一旦被延缓，也是有风险的。自己缓办的结果，说不定是竞争同业赶在前头了。政治家或政府机构的首长对此尤其敏感，决定缓办某一政策，谁也不能保证不会因此掀起政坛的轩然大波。

例如有关民权问题，艾森豪威尔总统没有视为优先，肯尼迪总统也没有视为优先。又例如约翰逊总统在就任之初，很明确地指出越战问题及其有关外交事务乃属"置后"事项。后来情况变化，连当初支持约翰逊总统、以"与贫穷作战"为优先政策的自由派人士，也掀起了激烈的反应。

决定延缓一项工作，并不是一件愉快的事情。因为我们的"置后"，往往是别人的"优先"。列举一份第一优先的工作单，事事都办，但均浅尝辄止，显然容易得多。这样经常能使人人皆大欢喜，结果却是一事无成。

如何决定优先次序，研究起来确实很复杂。不过我们可以说，在决定哪些应该优先、哪些可以延缓这个问题上，最重要的并不是分析，而是拿出应有的勇气来。

以下是几条可帮助确定优先次序的重要原则，每条都与勇气密切相关：

- 重将来而不重过去；
- 重视机会，不能只看到困难；
- 选择自己的方向，而不盲从；
- 目标要高，要有新意，不能只求安全和容易。

试看许多在研究方面卓然有成的科学家的成就，与其说是他们的研究能力决定了研究的成果，倒不如说是他们寻求机会的勇气决定了研究的成果（当然，像爱因斯坦创相对论，玻尔创原子结构，或普朗克创量子论这样的天才除外）。大凡从事研究的科学家选择研究课题时，如果着眼于易于成功而非着眼于接受挑战，那他们纵然能够成功，其成功也相当有限。他们的成功，也许可以使他们的名字在别人的论文中出现，却不能创造出一条以他们的姓名命名的"某某氏定律"来。所以真正的成就，只属于那些善于抓住机会选定研究课题的人，属于那些能把别人确立的准则只当作制约因素，而不当作决定因素的人。

同样的道理，在企业经营方面，成功的事业，不是迁就现有产品线来开发新产品的事业，而是以开发新技术或开发新事业为宗旨的事业。当然，如果说创新有风险、有艰辛、有不确定性，那么不管创新是大是小，同样是有风险、艰辛和不确定性的。化机会为成果，肯定比解决旧问题更有生产性。解决旧问题，总不过是恢复昨天的平衡而已。

优先与延缓的问题不是一成不变的，根据实际情况的变化，经常需要对这种先后次序进行重新考虑和修正。例如，哪位美国总统都不会有一成不变的优先处理某些事项的计划。其实，在完成必须优先处理的事项的过程中，哪些应该优先，哪些可以挪后，也总是在不断变化的。

换言之，一位有效的管理者，会把主要精力集中在当前正在进行的工作上，而不会再去兼办其他工作。完成一件事情之后，他会根据情况的变化，再决定下一步的优先事项。

要想集中精力，全神贯注于一项工作，首先要有足够的勇气，要敢于决定真正该做和真正先做的工作。这是管理者唯一的希望，只有这样，管理者才能成为时间和任务的"主宰"，而不会成为它们的奴隶。

第6章 | CHAPTER 6

# 决策的要素

　　管理者的任务繁多，决策只是其中一项。管理者在做出决策时通常并不需要花很多时间，但决策却是身为管理者特有的任务。所以，决策问题值得做特别的讨论。

　　只有管理者才需要做决策。管理者之所以为管理者，正是由于他拥有特殊的地位和知识，所以人们期望他能做出对整个组织、绩效和成果具有特殊影响的决策。

　　因此，卓有成效的管理者，做的是有效的决策。

　　他们的决策，是一套系统化的程序，有明确的要素和一定的步骤。我们常常读到有关决策的著作，然而管理者做出决策时实际采用的程序，与那些著作讨论的程序几乎完全不同。

　　有效的管理者不做太多的决策。他们所做的，都是重大的决策。他们重视的，是分辨什么问题为例行性的，什么问题为战略性的，而不重视"解决问题"。他们的决策是最高层次的、观念方面的少数重大决策，他们致力于找出情势中的常数。所以，他们给人的印象，是决策往往需要宽松的时间。

他们认为操纵很多变数的决策技巧,只是一种缺乏条理的思考方法。他们希望知道一项决策究竟涵盖什么,应符合哪种基本的现实。他们需要的是决策的结果,而不是决策的技巧;他们需要的是合乎情理的决策,而不是巧妙的决策。

有效的管理者知道什么时候应依据原则做决策,什么时候应依据实际情况的需要做决策。他们知道最棘手的决策,是正反两面折中的决策,他们能分辨正反两面的差异。他们知道在整个决策过程中,最费时的不是决策的本身,而是决策的推行。一项决策如果不能付诸行动,就称不上是真正的决策,最多只是一种良好的意愿。也就是说,有效的决策虽然是以高层次的理性认识为基础,但决策的推行却必须尽可能地接近工作层面,必须力求简单。

## 有关决策的案例研究

在美国商业史上,有一位不大为人所知的企业家,他也许是一位最有效的决策人。他就是20世纪初美国贝尔电话公司的总裁费尔先生。费尔担任该公司总裁,是从1910年之前,直到20世纪20年代中期,前后将近20年。在这段时期中,费尔创造了一个世界上最具规模、发展得最大的民营企业。

电话系统应该民营,在今天的美国看来是理所当然的。然而在世界发达国家的电话系统中,只有贝尔公司经营的北美洲(包括美国以及加拿大的魁北克和安大略两省)不是由政府经营。尽管享有垄断,而且原有市场也已饱和,但是作为一家公用事业公司,能经得起风险并能在风险中飞速成长的,只有贝尔公司。

贝尔公司为什么能有这样的成就?绝非由于幸运,也绝非由于所谓"美国人的保守作风"。主要的原因,在于费尔担任该公司总裁将近20年的时间里，做了四项"战略决策"。

起初，费尔看清了一个电话公司如果想保持其民营形态，自主经营，必须有突出而与众不同的局面。当时，欧洲各国的国营电话公司都经营得很稳健。费尔想，贝尔公司如果也认为"平安就是福"，就能不被政府收归国营，那是靠不住的，迟早难以避免政府的接收。他认为仅采取防守政策，最后结果肯定是失败，而且防守政策将麻痹管理层的创造力。因此，费尔有了第一个重要观念：贝尔公司虽是民营企业，但是应该比任何政府机关都更加照顾社会大众的利益，而且更为积极。出于这样的考虑，费尔做出了第一项大决策：贝尔电话公司必须预测并满足社会大众的服务需求。

所以，费尔担任公司总裁后，提出了"为社会提供服务是公司的根本目标"的口号。在20世纪初期，这是绝难被人接受的口号。而且，费尔并不以提出这句口号为满足，也不以管理层应确能兼顾服务与盈利为满足。他还制定出了用以衡量管理人员及经营水平的统一尺度，用以衡量服务工作的好坏，但他从来不强调利润完成的情况。经理只对服务情况负责，至于公司的管理和资金的筹集，那是公司高层的任务，他们要负责把公司的最佳服务转化为适当的收益。

与此同时，费尔还有一项新认识：一个全国性的电信事业，绝不能是传统的自由企业，换言之，绝不是一个无拘无束的事业。他认为如果想避免政府的收购，唯一的方法便是所谓的公众管制。所以，一项有效的、公正的和有原则的公众管制，是符合贝尔公司的利益的，而且事关公司的存亡。

所谓公众管制，在当时的美国虽然不是个生疏名词，但在费尔先生提出这项结论时，公众管制并无力量。当时企业界坚决反对，法院方面也不支持，所以有关公众管制的法律条文无法实施。公众管制委员会的人手和经费都不足，所以委员一职都成了第三流政客无所事事的闲差。

但是费尔先生却决定把实现公众管制作为贝尔公司的目标。他将这一目标交付给各地区的子公司总经理，责成各子公司设法恢复各管制机构的活力，倡导管制及等级审定的观念，以期能有公平合理的公众管制，一方面确保公众利益，另一方面又能使贝尔公司顺利经营。由于贝尔公司的高层管理成员包括子公司的总经理，所以整个公司及其所属每一个子公司，都能朝向这一目标而努力。

费尔先生的第三项大决策，是为公司建立了贝尔研究所，并使之成为企业界最成功的科学研究机构之一。他的这项决策，也是以一个垄断性民营企业必须自强不息才能保持活力的观念为出发点。他在做这项决策时，曾经自问："像贝尔公司这样的垄断性企业，应该如何永保其雄厚的竞争力？"当然，他所说的竞争力，并不是通常在有同业竞争情况下的竞争力。但是他知道，一个垄断性的企业如果没有竞争力，就很容易变得刻板和僵化起来，无法适应变化，无法谋求自身的发展。

在费尔看来，一个垄断性的企业当前虽然没有对手，但是应该以将来作为对手。电信事业以技术最为重要，有无前途，都视其技术能否推陈出新。贝尔研究所就是在这一观念下成立的。老实说，贝尔研究所绝不是企业界所设立的第一个研究机构，却是第一个以淘汰现有产品为己任的研究机构，尽管那些产品当时的收益都还不错。

贝尔研究所于第一次世界大战期间正式成立的时候，确是当时企业界一项令人颇感困惑的创新。即使在今天，恐怕也没有多少人能了解其所谓研究，其实是"旧世界的破坏者"和"今天的否定者"，目的是创造一个不同的明天。大多数研究机构进行的都是防御性的研究，但求能维持"今天"的现状，而贝尔研究所一开始就放弃了防御性的研究。

后来，费尔的观念已由事实证明了其正确性。贝尔研究所第一步发展的通信技术，已使整个北美洲成为一个巨无霸似的自动通信网，后来更发展到连当初费尔本人也没有梦想到的领域中了，例如电视节目的转播、电脑资料的传送以及通信卫星等，都是成长很快的通信技术。今天种种科学和技术的发展，包括信息处理的数学理论，以及诸如晶体管、电脑逻辑设计等的新产品及新方法，大部分都得归功于贝尔研究所之首开其端。

在费尔任期的最后阶段中，他又做了第四项重大决策。那已是20世纪20年代初了，他开创了一个大众资本市场。这项大决策的出发点，依然是为了要贝尔公司作为民营企业能继续生存下去。

> 许多企业之所以被政府接管，多半是由于无法取得所需的资金。1860～1920年，欧洲的许多铁路公司被政府接管，主要就是由于这个原因。英国的煤矿和电力公司由政府收归国营，也是因为缺乏推行现代化所需的资金。第一次世界大战后的通货膨胀期间，欧洲大陆的许多电力公司也是因同样的原因被政府接管。当时各公司在货币贬值的情况下不能提高电费，结果弄得虽然有心改善经营，却无法筹措资金。

费尔做这项大决策时，他本人是否已经看到了这个问题，现已无法查证。不过，他确实已经了解到贝尔公司需要大量资金的供应，而这些资本又不能从当时的资本市场取得。20世纪20年代的资本市场只是投机者的市场，当时许多公用事业尤其是电力公司，都曾经设法发售股票，以期吸引投机者。他们组成了控股公司，设法使公司普通股具有较佳的股息，但公司所需的营运资金，仍要按传统方式从保险公司之类的金融机构获取。费尔认为，把企业的资金来源建立在这样的基础上，风险是很大的。

费尔的构想，是发行一种 AT&T（美国电话电报公司）普通股。但他设计的这种股票，与当时的投机性股票完全不同。他的设计着眼于社会大众，尤其是当时新兴的所谓"莎莉姑妈"的中产阶层的主妇。"莎莉姑妈"手头拥有游资，想投资，但担不起风险。费尔设计的 AT&T 普通股，正是针对"莎莉姑妈"的意愿：这种股票股息有保证，完全符合她们的需要。而且，这又是一种普通股，能享有资产增值带来的好处，还可避开通货膨胀的威胁。

但是严格说来，所谓"莎莉姑妈"型的投资人在当时事实上尚未完全形成。拥有资金和购股能力的中产阶层当时才刚刚出现，他们仍沿袭传统的习惯，有余钱都存入银行或用于购买保险，敢于冒风险的，就进入投机股票市场。当然，这并不是说费尔创造了"莎莉姑妈"。这只是表示他诱导当时的"莎莉姑妈"成为投资人，动用她们的储蓄，符合她们的利益，也符合贝尔公司的利益。这一决策使贝尔公司在后来数十年间，一直拥有充裕的资金来源。直到今天，AT&T 普通股仍旧是美国和加拿大中产阶层投资的对象。

而且，费尔也设计了自己的一套实施办法。在那些年，贝尔公司一直没有依赖华尔街，公司本身成为股票的承兑人和包销人。当初费尔的财务助理季福特是这一制度的主要设计人，后来他接替费尔出任贝尔公司的总裁。

费尔先生的四项重大决策都是有针对性的，都是为了解决公司和他当时所面临的问题。这些大决策的思想，充分体现了什么才是真正的、有效的决策。

我们再举一个例子来说明。斯隆先生 1922 年出任通用汽车公司总裁，其时正当费尔先生退休之前不久。斯隆也跟费尔相似，设计和构建了一个举世无双的大企业。他不是费尔，他的时代也不是费尔的时代，但是他所做的一项令人难忘的大决策——使通用汽车公司采取分权组织制度，跟费尔所做的大决策相比，同样是了不起的大手笔。

斯隆先生著有一本回忆录，书名是《我在通用汽车的岁月》（*My Years with General Motors*）。书中说他在1922年接任时，通用汽车公司的组织简直就是一盘散沙，各自为政。通用汽车公司原是由几个企业合并而成，但是在合并后，各部门的主管，都像是独立部落的酋长，完全不听"王命"。

  解决这样的问题，传统上不外有两种办法。第一种办法，是把这些"强有力的酋长"调离。这就是洛克菲勒建立标准石油公司，和摩根建立美国钢铁公司的办法。第二种办法，是留任这些"酋长"，仍由他们指挥"他们的"事业，而总公司尽量不加以干预。其实这哪里是解决办法，只是靠股票期权维系的无政府状态，只有寄望于"酋长们"会因他们本身的经济利益，而顾到总公司的整体利益而已。事实上通用汽车公司的创办人杜兰特和斯隆的前任杜邦，都是采取这种办法。而在斯隆接任时，通用汽车公司败象已露，"酋长们"的不合作，已使得公司濒于关门大吉的边缘了。

斯隆先生看清了问题的根本，认为这并不是因为合并才发生的过渡期间的问题，而是一个大型企业常见的问题。他认为一个大型企业，需要有一个统一的方向和一个管制中心；需要有责权的高层管理；也需要积极进取和干练的运营人员。他们应该有选择其经营方法的自由，应该有确切的责任和履行其责任的职权，应该有足以使他们发挥所长的范围，应该使他们的成就得到应得的鼓励。斯隆先生看到了这些需要，其实何止是当时的通用汽车公司有此需要，随着公司的逐渐老化，任何一家依赖于主管才干的公司，又何尝不有此需要。

在斯隆先生之前，事实上人人都看到了这个问题，都认为是一项人事问题，必须靠权力的明争暗斗，出现一个最后胜利者之后才能解决。然而斯隆却认为这是一个制度上的问题，只有通过建立新的组织结构才能解决，所以他构想了分权制度，这既可以保证分公司的经营自主权，又可以体现总公司的方向及政策指导。

斯隆这一设计是否有效，不妨用"反证法"来说明。那就是说，我们不妨看看通用汽车公司在什么地方没有杰出的成就。自20世纪30年代以来，通用汽车公司最差劲的一步，是他们对美国人的政治兴趣，以及美国政府的方针和政策的预测都不准。而这恰恰是公司没有采用"分权制度"的唯一领域。自从1935年以来，通用汽车公司要求每一位高级主管，都必须是保守的共和党党员，从这一点就不难看出问题所在了。

上文介绍贝尔公司的费尔和通用汽车公司的斯隆两人的重大决策，内容各不相同，所解决的问题也各不相同，但两人的重大决策，却有几项相同的特性，那就是：他们解决问题，都着眼于最高层次的观念性的认识。他们先透彻地思考该决定的是什么，然后研究制定决策时应采用的原则。换句话说，他们的决策，不是为了适应当时的临时需要，而是战略性的考虑。所以，他们做了创新性的重大决策。当然，他们的大决策，也因此引发了很多争议。事实上他们那些决策，都与当时"众所周知"的看法大不相同。

以贝尔公司的费尔来说，竟曾遭到贝尔公司董事会的解聘。他提出"为社会提供服务是公司的根本目标"的观念，被人指责为精神不正常，因为谁都认为企业的目的在于盈利。然而，若干年后，美国出现了将电话收归国营的警报，董事会又急忙请费尔先生回来。此外费尔决定投下一笔经费建立研究所，用来更新公司现有的技术与工艺，而公司的现有技术与工艺，当时正为公司带来极大的盈利。同时他又拒绝利用当时的资本市场来筹措资金。这两大决策都同样遭到董事会激烈的反对，认为是费尔无可理喻的怪想法。

同样地，斯隆的分权制度计划，也曾饱受抨击，谁都认为是行不通的事。

在当时的美国企业家中，自然也有不少思想较前卫的人物，福特就是其中一位。但是即使在福特看来，费尔和斯隆的决策也都过于大胆了。福特曾经坚信他们开发的一种"T型"车，必将是永远受欢迎的车型。因此，费尔有意要让贝尔公司的现有生产技术过时的努力令福特大为不解。而且，福特坚信只有最严格的集权才能产生效率和成果，所以斯隆的分权计划，在福特看来，恐怕也是被认为是自寻死路。

## 决策的五个要素

费尔和斯隆的决策，其主要的意义，绝不是表示决策应标新立异，也不是表示决策应有引人争议的特性，而是表示出决策的以下五点特征。

（1）要确实了解问题的性质，如果问题是经常性的，那就只能通过一项建立规则或原则的决策才能解决。

（2）要确实找出解决问题时必须满足的界限，换言之，应找出问题的"边界条件"。

（3）仔细思考解决问题的正确方案是什么以及这些方案必须满足哪些条

件，然后再考虑必要的妥协、适应及让步事项，以期该决策能被接受。

（4）决策方案要同时兼顾执行措施，让决策变成可以被贯彻的行动。

（5）在执行的过程中重视反馈，以印证决策的正确性及有效性。

这就是有效决策的五个要素。以下我们一一予以较详细的说明。

有效的决策人首先需要辨明问题的性质：是一再发生的经常性问题呢，还是偶然的例外？换言之，某一问题是否为另一个一再发生的问题的原因？或是否确属特殊事件，需以特殊方法解决？倘若是经常性的老毛病，就应该建立原理原则来根治；而偶然发生的例外，则应该按情况做个别处置。

按问题的发生情况来说，细究起来，不只有"经常"和"例外"两类，一般可以分成四类。

第一类，是真正经常性的问题。发生的个别问题，只是一种表面现象。

管理者日常遇到的问题大部分都属于此类。例如生产上的库存决策，严格说来不能称为决策，只能说是一种措施。这类问题是经常性的，生产方面的许多问题，大都属于这种性质。

工厂中的生产管制及工程单位所处理的这类问题极多，每月要有好几百件。然而，分析起来，这类问题绝大部分只是一种表面现象，是一些反映基本情况的表面现象。但是，生产部门的程序工程师及生产工程师往往很难看透这一层，他们是"身在此山中"，所以"不识庐山真面目"。有时候，也许他们每个月都会碰到类似问题，如输送蒸汽或流体的管子接头坏了。这样的问题，只有经过较长时间的分析之后，才能显示其为"经常"的性质。这时他们才能发现究竟是否由于温度或压力过高，超过设备的负荷，需将接头重新设计。但是在得出这一结论前，生产部门往往早已花了不少修理管子接头的时间了。

第二类问题虽然是在某一特殊情况下偶然发生，但在实质上仍然是一项经常性问题。

例如某公司接受另一公司的建议，两家合并为一。如果该公司接受这一建议，就永远不会再接到第二次同样的建议了。对这家公司来说，对其董事会及管理机构而言，接受这种建议只能是一次性的，是一种特殊的问题。但是，细究这一问题的本质，却的确具有"经常"的性质，企业界随时可能出现这种问题。因此在考虑是否接受时，应以某些原则为基础，必须参考他人的经验。

第三类问题，才是真正偶发的特殊事件。

在1965年11月间，美国的整个东北部地区，从圣劳伦斯到华盛顿一带，发生了一次全面停电。根据初步的调查，这的确是一个真正的特殊偶发事件。又例如20世纪60年代初期，因孕妇服用"沙利度胺"而产生畸形婴儿所造成的悲剧，也属于此类。但是这一类偶发事件，发生的概率只有千万分之一或亿万分之一，发生过一次之后，就不太可能再发生第二次。就像我们坐的椅子忽然间自动分解成碳、氢、氧等元素一样，是根本不可能发生的。

真正偶然性的例外事件实在少之又少。但是，一旦发生时，我们必须自问：这究竟是一次"真正的偶发事件"，还是另一种"经常事件"的首次出现？

这也就是我们要介绍的第四类问题：首次出现的"经常事件"。

以上文所举两例来说：美国东北部地区的停电和沙利度胺引致婴儿畸形，直到今天我们才判定其均为"经常事件"之首次出现。我们已具备现代化电力技术和医学知识，如果能寻求"经常性的解决方法"，这种停电事件和畸形婴儿的悲剧，应该不至于一再发生。

除了上述第三类"真正偶发的特殊事件"外，其余三类问题均需要一种"经常性的解决方法"。换言之，需要制定一种规则、一种政策或一种原则。一旦有了正确的原则，一切类似问题的解决就将易如反掌。换句话说，问题再度发生时，即可根据原则去处理了。只有第三类"真正偶发的特殊事件"才必须个别对付，没有原理原则可循。

有效的决策人常需花费不少时间来确定问题的属性。如果问题的属性判断错了，其决策必为错误的决策。

我们常犯的错误，便是误将"经常问题"视为一连串的"偶发问题"。换言之，没有了解问题症结所在的基础，对问题缺乏经常性的认识与原则，其结果自然是失败与无效。

在美国肯尼迪政府时代，许多内政政策的失败，都是由于这项错误。肯尼迪总统手下自然有不少高手，但他们只做了一件成功的工作，那就是古巴导弹事件的处理。如果他们没有这一项表现，肯尼迪政府真称得上是一事无成了。主要的原因就在于他们自己所称的所谓"实用主义"。他们没有建立原则，坚持"兵来将挡、水来土掩"。然而人人都看得很清楚，甚至他们自己也看得很清楚：他们所赖以制定政策的那些基本设想，他们对战后局势的基本估计，已越来越脱离当时外交和内政的实际。

另一种常犯的错误,是误将真正的新问题视为旧病复发,因而仍旧应用旧原则。

美国东北部的停电即为一例。当初的停电,本来只限于纽约和加拿大安大略一带,后来范围越来越广,滚雪球似地扩展到整个东北部。纽约市的电力工程师起初运用了只适用于正常负荷情况的"旧原则"来处理。后来他们经过详细检查,发现了非比寻常的现象,才知道不能使用平常方法,必须用非常方法来解决。

反之,肯尼迪总统处理古巴导弹事件之所以成功,就是因为看准了这是一件"非常事件",应以"非常"手段来处理。肯尼迪总统对问题的属性做出正确的判断之后,他的智慧和勇气才得以发挥力量。

第三种常见的错误,是对某些根本性问题的界定似是而非。以下是一个例子。

自从第二次世界大战结束以来,美国军方常感到他们留不住高素质的医务人员。军方曾屡次研究这一问题,提出了不知多少建议。但是,所有的研究工作,都是以一项听来头头是道的假定为基础的——认为问题在于待遇不够,殊不知真正的原因在于军医的传统制度。美国的军医组织一向重视普通医师,然而今天的潮流已经是分科精细,重视专科医师了。照军方的系统,军医在人事晋升的阶梯上,只能转向行政方面,最后导致与医学研究相脱节。年轻一代的医务人员感到他们在军中服务的结果,最后不是升官,便是永远做普通医生,这对于他们的所学所长不免是一种浪费。他们真正的需要，是能有发展医学才干、成为一位专科医师的机会。

老实说，美国军方到今天也还没有正视这一根本问题。难道说他们愿意使军医水平一直停滞在第二流医疗机构的阶段，只让那些不能成为一流人才的医师留在军方医院里吗？或者，他们是否已打算对军队的医疗机构进行彻底改革？我看除非军方能接受这项观念，认为这是一项重要决策，否则年轻有为的医生始终会外流的。

最后一种错误，是只看到问题的部分，而没有看清全貌。

1966年，美国汽车工业忽然受到攻击。社会各界纷纷指责美国的汽车不安全，而业界本身竟一时惊慌失措。但是，事实上美国汽车业界不但重视车辆本身的安全，也关注了公路工程和驾驶人员的训练。社会上说车辆肇祸的原因，一在于道路不良，一在于驾驶不慎，这种说法极为动听。凡是与车辆安全有关的机构，从公路警察到驾驶学校，都以安全第一为共同的目标；而且这项安全运动确实已收到了效果：重视行车安全的公路，车祸次数明显较少；受过安全训练的驾驶人员，其肇事事件也同样很少。但是，事实上的证据是：以每1000辆汽车或者以每行驶1000公里来计算的肇事比率，虽然一直不断下降，但车祸总数及车祸损害程度，仍在继续上升。

很久以来我们都知道，在所有肇事事件中，酒醉驾驶或极少数有"行车肇事倾向"的驾驶人员所引发的车祸，往往占车祸数的3/4左右；而这种车祸，确实不是驾驶学校所能负责，也不是公路不良所造成的。很久以来我们也知道，努力的重点，其实在于应针对那些非交通安全法规和训练所能控制的车祸。就是说，除了公路安全和驾驶训练，还得同时在技术方面设法，使得万一发生车祸，伤亡情况可以减轻。汽车制造业应该做的，是在技术方面不但使车辆在"正常驾驶"下能确保安全，而且在"不正常驾驶"下也能够提高车辆的安全性。但美国汽车制造业竟没有看到这一层。

由上面这个例子，我们可以知道"一知半解"有时比"全然不知"更为可怕。凡属与交通安全有关的机构，包括汽车制造商、公路安全委员会、驾驶员协会以及保险公司等，都有一种误解，不敢承认车祸绝对不能避免，而以为凡有车祸即是因为忽略了安全。这种情况，正像我们上一代的老祖母一看见专治性病的医师，就认为这种医师在鼓励不道德的性关系一样。这是将"是非"和"道德"混淆在一起了。正因为人都免不了有时会混淆不清，以至于产生了不周全的假定，这才是最危险和最难于改正的。

一位有效的决策者碰到问题，总是先假定该问题为"经常性质"。他总是先假定该问题是一种表面现象，另有根本性的问题存在。他要找出真正的问题，不会只满足于解决表面现象。

即使问题确实是偶发性的，有经验的决策者也会先怀疑这是不是另一项新的经常问题的首次出现。

所以，一位有效的决策者，第一步总是先从最高层次的观念方面去寻求解决方法。如果公司资金不足，他不会马上想到发行最容易售出的债券；如果他认为在可预见的未来，有赖资本市场的协助，他会创造一类新的投资人，设计一种也许目前根本还不存在的大众资本市场的新证券。如果公司的各部门主管都非常干练，但是不肯听命，他也不会马上想到杀鸡儆猴，而会从更根本的立场建立一种大组织的观念。

社会生活及政治生活中最显著的一项事实是：暂时性的事物往往具有永久性。这类的例子很多，比如英国的旅馆登记制、法国的房屋租赁管制以及美国政府中的许多"临时建筑",都是在第一次世界大战时草草创设的。当时都以为最多三五个月就会取消,可是经过几十年,这些临时措施还是屹然不动。有效的管理者都懂得这个道理。当然,这并不是说有效的管理者永远不会采用临时措施。不过,他会问自己:"如果这个临时办法被长期执行下去,我会愿意吗?"如果他的回答是否定的,他就会从更基本、更理性及更广泛的观念上去谋求解决之道。换言之,他会建立一项正确的原则。

因此,有效的管理者所做的决策一般不会太多。但这并不是因为做一项原则性的大决策需要很长的时间。事实上原则性的决策,通常不会比头痛医头、脚痛医脚的决策所需的时间更长。有效的管理者实际上没有做太多决策的必要。他既然已经设计了一套规则和政策来解决经常事件,就可以运用有关的规则来解决绝大多数的问题。西方有一句谚语说:"法律越复杂,律师越无能。"在那样的国家里,每一个案件都将是一个独特的案件,而不是一般法理下的案件。同样的道理,一位管理者如果天天要做决策,时时要做决策,那恰恰说明他是个疏懒和无效的人。

决策者也常常要留意是否有非常事件出现。他一定经常自问:"这一解释能说明某些事件吗?能说明所有同类的事件吗?"他一定经常想,这个问题的解答,可能引发什么结果?例如能否消除车祸?然后观察是否果然消除了车祸。最后,当出现了别的非常事件时,当出现了他的解答所不能解释的事件时,或者当发生的结果竟与预期不符时,他又回过头来重新检讨原来的问题。

事实上这样的步骤,早在2000多年前希腊医学家希波克拉底就提出来了,也正是希腊哲人亚里士多德所提倡的科学方法,也是300多年前科学家伽利略所应用的方法。换言之,这些步骤是自古以来的学人早已经说过、用过且经过时间考验的规则,人人能学会,人人也能有系统地应用。

决策的第二个要素,在于确实了解决策应遵循的规范。决策的目标是什么？换言之，最低限度应该达成什么目的？应该满足什么条件？用科学的术语来说，这就是所谓"边界条件"。一项有效的决策必须符合边界条件，必须足以达成目的。

边界条件说明得越清楚和越精细，据以做出的决策越有效，越能达成决策的目的。反过来说，边界条件不够明确，则所做的决策不论看起来如何了不起，都肯定是一项无效的决策。

通常，探求边界条件的方法，是探求"解决某一问题应有什么最低需要"。通用公司的斯隆在1922年接任总裁时想必做过这样的检讨："如果解除各独立部门的自主权，能满足本公司的需要吗？"他的答案是不能。他的问题的边界条件，在于使各经营部门都具备经营能力，负起经营责任。此外，他还需要一个统一的中央管制。所以，归结起来，根据对边界条件的了解，他的问题是公司组织结构的问题，不是人事协调的问题，这使他获得了最后的结论。

边界条件往往不容易找出来，而且每个人所看到的边界条件往往也不尽相同。

美国大停电的那天早上，除了《纽约时报》，纽约市所有报纸都没有出版。原来那天停电时，《纽约时报》立刻把报纸改在赫德逊河对岸的纽瓦克印刷，当时纽瓦克还没有停电。当地的印刷厂除印刷本地的《纽瓦克晚报》外，还有很大的剩余劳动力。《纽约时报》本预订要印100多万份，结果却只印出了不到一半。这其中有个原因：据说就在《纽约时报》上了印刷机之后（这是当时许多人都知道的一个插曲），总编辑忽然跟他的三位助手起了争执，他们争论的问题只是某一个英文单词如何分节。这一争论据说花费了48分钟之久，正是该报所能享有印刷时间的一半。原来是《纽约时报》自己订了一套英文写作的标准：他们印出的东西绝不容许有任何文法上的错误。

我们不知道《纽约时报》这段故事是否属实——我本人就不大相信，但是任何人恐怕都会奇怪，为什么《纽约时报》管理当局会有那样的规定。不过，既然报纸有了那样的规定，总编辑坚持不容许文法错误，这一决定总是对的。总编辑的心目中所看到的边界条件，不是报纸每天应该发行多少份，而是不得出现任何错误，以保持《纽约时报》英文文法的权威。

有效的管理者明白，一项不符合边界条件的决策，肯定是无效和不适当的决策。不符合边界条件的决策，有时比一项符合"错误的边界条件"的决策更加误事。当然，不符合边界条件与符合错误的边界条件，两者都是错误的决策。不过，边界条件错了，还可能有修正的余地，决策仍可能成为有效的决策。如果根本与规范相反，那就难于补救了。

事实上，我们对边界条件必须保持清醒的认识，这能提醒我们一项决策什么时候应该抛弃。这里我们可以举出两个实例来说明。第一个实例，是边界条件含糊不清的决策；第二个实例，则是边界条件清晰明确，因而决策人能够立即以新决策来取代不合时宜的决策。

第一个实例，是关于第一次世界大战时德军参谋本部所做的"舒利芬计划"。所谓舒利芬计划，是德军在东西两面同时作战的战略。根据这一计划的构想，德军对付俄军，只需用小部分兵力来牵制，因为当时俄军力量较弱；但对付法军则要全力作战，期望以闪电战一举歼灭法军，然后再转而对付俄军。按照这一计划，自然在作战初期，德军要让俄军深入德境，等到对法之战获胜之后，再开始对俄军反攻。不料事出意外,俄军侵入德境的速度太快,1914年8月,东普鲁士已全面告急了。

当初舒利芬将军拟订作战计划时胸有成竹,一切边界条件都十分明确。然而他的继任将领,只擅长作战而拙于决策和战略。所以,德军后来竟抛弃了舒利芬计划中最基本的原则:德国的军力应集中而不应分散。按理来说,此时德军可以将舒利芬计划完全抛弃。然而他们却固执于原计划,遂使原定目标不可能达成。其结果是,德军在西边的兵力调走了,使对法之战的胜利无法贯彻到底;而在东边的兵力,又不足以对抗俄军。终于造成舒利芬计划中,原欲竭力避免的一种"僵持战局"产生了。僵持战局是兵力的消耗,靠人力才能取胜,而不能依靠优秀的战略。所以,从此以后,德军的作战完全走了样,只能靠随机应变,靠鼓励士气和奇迹,而不是靠最初所订的战略了。

现在再举第二个例子,是1933年罗斯福总统的故事。罗斯福总统当初在竞选活动中提出的口号是"经济复兴"。他拟订了一套经济复兴计划,原是以1933年时美国财政的保守政策和预算平衡为基础的。可是不巧在罗斯福总统接任之前,美国的经济几乎整个要垮了。当然,发生了这种变化,罗斯福的经济政策也许在经济上仍然可以行得通,但是在政治上明显是很难搞下去了。

于是,罗斯福立刻另提了一项政治目标,来代替当初的经济目标。他原先计划的是"复兴",现在马上转变为"改造"。新规范要求有政治上的动力,因此,起初以保守为基础的经济政策,现在一变而成为激烈的革新政策了。边界条件变了,罗斯福总统真是反应敏锐,不愧是一位伟大的决策者,能断然放弃原定计划,以保证施政的有效。

在各种不同的可能决策中要识别出哪项决策最危险（所谓最危险的决策，就是勉强可行的决策，即唯有在一切顺利的情况下，才可能达成的决策），也必须了解边界条件。几乎每一项这种决策都有其意义，但是当我们进一步探究其必须满足的规范时，便可能发现各项规范之间存在互相冲突的情况。这样的决策纵然不能说是不可能成功的，最多也只能说成功机会很小而已。若成功需寄望于奇迹，则问题不是奇迹出现的机会太小，而是我们不能依赖奇迹。

不过，对重要的决策而言，要确定边界条件和提出规范，光靠"事实"是不够的，还要看我们如何理解问题，这是一种充满风险的判断。

任何人都可能做出错误的决策，事实上任何人也确实会做出错误的决策。但是，任何人做决策，都不能不顾及边界条件。

决策的第三个要素，是研究"正确"的决策是什么，而不是研究"能为人接受"的决策是什么。人总有采取折中办法的倾向，如果我们不知道符合规范及边界条件的"正确"决策是什么，就无法辨别正确的折中和错误的折中之间的区别，最终不免走到错误的折中的方向去。

那是在1944年，我第一次承接一件最大的管理咨询项目时得到的教训。

当时我负责研究通用汽车公司的管理结构和管理政策，斯隆先生是该公司董事长兼总裁。开始工作的第一天，斯隆先生便请我到他的办公室，对我说："我不知道我们要你研究什么，要你写什么，也不知道该得到什么结果，这些都应该是你的任务。我唯一的要求，只是希望你将你认为正确的部分写下来。你不必顾虑我们的反应，也不必怕我们不同意。尤其重要的是，你不必为了使你的建议容易为我们接受而想到折中。在我们公司里，谈到折中，人人都会，不必劳你驾来指出。你当然可以折中，不过你必须先告诉我们什么是'正确的'，我们才能有'正确的折中'。"

斯隆先生的这段话，我认为可以作为每一位管理者做决策时的座右铭。

所谓"折中"，实际上有两种。第一种"折中"，即俗语所谓"半片面包总比没有面包好"。第二种"折中"，则可用古代所罗门王审判两位妇人争夺婴儿的故事来说明："与其要回半个死孩子，不如保全婴儿性命，将婴儿送与对方好。"第一种"折中"，仍能符合边界条件，因为面包本是为了充饥，半片面包仍然是面包。但是第二种"折中"，却完全不符合边界条件了：婴儿是一条生命，半个婴儿就没有生命可言，只是半个尸体了。

关于决策是否容易被他人接受的问题，如果老是要考虑决策如何才能被他人接受，又怕他人会反对，那就完全是浪费时间，不会有任何结果。世界上的事，你所担心的往往永不出现；而你从来没有担心的，却可能忽然间变成极大的阻碍。这就是说，如果你一开头就问："什么是能让人接受的决策？"那你永远不会有结果。因为在你这样考虑时，通常总是不敢提出最重要的结论，所以你也得不到有效和正确的答案。

决策的第四个要素，是化决策为行动。考虑边界条件，是决策过程中最难的一步；化决策为行动，则是最费时的一步。然而打从决策开始，我们就应该将行动的承诺纳入决策中，否则便是纸上谈兵。

事实上，一项决策如果没有列举详细具体的行动步骤，并指派为某人的工作和责任，那便不能算是一项决策，最多只是一种意愿。

过多的政策说明令人困扰，尤其是在企业机构里更是如此：决策中没有行动的承诺，没有指定何人负责执行。所以，组织的成员看到颁布的政策时，总不免是你看看我、我看看你，以为上级只不过是说说罢了。

若要化决策为行动，首先必须明确无误地回答下面几个问题：谁应该了解这项决策？应该采取什么行动？谁采取行动？这些行动应如何进行，才能使执行的人能够执行？特别是第一个和最后一个问题，通常最容易被人忽略，以至于即使有了结果，也是灾难性的。

这里我们可以用一个故事，来说明"谁应该了解这项决策"的重要性。某一制造生产设备的大厂家，几年前决定停产某一型号的设备。这种设备本是生产线上多年来的标准设备，迄今仍在普遍使用，有关这种设备的订单很多，因此公司决定在未来3年继续向老客户提供这种设备。3年之后，公司才停止生产和销售这种设备。整个公司上下，谁也没有想到这一决策应让什么人知道，甚至公司采购部门也不知道，因此仍然继续订购这种设备的零件，采购人员只知道按销货金额的一定比率购进零件。结果到了公司正式停产的那一天，库房竟积存了足够使用8～10年的零件库存。这笔损失真是相当可观。

决策行动还必须与执行人员的工作能力相适应。

某一化学公司几年前曾发生大批资金冻结于非洲某两个国家，无法汇出之事。该公司为了保护这批资金，决定投资于非洲当地的企业。他们选定的企业，第一，对非洲当地的经济发展确有贡献；第二，不必从外面进口别的资源；第三，该企业将来成功后，一旦该国外汇解冻，应有希望转售于当地企业家，而将资金汇出。因此，该公司便积极着手筹备设厂，发展了一种简单的化学处理程序，加工当地出产的热带水果。那种水果，在那两个国家中都有丰富的产量，但过去因没有加工而腐烂率极高，不能远销西方市场。

经过一番努力，两个国家的工厂都经营得非常成功。但是其中一个厂的厂长过于卖力，设定了过高的技术和管理水平，结果在当地找不到适当人选来接管。而另一个厂的厂长却能充分考虑到当地人员的水平，故加工程序较为简单，管理也较为容易。结果全厂自下而上，都能聘到可用的当地人才。

几年过去，两个国家都可以将外汇汇出了。在这时，公司准备将两家工厂转售当地的企业家。然而，那家有声有色、水准极高的加工厂，由于当地没有适合的技术和管理人才始终无法售出，结果该厂只落得清算了事。而另一家水准平平的工厂，当地投资人都竞相购买，公司不但收回了原先投下的资金，而且还大获其利。

事实上两厂的加工程序和经验方式基本上是相同的，问题只是第一家工厂当初在决策时，没有考虑到："这一决策应由谁来执行才能有效？他们能做些什么？"所以，终于失败了。

尤其是为推行某一决策执行人员必须改变其行为习惯和态度时，化决策为行动更是最重要的考虑。在这种情况下，不但行动责任必须明确指定，执行人员必须确有能力，而且绩效的衡量及标准和有关激励的制度，也都需要配合改变。否则，工作人员就会困于情绪的冲突之中。

例如贝尔电话公司的总裁费尔，当初提出"以服务为目的"的新决策时，如果没有同时设计出可以用于衡量管理绩效的服务标准，则这一决策必将落空。在那以前，贝尔公司一向以盈利或成本作为衡量绩效的标准。由于费尔总裁提出了新标准，所以新目标才能顺利被人接受。

另一个相反的例子，是美国某公司总裁提出了一项新的组织结构和目标，结果失败了。该公司规模庞大，历史悠久，人人都引以为豪，而且人人都认为有变革的必要。这家公司多年来一直在同业中居于领先地位，近年来已呈现老化的迹象。同业中许多规模较小，但更积极的新公司不断兴起，成为该公司的竞争对手。这时董事长为了使变革计划能为人接受，特别将几位老派的代表人物提升到重要职位，坐享高薪，尤其是三位副总裁，也改由老派人物出任。结果这项变革计划终于落空，公司里的人都说："他们不是真想变革！"

所以，如果某一新计划应有某项行为，实际上却在鼓励另一类行为的话，则人人都会明白：原来高层的期望不过如此，所谓变革只是空口说说而已。

当然，要想每一个管理者都能做到像费尔先生一样，能将决策的执行融合于决策本身，那是不容易的。可是，我们至少应该思考，某一决策需要怎样的行动承诺，需要怎样的工作划分以及有些怎样的人才可用。

决策的最后一个要素，是应在决策中建立一项信息反馈制度，以便经常对决策所预期的成果做实际的印证。

决策是人做的，人难免会犯错误。再了不起的决策，也不可能永远正确；即使是最有效的决策，总有一天也是会被淘汰的。

你如果不相信决策会过时失效，费尔和斯隆两位先生的决策可以证明。他们两人的创新力和魄力，可说是无人所能企及，但他们所做的几项大决策，到今天只有一项仍然可用，那就是费尔的"贝尔公司以服务为目的"。费尔当初设计的AT&T普通股，早在20世纪50年代就因情况改变而大为更改了。当时兴起了所谓"机构投资人"，例如养老信托及互助基金等，这些基金便成了中产阶级人士投资的新方式。

再说贝尔研究所，虽然今天仍享有极其优越的地位，可是后来由于科学和技术的神速发展（特别是空间技术和激光的发展），任何一家通信公司都无法独立进行现代的研究工作了。而且，通信技术发展得太快，使电话在75年来头一次出现了许多劲敌。例如信息处理方面的发展，已造成了一种任何通信媒介均无法居于压倒性优势的形势；贝尔公司仅以长途电话通信为主，自然不能再独占通信市场了。至于费尔构想的所谓公众管制，固然今天仍不失为保卫私营电信事业的手段，但是费尔当初费尽心力推动的各州单独立法，也已经日渐不合今天全国性甚至国际性通信系统的时代了。而且贝尔公司当年并没有促成美国联邦政府的立法管制，反而被费尔一直小心避免的延迟方法策略所阻滞。

再说斯隆先生设计的通用汽车公司分权制度，虽然该公司今天仍在采用，但显然有待重新检讨了。当初他设计这一制度的基本原则，多年来已屡经修改变得面目全非了。例如当年独立经营的各汽车部门，今天已演变成无法完全控制其制造与装配的局面，所以自然无法对其经营成果负责。斯隆时代的各种品牌，从雪佛兰到凯迪拉克，也已不像当年斯隆构想的，可以代表车主的不同身价了。尤其重要的是，当年斯隆所设计的是一家"美国公司"，后来虽然增设了国外子公司，但在组织及管理结构上，毕竟仍然是一家"美国公司"。可是到了今天，通用汽车公司已成为一家"国际公司"了。该公司的成长和机会，早已经走出了美国的领域，尤其是在欧洲的发展更远远出乎当年之所料。以今天的情况来看，通用汽车公司的前途，实系于该公司是否具有跨国公司的原则和组织。斯隆1922年所做的努力，今天已到了必须再努力一次不可的地步。我们可以预料，如果汽车工业遇到经济困难，这一努力恐怕将更为迫切。如果今天该公司再不彻底重新检讨的话，斯隆的计划必将变成通用汽车公司的绊脚石，阻碍其发展。○

艾森豪威尔当选美国总统时，他的前任杜鲁门总统曾说："可怜的艾克，他是军人，下达命令后必有人执行；现在他要坐在这间大办公室里了，只怕他发布命令之后，一件事也做不成。"

为什么美国总统发布的命令不能贯彻，这不是因为军事将领比总统的权力更大，其实是因为军事组织早就知道仅仅发布命令是没有用的，必须同时建立反馈制度，可以检讨命令的执行；而最可靠的反馈，在于亲自视察。○ 然而当了总统，通常只能批阅报告。批阅报告有什么用呢？在军队里，长官发了命令，总得亲自检查命令的执行，至少也得派遣代表去检查，而不会坐在总部等候报告。这不是说军人不信任下属，而是经验告诉他们，"报告或沟通"不一定靠得住。

---

○ 2009年，通用汽车申请破产保护。经过一年半的改革和精简，2010年11月18日，通用汽车重返华尔街。——编者注

○ 这种制度其实在很久以前就由我们的祖先建立起来了。古希腊的历史学家修昔底德（约公元前460—前400年）和色诺芬（约公元前431—前350年）都视这一点为理所当然，中国古代的军事教科书也如是说——连恺撒大帝也是这样做的。

这就是为什么营长常到食堂去亲自品尝菜肴。照理说，他只要看看菜单，指示一番就可以了。但是他没有这样做，他总是要自己到食堂去，看看他的官兵究竟吃些什么。

自从电脑问世以来，这个问题更加重要了。因为有了电脑，决策者和执行者之间的关系可能更加疏远。所以，如果管理者老坐在办公室，不到工作现场，他和实际情形必将越来越脱节。电脑处理的只是抽象资料，抽象资料只有经过实践的检验之后才是可靠的。否则，电脑必将引人走入歧途。

若想了解赖以做出决策的前提是否仍然有效，或者是否已经过时，亲自检查才最为可靠。而且，这种前提迟早是要过时的，因为现实绝不会一成不变。

我们看到许多早该修改的措施始终没有修改，其原因主要就是管理者不肯亲自去了解情况。企业的决策如此，政府的政策也是如此。

我们需要组织化的信息作为反馈。我们需要数字，也需要报告。可是如果反馈不能反映实际情况，我们又不肯亲自察看，那么我们缺乏有效性也就不该怨谁了。

以上所述，就是决策的要素。

至于决策本身究竟应该如何才能有效，我们在下章讨论。

# CHAPTER 7 | 第 7 章
# 有效的决策

## 个人见解和决策的关系

决策是一种判断,是若干项方案中的选择。所谓选择,通常不是"对"与"错"间的选择,最多只是"大概是对的"与"也许是错的"之间的选择。而绝大多数的选择,都是任何一项方案均不一定优于其他方案时的选择。

大部分关于决策的著作,开宗明义,第一步总是说"先搜集事实"。但是卓有成效的决策者都知道,决策的过程往往不是从搜集事实开始的,而是先从其本人的见解(opinions)开始的。所谓见解,乃是"尚待证实的假设";见解不能获得证实,就毫无价值可言。但要确定什么才是事实,必须先确定相关的标准,尤其是有关的衡量标准。决策有效与否,这是关键所在,也是常引起争论的地方。

许多教科书又说,决策来自大家一致的意见,其实这也不然。有效的决策,常自多种不同且互相冲突的见解中产生,常自多种旗鼓相当、优劣互见的方案中产生。

先要搜集事实是很难做到的。因为没有相关的标准,就不可能找到什么事实。事件本身并非事实。

> 对物理学家而言,物体的"味"和"色"均非事实。但在厨师看来,"味"是他所重视的事实;在画家看来,"色"是他所重视的事实。这就是说,物理学家、厨师和画家,各有其不同的判断标准,故其认定的事实各不相同。

有效的管理者都知道一项决策不是从搜集事实开始,而是先有自己的见解。这样做是正确的。因为凡在某一领域具有经验者,都应该有他的见解。假如说一个人在某一方面经验丰富,而竟然没有见解,那就说明此人没有敏锐的观察力,头脑迟钝。

人总是从自己的见解开始,所以要求决策者从搜集事实开始,是不符合实际的。其结果是,他像所有人一样,往往很容易不假思索地去寻找符合他自己心中结论的事实;他既然先有了结论,必能搜集到许多事实。干过统计工作的人都能体会到这一点,所以往往最不相信统计数字。统计工作人员也许知道提供数字者的立场,也许不知道提供数字者的立场,但是他知道数字的可疑。

因此唯一严谨的方法,唯一可以印证某一见解是否符合实际的方法,应该以明确承认"见解为先"作为基础——这是必要的做法。有了这样的认识,才能知道我们是以"尚待证实的假设"为起点——决策程序如此,科学研究也如此。我们都知道:假设是不必辩论的,却必须经得起验证。经得起验证的假设才值得我们重视,经不起验证者,就只有放弃了。

有效的管理者鼓励大家提出见解。但在鼓励的同时,他也会叫大家深思其见解，认清其见解经过实证后的结果。因此，有效的管理者会问："要验证某一假设是否为真，我们该知道些什么？""要验证某一见解，应有些怎样的事实？"他会培养出一种习惯：他自己这样问，也使与他共事者这样问，认清需要观察些什么，需要研究些什么以及需要验证些什么。他会要求提出见解的每一个人，负责理清他们可以并且应该期待和寻找什么样的事实。

但是最关键性的问题应该是："相关的标准是什么？"由这一问题，很自然地会转到关于衡量的课题：问题本身的衡量和决策的衡量。只要分析一下一项真正有效的决策是如何达成的，一项真正适当的决策是如何达成的，我们就能发现我们为决定衡量方法所耗用的时间和精力极多。

贝尔公司总裁费尔先生获得该公司应以服务为目的的结论，便是经过这样的思考。

有效的决策人通常必先假定传统的衡量方法并非适当的衡量方法。否则，他就用不着做决策了，他只略做简单的调整就可以了。传统的衡量方法反映的是昨天的决策。我们之所以需要一项新决策，正表示过去的衡量方法已不适于今天了。

自从朝鲜战争以来，美国军用物资的采购和库存政策一直不理想。军方也曾为这个问题绞尽脑汁，做过许多研究，但情况不但没有好转，反而每况愈下。直到麦克纳马拉出任国防部长，才向军需库存的传统衡量方法发起了挑战。在过去，军需物资的采购和库存，一直以物资项目的总项数和总金额为衡量的基础。麦克纳马拉一反此项传统，改用另一种衡量方法。他发现在所有军需物资中，有极少数的项目（也许只占总项数的4%）是高价物资，它们的采购金额占采购总金额的 90% 以上。

同样地，他又发现有极少数的项目（大约也只占总项数的 4%）是重要物资，足以维持 90% 的战备。在这两项物资（高价物资和战备物资）中，尚有部分重复者，所以合并起来，全部重要物资只不过占总项数的 5% 或 6% 而已。

麦克纳马拉极力主张这类物资应予分别管理，严加管制。至于其余的 95% 的物资，论金额不大，论重要性也不致对战备产生重大影响，他主张按照所谓"例外原则"来管理。麦克纳马拉这种一反过去传统的新衡量方法，立刻成为军需物资采购和库存的高度有效决策，也使整个后勤制度为之改观。

那么如何才能找出适当的衡量方法呢？一如本书前文所述，只有依靠"反馈"的制度。不过这里的所谓反馈，是决策前的反馈。

人事方面的许多问题都用"平均"数字来衡量，例如"平均每百人发生停工事故数""缺勤率""病假率"等。但是一位管理者如果肯亲自出去看一看，就能发现他需要的是另一套衡量方法。"平均数"适用于保险公司的需要，但是对人事管理的决策没有意义，有时甚至还会误导人们。

以"停工事故"而言，可能大多数意外事件均发生在工厂内某一两个部门里。至于"缺勤率"，也可能大部分出在某一个单位。"病假率"，也不见得每一部门都与"平均数"相近，可能只局限于某一部分人，例如年轻女性。所以，有关人事方面的措施，如果仅以"平均数"为依据——例如据以推动全厂性的安全运动，就不见得能收到预期的效果，甚至可能使情况更糟。

同样的道理，汽车制造业人士没有亲身查看，也正是该行业未能及早发现应该改善车辆安全设计的原因。汽车行业一向采用惯用的衡量方法，如"平均每行车公里交通事故件数"。如果他们能亲身查看，就会发现交通事故应该改以"人体伤残情况"来衡量。如果能这样做，他们就能知道这项"安全运动"的重点，该放在"一旦发生事故时如何使损伤减至最低"方面，也就是说，应该改良车辆的设计。

找出适当的衡量方法不是数学方法所能解决的，这是一项带有风险的判断。

说到判断，必须先有两项以上的方案，从其中选择一项。而且，如果说一项判断可以斩钉截铁地定其"对"与"错"，那也不称其为判断了。唯有在多项方案中，我们需凭借深入研究判断才能有所决定时，才称之为判断。

因此，有效的管理者一定要求先有若干种不同的衡量方案，再自其中选取最适当的一种。

以企业投资为例，通常都有多种衡量方法。其一，衡量投入资金需要多久才能收回；其二，衡量投资的获利能力；其三，衡量投资收益的"现值"。此外还有其他方法，但有效的管理者不会仅以其中某一方法为满足。即使会计部门强烈地推荐某一种方法最科学，有效的管理者也知道，任何方法都只能显示投资决策的某一层面。所以，除非他对每一角度都看得清清楚楚，否则不会轻易判断哪种方法最适合。会计部门也许不胜其烦，然而有效的管理者仍必须坚持分别用三种不同方法加以计算，他才会判定"某一衡量方法对这个投资决策来讲是最适合的"。

如果没有考虑每一个可能方案，就是偏颇。

这也正说明了有效的决策者，为什么故意不遵循教科书原则。教科书上说，决策需寻求"意见的一致"，但是他们却有意"制造"互相冲突的不同意见。

换句话说，管理者的决策不是从"众口一词"中得来的。好的决策，应以互相冲突的意见为基础，从不同的观点和不同的判断中选择。所以，除非有不同的见解，否则就不可能有决策。这是决策的第一条原则。

> 据说，通用汽车公司总裁斯隆曾在该公司一次高层会议中说过这样一段话："诸位先生，在我看来，我们对这项决策已经有了完全一致的看法了。"出席会议的委员们都点头表示同意。但是他接着说："现在，我宣布会议结束，这一问题延到下次开会时再行讨论。我希望下次开会时能听到相反的意见，只有这样，我们才能得到对这项决策的真正了解。"

斯隆做决策从来不靠"直觉"，他总是强调必须用事实来检验看法。他反对一开始就先下结论，然后再寻找事实来支持这个结论。他懂得正确的决策必须建立在各种不同意见充分讨论的基础之上。

在美国历史上，每一位有效的总统，都各有其一套激发反对意见的办法，以帮助自己做出有效的决策。林肯、西奥多·罗斯福、富兰克林·罗斯福、杜鲁门，都各有他们的方式。他们共同的秘诀在于激发反对意见，以便从各种角度去了解决策的真正含义。据说华盛顿总统最不愿见到冲突和争辩，希望有一个意见一致的内阁。但是实际上华盛顿在处理重要问题时，常分别去征求汉密尔顿（Hamilton，华盛顿时代的财政部长）和杰斐逊（Jefferson，美国第三任总统）的意见，以便得到不同的看法。

最懂得运用不同意见的美国总统，当首推富兰克林·罗斯福。每次遇有重大事件时，他总是约请他的一位助理，说："你研究一个问题，但是请你保守机密。"（罗斯福当然知道，他请助理"保守机密"，必然会使这个问题很快传遍华盛顿。）然后他再约请几位助理，明知道这几位助理一向跟第一位助理意见不同，也同样嘱咐他们去研究那同一问题，而且也同样要求他们"保守机密"。这样，罗斯福就能搜集到各种不同的意见，也可以从各种不同的角度去看一个问题。当然，罗斯福这样做，他自有把握不会被任何人的意见所困。

罗斯福总统这一手，曾经遭到一位内阁成员的激烈批评。那是罗斯福总统的内政部长伊基斯，他批评罗斯福的政权是最无聊的政权。在伊基斯的日记中，充满了指责罗斯福的种种形容词，"懒散""轻率"，甚至"误国"。然而，罗斯福自有他的看法，他认为身为美国总统，主要任务不在于维持政权，而在于做决策，做正确的决策。而要做正确的决策，最好的办法就是仿效法院的判案方法，从两边的辩论中去求取事实真相，使全部有关的事实都能摆在法官面前。

## 反面意见的运用

为什么该有反面意见，主要有三项理由。

第一，唯有反面意见，才能保护决策者不致沦为组织的俘虏。在一个组织中，所有人都必有求于决策者，每个人都各有所求，都希望主管的决策能对自己有利。上至美国总统，下至企业机构中一位初级工程师修改某一工程设计莫不如此。

唯一能突破这一陷阱，使决策者不致成为某方面的俘虏的办法，就在于引起争辩、掌握实据和经过深思熟虑的反面意见。

第二，反面意见本身，正是决策所需的"另一方案"。决策时只有一种方案，别无其他选择，无论多么深思熟虑，那与赌博何异？只有一种方案，失败的概率必高。也许是这决策打从开始就错了，也许是其后因情况变化而使决策错了，如果在决策过程中原有若干方案可供选择，则决策者进可攻、退可守，有多方思考和比较的余地。反之，舍此以外别无他途，决策人在遇到该决策行不通的时候，就只有背水一战了。

本书第6章曾介绍1914年德国的舒利芬战略计划和罗斯福总统的经济计划的故事。在这两个故事中，原来的计划到了应该发生效果的紧要关头，都忽然起了变化。

先说德军的作战计划，到头来走不通了，德军始终没有第二套战略方案，所以只好痛苦地撑持下去，走一步改一步。这实在是无可奈何的不幸。实际上前后25年，德军参谋本部从来没有想到拟另一套计划。参谋本部的力量，全部耗用在研究舒利芬计划的细节上了。等到舒利芬计划失败时，再也找不出第二条可行之路了。

德军所有将领虽然都受过严格的战略训练，可是在那种情况下也只有随机应变。换言之，他们只能时而向东，时而向西，始终不明白到底是为了什么。

1914年另有一次事件，也足以说明"别无选择"的危险。在当时俄军下动员令后，俄国沙皇另外有了一套构想。沙皇召见他的参谋长，命他解除动员令。然而参谋长答复说："不可能了。动员令已下，不能解除了，我们也没有准备解除动员令的计划。"虽然俄军在那最后关头如果能够停止军事行动，第一次世界大战的局面也不见得就有所改观，但我相信或许会有一次最后的清醒机会。

罗斯福总统的故事与上面所说的正好相反。在他当选就任总统之前，竞选活动全以正统的经济计划为基础。但是同时，罗斯福总统还有另一批后来被称为"智囊团"的人才，专门研究"替代方案"。那套替代方案以早年西奥多·罗斯福总统时代进步党的建议为基础，是一种根本不同的政策，以经济和社会的全面改革为目的。那一批研究"替代方案"的人才，后来都成了罗斯福总统的智囊团。因此，罗斯福接任总统后，美国金融制度起了变化，在当初的正统经济计划行不通的时候，他立刻胸有成竹地提出了第二套计划。所以，他才有一项有效的政策。

反过来说，如果罗斯福当初没有另一方案，恐怕他肯定会像德军参谋本部和俄国沙皇一样，要迷惘而不知所措了。罗斯福在就任之初，提出的计划是以19世纪传统的国际经济理论为基础的。他在1932年11月当选，第2年3月就职。谁知道就在这短短的4个多月中间，国际经济和国内经济都一落千丈。罗斯福看得很清楚，在这样重大的变化之下，如果提不出另一套方案，他就只有听天由命了。罗斯福纵然有天大的本领，也只能在骤然阴云密布之中摸索前进，也只能从一个极端到另一个极端摇摆不定，也只能听任那些贩卖经济政策狗皮膏药的郎中的摆布，一会儿说该使美元贬值，一会儿又说该恢复银本位制了，而两者都与真正的问题无关。

另一个例子，是1936年罗斯福再度全胜当选总统后，他计划改组最高法院，却遭到了失败。当时他以为自己能控制国会，想不到事与愿违，提出的计划受到国会的强烈反对。然而，这一次他却提不出别的方案了。结果不但无法推行他的改革计划，甚至他的政治控制力也受到了影响（虽然他当时仍拥有极高的声望）。

最后第三个理由，是反面意见可以激发想象力。当然，纯粹为了某一问题去找答案,并不一定非有想象力不可,只有解决数学问题才最需要想象力。但是一位管理者处理问题时,不论是政治、经济、社会问题,还是军事问题,通常总是"不确定性"极高,此时就需要有"创造性"的解决方案,来开创新的局面。这就是说,我们需要想象力,因为缺乏想象力的管理者不可能从另一个不同的、全新的角度去观察和理解。

我得承认,有丰富想象力的人并不是太多,但他们也不像人们认为的那么稀少。想象力需要被激发后才能充分发挥出来,否则它只能是一种潜在的、尚未开发的能力。不同意见,特别是那些经过缜密推断和反复思考的、论据充分的不同意见,便是激发想象力的最为有效的因素。

> 童话故事中的"矮胖子"诡计多端,早餐尚未用完便想到了许多不可能的事。我们当然很少有人能像"矮胖子"的创造人——《艾丽丝漫游奇境记》的作者卡罗尔那样富有想象力。但是孩子们读《艾丽丝漫游奇境记》,都读得津津有味,分享艾丽丝的乐趣。近代心理学家布鲁纳曾说:8岁的儿童也能看出"4×6等于6×4",可是"威尼斯盲人(a blind Venetian)却不等于软百叶窗帘(a Venetian blind)"。⊖这才是高级的想象力。在我们成年人的决策中,确实有不少是以"威尼斯盲人等于软百叶窗帘"的假定为基础的。
>
> 另一个老故事说,维多利亚时代南海某小岛的一位岛民前往西方旅行,归来后对岛上亲友畅谈他在西方所看到的"奇迹"。他说西方人的家中竟没有水喝。而在他们的小岛上,用水都是用半截竹筒引进来,所以家中可以"看见"流水。可是西方人家中是否真没有水呢?那只是因为西方国家用的是自来水,用水时需打开水龙头。但这位岛民在西方旅行时,谁也没有告诉他扭开水龙头即可有水。

---

⊖ 引自布鲁纳的著作 *Toward a Theory of Instruction* 第64页。

每次我听到这段故事，就会联想到人的想象力。想象力正像水一样，必须扭开"水龙头"才会流出。而激发争辩的"反面意见"，正是想象力水管的水龙头。

所以，有效的管理者会运用反面意见。只有这样，他才能避免为"似是而非"的看法所征服；他才能得到"替代方案"，以供他选择和决定；他也才能在万一决策行不通时不至于迷惘。同时，鼓励反面意见，可以启发他本人的想象力，启发与他共事者的想象力。反面意见能把"言之有理"者转化为"正确"，再把"正确"转化为"良好的决策"。

有效的管理者绝不认为某一行动方向为"对"，其他行动方向均为"错"。他也绝不坚持己见，以自己为"对"，以他人为"错"。有效的管理者第一步会先找出为什么各人有不同的意见。

当然，有效的管理者知道世上有蠢材，也有恶作剧的人。但是，他绝不会将持不同意见者轻易地视为蠢材或捣蛋者，他总是假定任何人提出不同的意见，必是出于至诚。所以，某人的意见纵然错了，也是由于此人所看到的现实不同，或他所关切的是另一个不同的问题。因此，有效的管理者会问："如果此人的立场果真正当、果真合理、果真有见地的话，此人的看法又将如何呢？"有效的管理者关切的是"理解"。只有在有了确切的理解之后，他才研究谁是谁非。⊖

> 某一律师事务所，给刚从法学院毕业的新手报到后分配的第一件工作，总是一个最棘手的案子。此办法对新手虽然太"苛"，可是却使他不能不静下心来，替当事人解决问题（当然，他在研究这桩案子时，自然不能忽视对方的律师也在研究）。同时，这也是对

---

⊖ 这当然并不是什么新观点，是玛丽·帕克·福列特在她的著作《能动管理》中，扩展了柏拉图在《斐德罗篇》中关于"修辞学"的讨论。

新手一种很好的训练。这样的训练，能使新手一开头就知道办案时不能"只求自己了解本案"，而必须考虑对方律师如何了解本案，这样，新手就能从两方面来看一个案子，而将一案当成两案来思考了。只有这样，他才能对他处理的案件有真正的了解。也只有这样，他才能学会准备各种不同的对策。

我们绝大多数人，不论是否身为管理者，大概都没有像上面这则故事那样做，我们大多仅是从问题的一面着手，也以为问题仅此一面。

　　美国钢铁工业界的巨头谁都不曾问过："为什么每次我们一提到'超额雇用'⊖这个名词，工会的人就会那样不满？"同样地，工会人员也从来没有反躬自问："为什么我们本没有什么行动，而管理当局会庸人自扰地提到'超额雇用'？"劳资双方都互相指责对方的错误。如果双方都能努力了解对方的立场，自然都能更为坚强，钢铁业界的劳资关系也自然会好得多。

身为管理者，不论他本身刻意求好之心如何迫切，也不论他如何自信看出了别人的错误，只要他打算做一项正确的决策，就会将了解"对方"作为他探求"另一方案"的方法。见解的冲突正是他的"工具"，运用这项"工具"，他才能保证自己看清问题的每一面。

　　最后，有效的管理者还得再问一个问题："我们是不是真的需要一项决策？"为什么要问这个问题呢？因为有时候什么都不做也是一种决策。
　　做一项决策像动一次外科手术。任何新的决策都不免影响既有的制度，

---

⊖ 超额雇用（featherbedding），指工会迫使雇主尽可能雇用多些工人的行动，尤其是反对采用节省劳动力的机器，或是要求以超额的工人来操作新的机器。——编者注

因此多少得冒风险。外科医师不到非动手术不可的时候绝不轻言开刀；同样地，不到非做决策的时候，也不宜轻易做出决策。每一位决策人也正像外科医师一样，各有不同性格。有的倾向于急进，有的偏于保守。但是大体上，他们信守的原则是一致的。

什么时候需要决策？如果继续保守成规，情况就会恶化，那就必须做出新的决策。遇有新的机会来临，而且这个新的机会至关重要、稍纵即逝的时候，也必须立刻做出新的决策。

在费尔担任贝尔公司总裁期间，许多人都看到了该公司有被政府接管的可能。大家都在力图挽救，但是大家挽救的方法只是就事论事。所以，有的反对这项或那项政府法案，有的反对这位国会议员和拉拢那位国会议员。但是只有费尔，了解这类办法肯定仍不能挽救公司的颓败，即使是打赢了每一仗，也不能打赢整个战争。所以，他认定了必须采取根本的办法，来创造一个新局面。只有他看清楚了应该建立一种"公众管制"，才是避免贝尔公司被政府接管的有效对策。

决策的反面是不做任何决策。有时候不做任何改变，事情也不会出问题。我们问："保持现状，会有什么后果？"如果答案是："不会有变化。"那我们又何必横生枝节？即使问题颇为恼人，但问题并不重要，也不致有什么严重后果，那我们也没有改变的必要。

了解这层道理的管理者恐怕不多。一位财务主管感到财务危机重重，大声疾呼要求降低成本，连细枝末节也不放过。然而从小处来降低成本，即使有成果，其成果也微不足道。举例来说，他也许发现公司里最难控制成本的地方在销售和物流部门。于是他用了种种办法，去帮助这两个部门控制成本。他发现某一部门"多"用了两三位老职员，于是大声叫嚷裁员，不顾别人对他的印象。别人说那两三位老职员已届退休之年，予以解雇也不会有多大差别，但他不听。他还说："为什么要留用这几位老职员，而使整个工厂受到影响？"

这次事件过去之后，公司同仁谁也不记得他当初挽救了公司，大家只记得他公报私仇，说他跟两三位与他合不来的老职员作对——而事实正是如此。其实，2000年前罗马律法就曾说过："行政长官不宜考虑鸡毛蒜皮之类的事情。"直到今天，我们的决策者还是需要好好学习这句话。

我们通常所做的决策，大部分都介于必须做决策与可以不做决策这两者之间。我们碰到的问题，大多数并不是"随他去吧，船到桥头自然直"，但也不至于严重到不做新决策便将无可救药的程度。我们的问题，通常多是如何改进，而不是如何做真正的变革和创新。当然，这类问题还是颇值得我们重视的。这就是说，对这类问题，虽不做新决策我们同样能够生存，但有了新决策，情况也许会变得更好。

在这种情形下，有效的管理者会做比较：做了新决策，可能有什么收获和风险；不做又可能有什么损失。至于如何比较，通常没有一定的公式。但是，实际上只要遵循下面两项原则就够了：

- 如果利益远大于成本及风险，就该行动；
- 行动或不行动，切忌只做一半或折中。

以外科医师为例，做一次切除扁桃体或切除阑尾（俗称割盲肠）的手术固然是冒险，但是如果只切除一半，同样是一大冒险。手术不成功，不但治不了病，反将引起更严重的后果。所以，开刀或不开刀，不能只开一半。同样地，有效的决策者，会采取行动或不采取行动，而不会只采取一半行动。只采取一半行动才是不折不扣的错误，是一项绝对不符合最起码的要求和不符合边界条件的错误。

一切条件具备，现在就只等着决策了。规范已经清楚了，不同方案已经想到了，得失也衡量了。一切都已经一目了然，应该采取什么行动，也已经清清楚楚。该采取什么决策，已是明摆着的了。

不幸的是，绝大多数决策是在此时流产的。决策者这才"恍然大悟"，原来决策那么难受，那么不受欢迎，那么不容易。到了这一步，不但需要判断，更需要勇气。俗话说良药苦口，这句话虽不见得是真理，但实际上良药却多苦口。同样地，我们不敢说所有的决策都会让人觉得痛苦，但实际上有效的决策执行起来往往会让人产生不愉快的感觉。

到了这一步，有效的管理者绝不会说："让我们再研究研究！"那只证明这位管理者缺乏胆识。没有胆识的人可能失败一千次，有胆识的人则只失败一次。面对"再研究研究"的呼声，卓有成效的管理者会问："是不是再做一次研究就能讨论出新方案来？即使研究出新的方案，它是不是一定比现有的方案好？"如果答案是否定的，那么管理者就不需要再去做任何研究，他绝不会因为自己的优柔寡断再去浪费别人的时间。

不过，如果他的确尚未了解清楚，他也不会冒冒失失地决策。有效的管理者都知道希腊哲人苏格拉底所说的"守护神"，那是潜藏在人身体内的"神灵"，他不断提醒我们："千万要小心！"但是，只要决策是正确的，就没有理由因其执行困难、因其可怕，或因其麻烦而退却。略加犹豫有时难免，但也仅仅是"略加"犹豫而已。在我认识的许多最佳的决策者中，就有这样一位，他常说："我通常总得停下来，多想一下。"

决策如果真有困难，十有八九是出在不必要的细节上。至于那第十次，也许是决策前的思考不周,忽略了问题中某一最重要的事实,也许是有某项疏忽或失误,也许是研究判断错了。但是,通常在最后总能"豁然开朗",半夜中想到了线索而突然起床,就像福尔摩斯在侦探小说中说的:"对了,为什么凶手出现时,巴斯克维尔猎犬没有叫?"

但是有效的决策者不会等得太久,也许一两天,最多一两个星期。只要"守护神"不在他耳朵边,他便会尽快行动。

组织雇用管理者并不是要他去做他自己喜欢做的事。管理者的责任是要把该做的事做好,具体地说,就是要进行有效的决策。

## 决策与电脑

今天我们有了电脑,上文所说有关决策的道理,是不是仍能适用?有人说,有了电脑,可以取代决策者了,至少可以取代中层管理部门的决策者了。再过几年,经营方面的决策会全部由电脑来取代,最后连战略方面的决策,也会全部由电脑来取代了。

但事实上,电脑问世以后,今天所见大部分的现场调节性的"决策",估计仍必须由管理者承担不可。而且,电脑的问世,使今天许多只是"奉命行事"的被动的管理者,也必将转变为真正的管理者和决策者。

电脑是管理者强有力的工具。电脑像锤头和铁钳——但不像轮子和锯子,人不能做的工作,电脑也不能做。但是电脑能做加减计算,而且远比人做得快。电脑只是工具,所以电脑不会厌烦,不会疲劳,也不会要求加班费。当然,人发明的工具,对某些工作能比人做得更好,也具有更大的工作能量。例如汽车、飞机、电视,能做人所不能做的事,使人的能力得到极大的增长。但是电脑也像其他工具一样,只能做一项或两项工作,也有能力的限制。电脑的这种局限性使我们的管理者不得不自己承担起做真正决策的责任，将目前这种调节性决策提高到真正决策的水平上来。

电脑的主要优点，在于它是一种"逻辑的机器"。交给电脑一个程序，电脑便能完全听命，而且快速无比。但电脑究竟只是笨脑，因为逻辑本身就是笨脑。电脑只能做简单和明显的工作。反之，人类不是逻辑的，而是具有感官的，因此，人会马虎，也会懒散。但是人有智慧和洞察力，因此能够根据现场的情况灵活反应。换言之，即使资料不足或根本没有资料，人也能推断全貌。而且，人不需要输入一套程序，自能记住许多事情。

一位传统的典型经理人常做的现场调节性的决策，就是有关库存和运输方法的决策。一位地区业务经理，肯定知道他的客户A的工厂生产程序排得很紧，所以如果对A送货不按时，A便将发生存料断档的麻烦了。而客户B的工厂通常存料充裕，所以送货即使延迟几天，B也不致有太大的困扰。他又知道客户C的工厂已开始抱怨，打算改向别家工厂采购原料了。他还知道某一产品缺货时该如何调配。他根据这类经验，自然能做适当的调节和适应。

可是电脑却办不到。除非能把所有的资料都输进电脑，告诉电脑公司政策是重视客户A还是B，电脑才能认识A和B的轻重。电脑能做的只是"听命"，只是按照输入的程序行事。与普通的计算器和收银机相比，电脑并不能多做什么"决策"。电脑能做的，只是计算而已。

若一家公司决定采用电脑来做库存控制，第一便是应制定一套规则，该公司必须有一套库存政策。但是，一旦制定了规则，也决定了政策之后，公司当局便会发现有关库存的决策，原来并不是什么库存决策，而是企业风险的决策。所谓库存决策，原来不过是各项风险的平衡：例如交货是否令客户失望的风险，生产程序是否稳定的成本和风险，存货积压资金的多寡以及存货变质、过时、损坏的成本和风险等。

传统上的种种政策，对电脑并没有太大的帮助。例如"本公司的目标，是要为90%的客户，完成90%的交货承诺"。这样的政策，以传统的眼光来看，应该是明确无比的了。但是如果交给电脑，却是全无意义——这项政策到底表示什么呢？是说凡是接到客户的订单，每一客户我们都只交货90%？还是说我们只对"好客户"如约交货？可是"好客户"又是什么意思？还是说凡属本公司任何产品，我们均只答允交货90%？还是说只对"重要的产品"我们如约交货？那么"重要产品"又是什么意思？某项产品我们认为不是"重要产品"，而客户却认为最为重要，那又该怎样处理？

上述每一问题，都各需要一项风险的决策，也都需要一项原则的决策。除非这些决策都已经明确地决定了，电脑才能有助于解决库存的问题。而且这些决策都是"不确定性情况下的决策"，而所谓"不确定性"，却往往无法明确界定，因此也往往无法输进电脑。

所以，要运用电脑，使其能按照我们的要求平稳运行，或使其能对发生的事件做出预定的反应（例如发现敌方核弹时，或发现原油中硫含量超过规定时，我们应采取的行动），则这类决策必须是能够预先安排的决策，这类决策必须是不能随机应变的决策，这类决策必须是不能一步一步地摸索而得的决策——每一步摸索，用物理学上的术语来说都是"虚拟的"，而不是"真正的"的决策。这类决策都必须是硬性原则的决策。

出现这种情况，原因并不在电脑，电脑仅是一种工具，工具不会是任何结果的原因。实际上电脑只不过是将种种早已发生多时的现象，明确地表现出来罢了。由逐步适应性的决策转变为硬性原则的决策，早已经存在多时了。第二次世界大战期间及战后，军事决策方面早已出现了这种转变。军事作战的问题，何其庞大和复杂，需要一套支援整个战区和整个三军部队的后勤体系。中层的司令官，日渐感到有了解总体战略的必要，他们需在不违背总体战略的要求下，分别针对局部情况来做真正的决策，而不仅是遵行上级的命令。在大战期间，许多著名将领，例如隆美尔、布雷德利、朱可夫等人，事实上都只是"中层的将领"，但他们必须做真正的决策，而不能像早期战争的骑兵一样，只知受命冲锋。

因此，电脑问世后，决策将不仅是高层中少数几个人的事了。同样地，今天组织中的每一位知识工作者都必须是一位决策者，至少也得在决策过程中担任一个积极的角色、智慧的角色和自主性的角色。从前，决策只是高度专业性的职能，只由极少数几位责任分明的人物承担——其他人只是贯彻执行。在今天新的社会机构和大规模的知识组织中，几乎每一个单位都得承担决策了，虽然不能说这是他们每天必有的任务，至少也已成为他们的正常任务了。每一位知识工作者有效决策能力的高低，决定其工作能力的高低，至少那些身负重责的知识工作者，必须做有效的决策。

我们还可以再举一例来说明决策的转变。我们常常讨论所谓PERT（项目计划评审技术）的新技术。所谓PERT，是对一项极为复杂的计划，提供一幅工作进行的"地图"，例如航天飞机的研制和建造等。其目的在于事先列举出该项计划需要执行些什么，其执行的顺序如何以及其每一工作项目的完成期限如何，以便控制整个计划的推进。有了这样的计划，则临时调节性的工作便能大为减少，取而代之的是高度风险决策的增加。作业人员绘制的 PERT 程序图，往往每一步判断都可能发生错误，其每一次通过临时调节所做的修正，都有赖于系统的风险决策。

对于战略性的决策，电脑也起着同样的作用。当然，电脑不能替我们做战略性的决策。电脑所能做的，只是针对某一不确定性的未来事件告诉我们，按照我们预设的假定将有什么结论，或者是按照某一既有的行动，告诉我们其背后所依据的是什么假定。电脑所能做的，仍只是计算而已。因此，电脑需要明确的分析，尤其是有关某一决策所需边界条件的分析。而这样的分析，都有赖于更高层次的风险判断。

但电脑对于决策，还是有更深一层的意义。举例来说，电脑使用得当，能使管理者把原用于组织内部事务的许多时间匀出来。因此他可以有较多时间用在外界，换言之，用在能够产生成果的地方。

此外，电脑还有助于改善决策上常犯的几项错误。我们常犯的一项错误，是误将"例行事件"视为一连串的"偶发事件"。换言之，我们常有"头痛医头、脚痛医脚"的习惯。而电脑只有处理"例行情况"的能力——电脑只懂逻辑。所以，有了电脑，这项错误就容易避免，说不定将来我们的错误，会是误将真正的"偶发事件"视为"例行情况"呢。

因为电脑有这种倾向，于是人们开始抱怨说，在军事决策上，绝不应该让电脑来取代那些经过考验的军事人员的判断。我们不应该把这种抱怨仅仅当成一些高级将领的牢骚。反对军事决策标准化的最有力的论据来自一位杰出的"管理科学家"朱克曼爵士。他是英国一位著名的生物学家，是英国国防部的科学顾问。他在开发电脑分析和运用研究的工作中发挥过重要的作用。

我们说过电脑的能力有限，这正是电脑对我们的冲击之所在。因为电脑能力有限，所以才使我们更需做决策，也才使中层主管不能不从决策的执行者转变为管理者和决策者。

这种转变早就出现了。例如通用汽车公司之类的企业组织，例如德军参谋本部之类的军事组织，他们最大的优点，便是他们早已经重新编组，把日常作业转变为真正的决策了。

大型组织的基本弱点之一，是中层人士很少有决策训练的机会，以致难以担任高层的决策职位。执行层的经理人，越早学会风险及不定情况下的判断和决策，这一弱点就能越早消除。如果我们在日常工作中，一直是只知适应而不知思考，一直是只凭感觉而不凭知识和分析，那么执行层的主管人员将永远难以进步，等到将来他们升迁到了高层职位，开始面对战略性的决策时，必会感到非常生疏。

但这并不是说有了电脑，普通职员就可以变成决策者了。这正像有了计算器，并不能使高中学生变成数学家一样。不过，有了电脑之后，至少能使我们早一天分辨出普通职员中谁可能发展为决策者。电脑将为潜在的决策者提供目标明确、讲求效果的决策学习机会。不过他必须敢于操作，并且把电脑操作好，否则电脑是不会自行运转的。

电脑的问世，确实掀起了世人对决策问题的兴趣。其原因确实很多，却绝不是因为电脑可以代替决策。那只是因为电脑能够计算，所以从此组织中的上下人员，不能不学会管理之道了，也不能不学会有效的决策之道了。

第8章 | CHAPTER 8

# 结论：管理者必须卓有成效

本书讨论的内容是以如下两项为前提的：

- 管理者的工作必须卓有成效；
- 卓有成效是可以学会的。

人们聘用管理者，就是希望他的工作卓有成效。管理者必须在他的组织里开展有效的工作，否则就对不起聘用他的组织。那么，管理者应该学些什么，应该做些什么，才不辜负其管理者的职责呢？在回答这个问题时，本书把组织和管理者的工作绩效作为两大目标。

本书的第二个前提是，卓有成效是可以学会的。所以本书探讨了管理者绩效的每一个层面，本书编排的顺序，有利于激发读者学会如何成为有效的管理者。本书并不是教科书，因为有效性虽然人人可学，却无人可教。有效性不是一门课程，而是一种自我训练。本书从头到尾，都不忘一个问题："是什么促成了组织和管理者的卓有成效？"但本书很少提到这样的问题："为什么需要卓有成效？"因为卓有成效对管理者来说是理所当然应该做到的。

回顾本书各章所提出的论点和论证结果，读者会发现管理者的卓有成效还有另一个完全不同的侧面。它对个人的提高，对机构的发展，对现代社会的生存和运作都是必不可少的。

（1）要做到卓有成效，首先要做的第一步，是记录好时间的使用情况。这是一件"机械性"的工作。时间的记录，并不一定要由管理者本人自己动手，最好是交由秘书或助手来做。但是，只要管理者确能这么去做，他就能有所收获。虽然不敢说能立竿见影，也一定进步很快。而且，只要持之以恒，这样做肯定能激发管理者进一步求取有效性的兴趣。

分析时间记录以及消除不必要的时间浪费，还需要管理者采取某些行动，需要管理者有初步的决策，也需要管理者在行为、人际关系和工作重心上做出一些改变。因此，接着的问题，是衡量各项耗用时间的工作项目的轻重，以及衡量各项工作目的的轻重。其结果，必将改变管理者的工作水平和质量。管理者也许得采用一种检查表，每隔几个月检查一次。这步工作着实攸关管理者对时间（管理者最稀缺的资源）运用的效率。

（2）第二步，是管理者应把眼光集中在贡献上。着眼于贡献，比第一步更深入了一层：由程序进入到观念；由机械性工作进入到分析性方法；由效率进入到成果。这一步是培养管理者的自省：为什么组织聘他为管理者？他应该对组织有什么贡献？要做到这一点并不复杂。管理者关于自省的问题，仍然是比较直截了当的问题，而且多少是形式上的问题。但是管理者在得到自省的答案后，却应该对自己提出更高的要求；应该想到自己的目标及组织的目标；应该进而关注个人及组织的价值。尤其重要的是，这些自省是要求管理者承担起责任，而不是要求管理者单纯地执行命令，只求上司满意。管理者如果能着眼于贡献，那么他所重视的就应当不仅是"方法"，而是"目标"和"结果"。

（3）第三步，充分发挥人的长处。这个步骤，基本上是一种行为的态度问题。这是对人的尊重：尊重自己，也尊重他人。这是管理者的价值观在行为上的体现。不过，充分发挥人的长处也需要"边做边学"，需要通过实践才能掌握。管理者如果能充分发挥人的长处，就能使个人目标与组织需要相融合，使个人能力与组织成果相融合，也能使个人成就与组织机会相融合。

（4）本书第5章"要事优先"，可以与第2章"掌握自己的时间"互为呼应。我们说，这两章的内容，实在是管理者有效性的两大支柱，缺一不可。但这一章讨论的不是管理者的时间资源，而是管理者的终极产品——管理者和组织的绩效。在这一章里，记录和分析的对象不是"管理者周围所发生的事情"，而是"管理者应该努力促成的事情"。所以，这一章没有讨论"信息"，而是讨论管理者的"性格特征"——诸如远见、自信和勇气。换句话说，这一章的主题是"领导力"，但所谓"领导力"，并不是指智慧和天赋，而是指人人皆可达成的专心、决心和目标。

（5）本书最后几章研究有效的决策，其重心在于合理的行动。关于这一问题，我们无法提出可供管理者遵行的明显和具体的步骤，但是本书提供了一些明确的标准，这些标准可以起到方向性和指导性的作用。举例来说，对管理者应该如何识别"例行事件"，进而找出决策所需的边界条件，本书并无具体说明。因为具体的方法，也需视个别情况而异。但是，应该做什么和应该按怎样的顺序去做，却已说得非常清楚。根据这些标准，管理者就能训练和发展他们的判断力。有效的决策，固然有赖于一定的步骤，也有赖于分析的能力。而有效的决策，在本质上却是一种行动的规范。

管理者的自我提高往往要比卓有成效的训练更为重要。管理者必须增进其知识与技巧，必须养成各种新的工作习惯，同时也必须放弃旧的工作习惯。但是话说回来，如果他不能先发展自己的有效性，那不管他有多少知识，有多好的技能和习惯，也不会对他有太大的帮助。

当一名管理者，并没有什么值得自豪的，因为管理者与其他千千万万人一样，都是做他自己应做的工作。即使已成为一位有效的管理者，我们仍然还有更高的人生境界。正因为有效的管理者并不是高不可攀的境界，我们才期望能到达这一境界。换言之，本书的目的，是希望在我们今天的社会和各种组织中，能培养出大量的卓有成效的管理者。反过来说，如果境界悬之过高，希望我们的知识组织中有圣贤、有大诗人、有第一流的学者，那大型组织恐怕也就存在不了啦。今天的组织，需要的是由平凡人来做不平凡的事业。这正是有效的管理者所应自勉的目标。这项目标并不高，我们只要"肯"去做，就一定"能"做到。有效的管理者的自我提高，是个人的真正发展。这种自我提高应该包括从技术性细节到工作态度、价值观、品格等各个方面，包括从履行工作程序到承担各项义务等各个领域。

有效的管理者的自我提高，是组织发展的关键所在。企业机构如此，政府机构如此，其他研究机构、医院以至于军事机构，都莫不如此。这是所有组织迈向成功的必经之路。管理者如能卓有成效，则整个组织的绩效水平肯定能够提高，而且个人的眼光也肯定随之提高。

这样，组织的工作不但能蒸蒸日上，而且能承担新的任务，追求新的目标。管理者有效性的发展，其实是对组织的目标和方向的挑战。有了这种挑战精神，我们就能转移视线：由专注于问题转而重视机会，由只见人之所短转而能用人所长。组织到了这一境界，就会对外界的优秀人才产生很大的吸引力，内部既有的人力也将获得更大的激励，做出更大的贡献。组织拥有优秀人才，并不一定能更为有效。组织之所以能拥有优秀人才是通过工作标准、行为习惯和团队氛围来鼓励自我提高的结果。而何以能有这种结果，那要靠组织中的每个人都能切实进行系统化、专门化、目的明确的自我训练，成为有效的管理者。

现代的社会是大型组织的社会。现代社会的运行不但有赖于大型组织的生存，也有赖于大型组织的有效性及其绩效和成果、价值观和标准，及自我要求的提升。

组织的绩效已不仅是经济方面的课题，诸如教育、保健及学术研究等社会领域情况也是一样。现代社会的大型组织已日益成为一种知识的组织。在这种知识的组织中，以知识工作者为主，其组成分子不分男女，都必须担当管理者的工作，也必须肩负整体成果的责任，并且由于他们的知识和工作的特殊，他们所做的决策将会影响到整个组织的绩效和成果。

然而环视我们的周围，有效的组织固然不多，有效的管理者尤其少见。当然，偶然也能出现几个辉煌的例子，但毕竟寥若晨星。我们敢说，大致说来，组织绩效还停滞在原始阶段。我们眼见大量的资源投进了现代的大型组织，投进了现代的政府机构、现代的医院、现代的研究机构；然而，这些现代的大型组织，其成就实在无足称道，其工作散乱无章，其努力仅着重昨天而规避决策和行动。组织及管理者都必须力求有效，都必须培养有效性的习惯。他们必须学会掌握良机，学会消除问题。他们必须能充分发挥人的长处，懂得衡量工作的优先，做重点的努力，而不能凡事均浅尝辄止。

管理者的工作卓有成效，这肯定是卓有成效的机构所必须具备的基本要求。而管理者的有效性本身，就是对组织发展最重要的贡献。

提高管理者的有效性，是促进现代社会经济增长的希望所在，也是现代社会得以生存和发展的一大保障。

本书曾反复提到：知识工作者已迅速成为发达国家的主要资源，知识工作者也是现代国家最重要的投资。任何投资都不及教育投资庞大，因此知识工作者又已成为一项重要的成本中心。一个高度发达的工业社会，经济上最迫切需要的，莫过于提高知识工作者的生产力。

自从第二次世界大战以来，我们虽然很明显地看出重心已经从体力工作转移到知识工作了，可是这种转移究竟产生了怎样的结果，我承认，至今还没有表现出来。我们试以衡量经济成果的生产力及利润这两项尺度来看，自第二次世界大战结束以来，这两方面的增加并不显著。当然，发达国家在各方面的进步也很可观，可是，在如何提高知识工作者的生产力这个问题上，我们还有很长的路要走，其关键还是在于管理者的有效性。因为管理者本身是最重要的知识工作者。管理者的水平、管理者的标准和管理者对自身的要求，都对其周围的其他知识工作者的激励、方向和奉献，具有决定性的影响。

尤其重要的是，管理者的有效性已成为今天的社会需要。我们社会的凝聚力和优势的发挥，有赖于知识工作者的心理需求和社会需求，能否与组织及工业社会的目标互相融和。

知识工作者本身不会成为社会的经济问题。知识工作者大部分生活富裕，他既有职业的安全，也有充分流动的自由。但是他在组织中服务，他的心理需求和个人价值必须能从工作上和职位上得到满足。他通常被视为专业人员，也自视为专业人员。但是在组织中，他却只是雇员的身份，处于"听命于人"的地位。他的工作虽然属于知识工作的领域之内，但是事实上他的知识权威性，却必须服从于组织的目的和目标。在知识工作的领域中并无上下级的关系，只有年龄的长幼。但是，组织却不能没有等级制度。这自然不是今天发生的新问题，军队和政府机构里的工作人员对这种等级制度很熟悉，他们早已知道解决的方法。但是，这些问题却是实实在在的问题。知识工作者并不是不能安贫乐道，问题是知识工作者常会厌烦、失意、消沉。用时髦的名词来说，就是他们会产生所谓的"疏离感"。

19世纪的发展中国家遇到的社会问题，是体力工作者的需求与经济发展的冲突。到了20世纪的今天，当时的那些国家已经成为发达国家了，它们的社会问题却是知识工作者的问题了，即知识工作者的职位问题、职能问题及其满足的问题。

这个问题不会因为我们否认它的存在而消失。声称只有经济和社会效益的问题才是"客观现实",也解决不了问题。近代社会心理学的新浪漫学派(例如耶鲁大学的阿吉里斯教授)也不能解决这一问题,他们认为组织的目标,绝不是在个人目标满足后即可自然达成,因此认为不如撇开组织目标。这种见解,又何尝是解决问题?事实上,我们既要通过组织的绩效来满足社会的需要,同时也要力求实现个人的成就,以满足个人的需要。

管理者在卓有成效方面的自我提高是解决这一问题的唯一可行办法。它可以使组织的目标与个人的需求很好地结合起来。想充分发挥自己及其他人长处的管理者,一定要使组织的绩效与个人的成就协调起来。他要设法让自己的知识成为促进因素,帮助机构抓住机遇并获得成功。通过强调贡献,他可以使自身的价值转化为组织的成果。

我们往往认为体力工作者只有经济的需要,能获得经济报酬即能满足——至少19世纪时有如此的看法。但是,据人际关系学派的人士看来,实际上绝非如此。对体力工作者而言,当其所获的报酬高达某一水平以上时,报酬便不一定再起作用了。以知识工作者来说,当然也需要经济报酬。但经济报酬也是对知识工作者的一种制约因素,光有经济报酬并不等于有了一切。知识工作者还需要机会、需要成就、需要实现、需要价值。知识工作者只有在成为一位有效的管理者之后,才能获得这些满足。

今天的社会有两种需要:对组织而言,需要个人为其做出贡献;对个人而言,需要把组织当成实现自己人生目标的工具。只有管理者的有效性,才能使这两种社会需要相辅相成。总而言之,卓有成效确实是必须学会的。

# The Effective Executive

| Preface |

Management books usually deal with managing other people. The subject of this book is managing oneself for effectiveness. That one can truly manage other people is by no means adequately proven. But one can always manage oneself. Indeed, executives who do not manage themselves for effectiveness cannot possibly expect to manage their associates and subordinates. Management is largely by example. Executives who do not know how to make themselves effective in their own job and work set the wrong example.

To be reasonably effective it is not enough for the individual to be intelligent, to work hard or to be knowledgeable. Effectiveness is something separate, something different. But to be effective also does not require special gifts, special aptitude, or special training. Effectiveness as an executive demands *doing* certain—and fairly simple—things. It consists of a small number of practices, the practices that are presented and discussed in this book. But these practices are not "inborn". In forty-five years of work as a consultant with a large number of executives in a wide variety of organizations—large and small; businesses, government agencies, labor unions, hospitals, universities, community services; American, European, Latin American and Japanese—I have not come across a single "natural": an executive who was born effective. All the effective ones have had to learn to be effective. And all of them then had to practice effectiveness until it became habit. But all the ones who worked on making themselves effective executives succeeded in doing so. Effectiveness can be learned— and it also *has* to be learned.

Effectiveness is what executives are being paid for, whether they work as managers who are responsible for the performance of others as well as their own, or as individual professional contributors responsible for their own performance only. Without effectiveness there is no "performance," no matter how much intelligence and knowledge goes into the work, no matter how many hours it takes. Yet it is perhaps not too surprising that we have so far paid little attention to the effective executive. Organizations—whether business enterprises, large government agencies, labor unions, large hospitals or large universities—are, after all, brand new. A century ago almost no one had even much contact with such organizations beyond an occasional trip to the local post office to mail a letter. And effectiveness as an executive means effectiveness in and through an organization. Until recently there was little reason for anyone to pay much attention to the effective executive or to worry about the low effectiveness of so many of them. Now, however, most people—especially those with even a fair amount of schooling—can expect to spend all their working lives in an organization of some kind. Society has become a society of organizations in all developed countries. Now the effectiveness of the individual depends increasingly on his or her ability to be effective in an organization, to be effective as an executive. And the effectiveness of a modern society and its ability to perform—perhaps even its ability to survive—depend increasingly on the effectiveness of the people who work as executives in the organizations. The effective executive is fast becoming a key resource for society, and effectiveness as an executive a prime requirement for individual accomplishment and achievement—for young people at the beginning of their working lives fully as much as for people in mid-career.

Claremont, California                                            Peter F. Drucker
New Year's Day, 1985

CHAPTER 1

# Effectiveness Can Be Learned

To be effective is the job of the executive. "To effect" and "to execute" are, after all, near-synonyms. Whether he works in a business or in a hospital, in a government agency or in a labor union, in a university or in the army, the executive is, first of all, expected to *get the right things done*. And this is simply that he is expected to be effective.

Yet men of high effectiveness are conspicuous by their absence in executive jobs. High intelligence is common enough among executives. Imagination is far from rare. The level of knowledge tends to be high. But there seems to be little correlation between a man's effectiveness and his intelligence, his imagination or his knowledge. Brilliant men are often strikingly ineffectual; they fail to realize that the brilliant insight is not by itself achievement. They never have learned that insights become effectiveness only through hard systematic work. Conversely, in every organization there are some highly effective plodders. While others rush around in the frenzy and busyness which very bright people so often confuse with "creativity," the plodder puts one foot in front of the other and gets there first, like the tortoise in the old fable.

Intelligence, imagination, and knowledge are essential resources, but only effectiveness converts them into results. By themselves, they only set limits to what can be attained.

## WHY WE NEED EFFECTIVE EXECUTIVES

All this should be obvious. But why then has so little attention been paid to effectiveness, in an age in which there are mountains of books and articles on every other aspect of the executive's tasks?

One reason for this neglect is that effectiveness is the specific technology of the knowledge worker within an organization. Until recently, there was no more than a handful of these around.

For manual work, we need only efficiency; that is, the ability to do things right rather than the ability to get the right things done. The manual worker can always be judged in terms of the quantity and quality of a definable and discrete output, such as a pair of shoes. We have learned how to measure efficiency and how to define quality in manual work during the last hundred years—to the point where we have been able to multiply the output of the individual worker tremendously.

Formerly, the manual worker—whether machine operator or front-line soldier—predominated in all organizations. Few people of effectiveness were needed: those at the top who gave the orders that others carried out. They were so small a fraction of the total work population that we could, rightly or wrongly, take their effectiveness for granted. We could depend on the supply of "naturals," the few people in any area of human endeavor who somehow know what the rest of us have to learn the hard way.

This was true not only of business and the army. It is hard to realize today that "government" during the American Civil War a hundred years ago meant the merest handful of people. Lincoln's Secretary of War had fewer than fifty civilian subordinates, most of them not "executives" and policy-makers but telegraph clerks. The entire Washington establishment of the U. S. government in Theodore Roosevelt's time, around 1900, could be comfortably housed in any one of the government buildings along the Mall today.

The hospital of yesterday did not know any of the "healthservice professionals," the X-ray and lab technicians, the dieticians and therapists, the social workers, and so on, of whom it now employs as many as two hundred and fifty for every one hundred patients. Apart from a few nurses, there were only cleaning women, cooks and maids. The physician was the knowledge worker, with the nurse as his aide.

In other words, up to recent times, the major problem of organization was efficiency in the performance of the manual worker who did what he had been told to do. Knowledge workers were not predominant in organization.

In fact, only a small fraction of the knowledge workers of earlier days were part of an organization. Most of them worked by themselves as professionals, at best with a clerk. Their effectiveness or lack of effectiveness concerned only themselves and affected only themselves.

Today, however, the large knowledge organization is the central reality. Modern society is a society of large organized institutions. In every one of them, including the armed services, the center of gravity has shifted to the knowledge worker, the man who puts to work what he has between his ears rather than the brawn of his muscles or the skill of his hands. Increasingly, the majority of people who have been schooled to use knowledge, theory, and concept rather than physical force or manual skill work in an organization and are effective insofar as they can make a contribution to the organization.

Now effectiveness can no longer be taken for granted. Now it can no longer be neglected.

The imposing system of measurements and tests which we have developed for manual work—from industrial engineering to quality control—is not applicable to knowledge work. There are few things less pleasing to the Lord, and less productive, than an engineering department that rapidly turns out beautiful blueprints for the wrong product. Working on the *right* things is what makes knowledge work effective. This is not capable of being measured by any of the yardsticks for manual work.

The knowledge worker cannot be supervised closely or in detail. He can only be helped. But he must direct himself, and he must direct himself toward performance and contribution, that is, toward effectiveness.

A cartoon in *The New Yorker* magazine some time ago showed an office on the door of which was the legend: CHAS. SMITH, GENERAL SALES MANAGER, AJAX SOAP COMPANY. The walls were bare except for a big sign saying THINK. The man in the office had his feet propped up on his desk and was blowing smoke rings at the ceiling.

Outside two older men went by, the one saying to the other: "But how can we be sure that Smith thinks soap?"

One can indeed never be sure what the knowledge worker thinks—and yet thinking is his specific work; it is his "doing."

The motivation of the knowledge worker depends on his being effective, on his being able to achieve.⊖ If effectiveness is lacking in his work, his commitment to work and to contribution will soon wither, and he will become a time-server going through the motions from 9 to 5.

The knowledge worker does not produce something that is effective by itself. He does not produce a physical product—a ditch, a pair of shoes, a machine part. He produces knowledge, ideas, information. By themselves these "products" are useless. Somebody else, another man of knowledge, has to take them as his input and convert them into his output before they have any reality. The greatest wisdom not applied to action and behavior is meaningless data. The knowledge worker, therefore, must do something which a manual worker need not do. He must provide effectiveness. He cannot depend on the utility his output carries with it as does a well-made pair of shoes.

The knowledge worker is the one "factor of production" through which the highly developed societies and economies of today—the United States, Western Europe, Japan, and also increasingly, the Soviet Union—become and remain competitive.

---

⊖ This is brought out in all studies, especially in three empirical works: Frederick Herzberg(with B. Mauser and B. Snyderman), *The Motivation to Work* (New York, Wiley, 1959); David C. McClellan, *The Achieving Society* (Princeton, N. J. , Van Nostrand, 1961); and Frederick Herzberg, *Work and the Nature of Man* (Cleveland, World, 1966).

This is particularly true of the United States. The only resource in respect to which America can possibly have a competitive advantage is education. American education may leave a good deal to be desired, but it is massive beyond anything poorer societies can afford. For education is the most expensive capital investment we have ever known. A Ph. D. in the natural sciences represents $100 000 to $200 000 of social capital investment. Even the boy who graduates from college without any specific professional competence represents an investment of $50 000 or more. This only a very rich society can afford.

Education is the one area, therefore, in which the richest of all societies, the United States, has a genuine advantage—provided it can make the knowledge worker productive. And productivity for the knowledge worker means the ability to get the right things done. It means effectiveness.

## WHO IS AN EXECUTIVE?

Every knowledge worker in modern organization is an "executive" if, by virtue of his position or knowledge, he is responsible for a contribution that materially affects the capacity of the organization to perform and to obtain results. This may be the capacity of a business to bring out a new product or to obtain a larger share of a given market. It may be the capacity of a hospital to provide bedside care to its patients, and so on. Such a man (or woman) must make decisions; he cannot just carry out orders. He must take responsibility for his contribution. And he is supposed, by virtue of his knowledge, to be better equipped to make the right decision than anyone else. He may be overridden; he may be demoted or fired. But so long as he has the job the goals, the standards, and the contribution are in his keeping.

Most managers are executives—though not all. But many nonmanagers are also becoming executives in modern society. For the knowledge organization, as we have been learning these last few years, needs *both* "managers" and "individual professional contributors" in positions of responsibility, decision-making, and authority.

This fact is perhaps best illustrated by a recent newspaper interview with a young American infantry captain in the Vietnam jungle.

> Asked by the reporter, "How in this confused situation can you retain command?" the young captain said: "Around here, I am only the guy who is responsible. If these men don't know what to do when they run into an enemy in the jungle, I'm too far away to tell them. My job is to make sure they know. What they do depends on the situation which only they can judge. The responsibility is always mine, but the decision lies with whoever is on the spot."

In a guerrilla war, every man is an "executive."

There are many managers who are not executives. Many people, in other words, are superiors of other people—and often of fairly large numbers of other people—and still do not seriously affect the ability of the organization to perform. Most foremen in a manufacturing plant belong here. They are "overseers" in the literal sense of the word. They are "managers" in that they manage the work of others. But they have neither the responsibility for, nor authority over, the direction, the content, and the quality of the work or the methods of its performance. They can still be measured and appraised very largely in terms of efficiency and quality, and by the yardsticks we have developed to measure and appraise the work and performance of the manual worker.

Conversely, whether a knowledge worker is an executive does not depend on whether he manages people or not. In one business, the market research man may have a staff of two hundred people, whereas the market research man of the closest competitor is all by himself and has only a secretary for his staff. This should make little difference in the contribution expected of the two men. It is an administrative detail. Two hundred people, of course, can do a great deal more work than one man. But it does not follow that they produce and contribute more.

Knowledge work is not defined by quantity. Neither is knowledge work defined by its costs. Knowledge work is defined by its results. And for these, the size of the group and the magnitude of the managerial job are not even symptoms.

Having many people working in market research may endow the results with that increment of insight, imagination, and quality that gives a company the potential of rapid growth and success. If so, two hundred men are cheap. But it is just as likely that the manager will be overwhelmed by all the problems two hundred men bring to their work and cause through their interactions. He may be so busy "managing" as to have no time for market research and for fundamental decisions. He may be so busy checking figures that he never asks the question: "What do we really mean when we say our market"? And as a result, he may fail to notice significant changes in the market which eventually may cause the downfall of his company.

But the individual market researcher without a staff may be equally productive or unproductive. He may be the source of the knowledge and vision that make his company prosper. Or he may spend so much of his time hunting down details—the footnotes academicians so often mistake for research—as to see and hear nothing and to think even less.

Throughout every one of our knowledge organizations, we have people who manage no one and yet are executives. Rarely indeed do we find a situation such as that in the Vietnam jungle, where at any moment, any member of the entire group may be called upon to make decisions with life-and-death impact for the whole. But the chemist in the research laboratory who decides to follow one line of inquiry rather than another one may make the entrepreneurial decision that determines the future of his company. He may be the research director. But he also may be—and often is—a chemist with no managerial responsibilities, if not even a fairly junior man. Similarly, the decision what to consider one "product" in the account books may be made by a senior vice-president in the company.⊖ It may also be made by a junior. And this holds true in all areas of today's large organization.

I have called "executives" those knowledge workers, managers, or individual professionals who are expected by virtue of their position or their knowledge to make decisions in the normal course of their work that have significant impact on the performance and results of the whole. They are by no means a majority of the knowledge workers. For in knowledge work too, as in all other areas, there is unskilled work and routine. But they are a much larger proportion of the total knowledge work force than any organization chart ever reveals.

---

⊖ On this see my *Managing for Results* (New York, Harper & Row, 1964)—especially chap. 2.

This is beginning to be realized—as witness the many attempts to provide parallel ladders of recognition and reward for managers and for individual professional contributors. ⊖ What few yet realize, however, is how many people there are even in the most humdrum organization of today, whether business or government agency, research lab or hospital, who have to make decisions of significant and irreversible impact. For the authority of knowledge is surely as legitimate as the authority of position. These decisions, moreover, are of the same *kind* as the decisions of top management. (This was the main point Mr. Kappel was making in the statement referred to above. )

The most subordinate manager, we now know, may do the same kind of work as the president of the company or the administrator of the government agency; that is, plan, organize, integrate, motivate, and measure. His compass may be quite limited, but within his sphere, he is an executive.

Similarly, every decision-maker does the same kind of work as the company president or the administrator. His scope may be quite limited. But he is an executive even if his function or his name appears neither on the organization chart nor in the internal telephone directory.

And whether chief executive or beginner, he needs to be effective.

Many of the examples used in this book are taken from the work and experience of chief executives—in government, army, hospitals, business, and so on. The main reason is that these are accessible, are indeed often on the public record. Also big things are more easily analyzed and seen than small ones.

But this book itself is not a book on what people at the top do or should

---

⊖ The best statement I know was made by Frederick R. Kappel, the head of the American Telephone & Telegraph Company (The Bell Telephone System) at the XIII[th] International Management Congress in New York, September 1963. Mr. Kappel's main points are quoted in chap. 14 of *Managing for Results*.

do. It is addressed to everyone who, as a knowledge worker, is responsible for actions and decisions which are meant to contribute to the performance capacity of his organization. It is meant for every one of the men I call "executives."

## EXECUTIVE REALITIES

The realities of the executive's situation both demand effectiveness from him and make effectiveness exceedingly difficult to achieve. Indeed, unless executives work at becoming effective, the realities of their situation will push them into futility.

Take a quick look at the realities of a knowledge worker *outside* an organization to see the problem. A physician has by and large no problem of effectiveness. The patient who walks into his office brings with him everything to make the physician's knowledge effective. During the time he is with the patient, the doctor can, as a rule, devote himself to the patient. He can keep interruptions to a minimum. The contribution the physician is expected to make is clear. What is important, and what is not, is determined by whatever ails the patient. The patient's complaints establish the doctor's priorities. And the goal, the objective, is given: It is to restore the patient to health or at least to make him more comfortable. Physicians are not noted for their capacity to organize themselves and their work. But few of them have much trouble being effective.

The executive in organization is in an entirely different position. In his situation there are four major realities over which he has essentially no control. Every one of them is built into organization and into the executive's day and work. He has no choice but to "cooperate with the inevitable." But every one of these realities exerts pressure toward nonresults and nonperformance.

1. The executive's time tends to belong to everybody else. If one attempted to define an "executive" operationally (that is, through his activities) one would have to define him as a captive of the organization. Everybody can move in on his time, and everybody does. There seems to be very little any one executive can do about it. He cannot, as a rule, like the physician, stick his head out the door and say to the nurse, "I won't see anybody for the next half hour." Just at this moment, the executive's telephone rings, and he has to speak to the company's best customer or to a high official in the city administration or to his boss—and the next half hour is already gone. ⊖

2. Executives are forced to keep on "operating" unless they take positive action to change the reality in which they live and work.

In the United States, the complaint is common that the company president—or any other senior officer—still continues to run marketing or the plant, even though he is now in charge of the whole business and should be giving his time to its direction. This is sometimes blamed on the fact that American executives graduate, as a rule, out of functional work and operations, and cannot slough off the habits of a lifetime when they get into general management. But exactly the same complaint can be heard in countries where the career ladder is quite different. In the Germanic countries, for instance, a common route into top management has been from a central secretariat, where one works all along as a "generalist." Yet in German, Swedish, or Dutch companies top management

---

⊖ This comes out clearly in Sune Carlson's *Executive Behavior* (Stockholm, Strombergs, 1951), the one study of top management in large corporations which actually recorded the time-use of senior executives. Even the most effective executives in Professor Carlson's study found most of their time taken up with the demands of others and for purposes which added little if anything to their effectiveness. In fact, executives might well be defined as people who normally have no time of their own, because their time is always preempted by matters of importance to somebody else.

people are criticized just as much for "operating" as in the United States. Nor, when one looks at organizations, is this tendency confined to the top; it pervades the entire executive group. There must be a reason for this tendency to "operate" other than career ladders or even the general perversity of human nature.

The fundamental problem is the reality around the executive. Unless he changes it by deliberate action, the flow of events will determine what he is concerned with and what he does.

Depending on the flow of events is appropriate for the physician. The doctor who looks up when a patient comes in and says: "Why are you here today?" expects the patient to tell him what is relevant. When the patient says, "Doctor, I can't sleep. I haven't been able to go to sleep the last three weeks," he is telling the doctor what the priority area is. Even if the doctor decides, upon closer examination, that the sleeplessness is a fairly minor symptom of a much more fundamental condition he will do something to help the patient to get a few good nights' rest.

But events rarely tell the executive anything, let alone the real problem. For the doctor, the patient's complaint is central because it is central to the patient. The executive is concerned with a much more complex universe. What events are important and relevant and what events are merely distractions the events themselves do not indicate. They are not even symptoms in the sense in which the patient's narrative is a clue for the physician.

If the executive lets the flow of events determine what he does, what he works on, and what he takes seriously, he will fritter himself away "operating." He may be an excellent man. But he is certain to waste his knowledge and ability and to throw away what little effectiveness he might have achieved. What the executive needs are criteria which enable him to work on the truly important, that is, on contributions and results, even though the criteria are not found in the flow of events.

3. The third reality pushing the executive toward ineffectiveness is that he is within an *organization*. This means that he is effective only if and when other people make use of what he contributes. Organization is a means of multiplying the strength of an individual. It takes his knowledge and uses it as the resource, the motivation, and the vision of other knowledge workers. Knowledge workers are rarely in phase with each other, precisely because they are knowledge workers. Each has his own skill and his own concerns. One man may be interested in tax accounting or in bacteriology, or in training and developing tomorrow's key administrators in the city government. But the fellow next door is interested in the finer points of cost accounting, in hospital economics, or in the legalities of the city charter. Each has to be able to use what the other produces.

Usually the people who are most important to the effectiveness of an executive are not people over whom he has direct control. They are people in other areas, people who in terms of organization, are "sideways." Or they are his superiors. Unless the executive can reach these people, can make his contribution effective for them and in their work, he has no effectiveness at all.

4. Finally, the executive is *within* an organization.

Every executive, whether his organization is a business or a research laboratory, a government agency, a large university, or the air force, sees the inside—the organization—as close and immediate reality. He sees the outside only through thick and distorting lenses, if at all. What goes on outside is usually not even known firsthand. It is received through an organizational filter of reports, that is, in an already predigested and highly abstract form that imposes organizational criteria of relevance on the outside reality.

But the organization is an abstraction. Mathematically, it would have to be represented as a point—that is, as having neither size nor extension. Even the largest organization is unreal compared to the reality of the environment in which it exists.

Specifically, there are no results within the organization. All the results are on the outside. The only business results, for instance, are produced by a customer who converts the costs and efforts of the business into revenues and profits through his willingness to exchange his purchasing power for the products or services of the business.

Similarly, a hospital has results only in respect to the patient. But the patient is not a member of the hospital organization. For the patient, the hospital is "real" only while he stays there. His greatest desire is to go back to the "nonhospital" world as fast as possible.

What happens inside any organization is effort and cost. To speak of "profit centers" in a business as we are wont to do is polite euphemism. There are only effort centers. The less an organization has to do to produce results, the better it does its job. That it takes 100 000 employees to produce the automobiles or the steel the market wants is essentially a gross engineering imperfection. The fewer people, the smaller, the less activity inside, the more nearly perfect is the organization in terms of its only reason for existence: the service to the environment.

This outside, this environment which is the true reality, is well beyond effective control from the inside. At the most, results are codetermined, as for instance in warfare, where the outcome is the result of the actions and decisions of both armies. In a business, there can be attempts to mold the customers' preferences and values through promotion and advertising. Except in an extreme shortage situation such as a war economy, the customer still has the final word and the effective veto power. But it is the inside of the organization that is most visible to the executive. It is the inside that has immediacy for him. Its relations and contacts, its problems and challenges, its crosscurrents and gossip reach him and touch him at every point. Unless he makes special efforts to gain direct access to outside reality, he will become increasingly inside-focused. The higher up in the organization he goes, the more will his attention be drawn to problems and challenges of the inside rather than to events on the outside.

An organization, a social artifact, is very different from a biological organism. Yet it stands under the law that governs the structure and size of animals and plants: The surface goes up with the square of the radius, but the mass grows with the cube. The larger the animal becomes, the more resources have to be devoted to the mass and to the internal tasks, to circulation and information, to the nervous system, and so on.

Every part of an amoeba is in constant, direct contact with the environment. It therefore needs no special organs to perceive its environment or to hold it together. But a large and complex animal such as man needs a skeleton to hold it together. It needs all kinds of specialized organs for ingestion and digestion, for respiration and exhalation, for carrying oxygen to the tissues, for reproduction, and so on. Above all, a man needs a brain and a number of complex nervous systems. Most of the mass of the amoeba is directly concerned with survival and procreation. Most of the mass of the higher animal—its resources, its food, its energy supply, its tissues—serve to overcome and offset the complexity of the structure and the isolation from the outside.

An organization is not, like an animal, an end in itself, and successful by the mere act of perpetuating the species. An organization is an organ of society and fulfills itself by the contribution it makes to the outside environment. And yet the bigger and apparently more successful an organization gets to be, the more will inside events tend to engage the interests, the energies, and the abilities of the executive to the exclusion of his real tasks and his real effectiveness in the outside.

This danger is being aggravated today by the advent of the computer and of the new information technology. The computer, being a mechanical moron, can handle only quantifiable data. These it can handle with speed, accuracy, and precision. It will, therefore, grind out hitherto unobtainable quantified information in large volume. One can, however, by and large quantify only what goes on inside an organization—costs and production figures, patient statistics in the hospital, or training reports. The relevant outside events are rarely available in quantifiable form until it is much too late to do anything about them.

This is not because our information-gathering capacity in respect to the outside events lags behind the technical abilities of the computer. If this were the only thing to worry about, we would just have to increase statistical efforts—and the computer itself could greatly help us to overcome this mechanical limitation. The problem is rather that the important and relevant outside events are often qualitative and not capable of quantification. They are not yet "facts." For a fact, after all, is an event which somebody has defined, has classified and, above all, has endowed with relevance. To be able to quantify one has to have a concept first. One first has to abstract from the infinite welter of phenomena a specific aspect which one then can name and finally count.

The thalidomide tragedy which led to the birth of so many deformed babies is a case in point. By the time doctors on the European continent had enough statistics to realize that the number of deformed babies born was significantly larger than normal—so much larger that there had to be a specific and new cause—the damage had been done. In the United States, the damage was prevented because one public health physician perceived a qualitative change—a minor and by itself meaningless skin tingling caused by the drug—related it to a totally different event that had happened many years earlier, and sounded the alarm before thalidomide actually came into use.

The Ford Edsel holds a similar lesson. All the quantitative figures that could possibly be obtained were gathered before the Edsel was launched. All of them pointed to its being the right car for the right market. The qualitative change—the shifting of American consumer-buying of automobiles from income-determined to taste-determined market-segmentation—no statistical study could possibly have shown. By the time this could be captured in numbers, it was too late—the Edsel had been brought out and had failed.

The truly important events on the outside are not the trends. They are changes in the trends. These determine ultimately success or failure of an organization and its efforts. Such changes, however, have to be perceived; they cannot be counted, defined, or classified. The classifications still produce the expected figures—as they did for Edsel. But the figures no longer correspond to actual behavior.

The computer is a logic machine, and that is its strength—but also its limitation. The important events on the outside cannot be reported in the kind of form a computer (or any other logic system) could possibly handle. Man, however, while not particularly logical is perceptive—and that is his strength.

The danger is that executives will become contemptuous of information and stimulus that cannot be reduced to computer logic and computer language. Executives may become blind to everything that is perception (i. e., event) rather than fact (i. e., after the event). The tremendous amount of computer information may thus shut out access to reality.

Eventually the computer—potentially by far the most useful management tool—should make executives aware of their insulation and free them for more time on the outside. In the short run, however, there is danger of acute "computeritis." It is a serious affliction.

The computer only makes visible a condition that existed before it. Executives of necessity live and work within an organization. Unless they make conscious efforts to perceive the outside, the inside may blind them to the true reality.

These four realities the executive cannot change. They are necessary conditions of his existence. But he must therefore assume that he will be ineffectual unless he makes special efforts to learn to be effective.

## THE PROMISE OF EFFECTIVENESS

Increasing effectiveness may well be the only area where we can hope significantly to raise the level of executive performance, achievement, and satisfaction.

We certainly could use people of much greater abilities in many places. We could use people of broader knowledge. I submit, however, that in these two areas, not too much can be expected from further efforts. We may be getting to the point where we are already attempting to do the inherently impossible or at least the inherently unprofitable. But we are not going to breed a new race of supermen. We will have to run our organizations with men as they are.

The books on manager development, for instance, envisage truly a "man for all seasons" in their picture of "the manager of tomorrow." A senior executive, we are told, should have extraordinary abilities as an analyst and as a decision-maker. He should be good at working with people and at understanding organization and power relations, be good at mathematics, and have artistic insights and creative imagination. What seems to be wanted is universal genius, and universal genius has always been in scarce supply. The experience of the human race indicates strongly that the only person in abundant supply is the universal incompetent. We will therefore have to staff our organizations with people who at best excel in one of these abilities. And then they are more than likely to lack any but the most modest endowment in the others.

We will have to learn to build organizations in such a manner that any man who has strength in one important area is capable of putting it to work (as will be discussed in considerable depth in Chapter 4 below). But we cannot expect to get the executive performance we need by raising our standards for abilities, let alone by hoping for the universally gifted man. We will have to extend the range of human beings through the tools they have to work with rather than through a sudden quantum jump in human ability.

The same, more or less, applies to knowledge. However badly we may need people of more and better knowledge, the effort needed to make the major improvement may well be greater than any possible, let alone any probable, return.

Fifteen years ago when "operations research" first came in, several of the brilliant young practitioners published their prescription for the operations researcher of tomorrow. They always came out asking for a polymath knowing everything and capable of doing superior and original work in every area of human knowledge. According to one of these studies, operations researchers need to have advanced knowledge in sixty-two or so major scientific and humanistic disciplines. If such a man could be found, he would, I am afraid, be totally wasted on studies of inventory levels or on the programing of production schedules.

Much less ambitious programs for manager development call for high knowledge in such a host of divergent skills as accounting and personnel, marketing, pricing and economic analysis, the behavioral sciences such as psychology, and the natural sciences from physics to biology and geology. And we surely need men who understand the dynamics of modern technology, the complexity of the modern world economy, and the labyrinth of modern government.

Every one of these is a big area, is indeed, too big even for men who work on nothing else. The scholars tend to specialize in fairly small segments of each of these fields and do not pretend to have more than a journeyman's knowledge of the field itself.

I am not saying that one need not try to understand the fundamentals of every one of these areas.

> One of the weaknesses of young, highly educated people today—whether in business, medicine, or government—is that they are satisfied to be versed in one narrow specialty and affect a contempt for the other areas. One need not know in detail what to do with "human relations" as an accountant, or how to promote a new branded product if an

engineer. But one has a responsibility to know at least what these areas are about, why they are around, and what they are trying to do. One need not know psychiatry to be a good urologist. But one had better know what psychiatry is all about. One need not be an international lawyer to do a good job in the Department of Agriculture. But one had better know enough about international politics not to do international damage through a parochial farm policy.

This, however, is something very different from the universal expert, who is as unlikely to occur as the universal genius. Instead we will have to learn how to make better use of people who are good in any one of these areas. But this means increasing effectiveness. If one cannot increase the supply of a resource, one must increase its yield. And effectiveness is the one tool to make the resources of ability and knowledge yield more and better results.

Effectiveness thus deserves high priority because of the needs of organization. It deserves even greater priority as the tool of the executive and as his access to achievement and performance.

## BUT CAN EFFECTIVENESS BE LEARNED?

If effectiveness were a gift people were born with, the way they are born with a gift for music or an eye for painting, we would be in bad shape. For we know that only a small minority is born with great gifts in any one of these areas. We would therefore be reduced to trying to spot people with high potential of effectiveness early and to train them as best we know to develop their talent. But we could hardly hope to find enough people for the executive tasks of modern society this way. Indeed, if effectiveness were a gift, our present civilization would be highly vulnerable, if not untenable. As a civilization of large organizations it is dependent on a large supply of people capable of being executives with a modicum of effectiveness.

If effectiveness can be learned, however, the questions arise: What does it consist in? What does one have to learn? Of what kind is the learning? Is it a knowledge—and knowledge one learns in systematic form and through concepts? Is it a skill which one learns as an apprentice? Or is it a practice which one learns through doing the same elementary things over and over again?

I have been asking these questions for a good many years. As a consultant, I work with executives in many organizations. Effectiveness is crucial to me in two ways. First, a consultant who by definition has no authority other than that of knowledge must himself be effective—or else he is nothing. Second, the most effective consultant depends on people within the client organization to get anything done. Their effectiveness therefore determines in the last analysis whether a consultant contributes and achieves results, or whether he is pure "cost center" or at best a court jester.

I soon learned that there is no "effective personality." ⊖ The effective executives I have seen differ widely in their temperaments and their abilities, in

---

⊖ As is asserted in an unpublished (and undated) talk which Professor Chris Argyris of Yale University made at the graduate business school of Columbia University. According to Professor Argyris, the "successful" executive (as he calls him) has ten characteristics, among them "High Frustration Tolerance," understanding of the "Laws of Competitive Warfare," or that he "Identifies with Groups." If this were indeed the executive personality we need, we would be in real trouble. There are not too many people around with such personality traits, and no one has ever known a way of acquiring them. Fortunately, I know many highly effective—and successful—executives who lack most, if not all, of Argyris' "characteristics." I also know quite a few who, though they answer Argyris' description, are singularly ineffectual.

what they do and how they do it, in their personalities, their knowledge, their interests—in fact in almost everything that distinguishes human beings. All they have in common is the ability to get the right things done.

Among the effective executives I have known and worked with, there are extroverts and aloof, retiring men, some even morbidly shy. Some are eccentrics, others painfully correct conformists. Some are fat and some are lean. Some are worriers, some are relaxed. Some drink quite heavily, others are total abstainers. Some are men of great charm and warmth, some have no more personality than a frozen mackerel. There are a few men among them who would answer to the popular conception of a "leader." But equally there are colorless men who would attract no attention in a crowd. Some are scholars and serious students, others almost unlettered. Some have broad interests, others know nothing except their own narrow area and care for little else. Some of the men are self-centered, if not indeed selfish. But there are also some who are generous of heart and mind. There are men who live only for their work and others whose main interests lie outside—in community work, in their church, in the study of Chinese poetry, or in modern music. Among the effective executives I have met, there are people who use logic and analysis and others who rely mainly on perception and intuition. There are men who make decisions easily and men who suffer agonies every time they have to move.

Effective executives, in other words, differ as widely as physicians, high-school teachers, or violinists. They differ as widely as do ineffectual ones, are indeed indistinguishable from ineffectual executives in type, personality, and talents.

What all these effective executives have in common is the practices that make effective whatever they have and whatever they are. And these practices are the same, whether the effective executive works in a business or in a government agency, as hospital administrator, or as university dean.

But whenever I have found a man, no matter how great his intelligence, his industry, his imagination, or his knowledge, who fails to observe these practices, I have also found an executive deficient in effectiveness.

Effectiveness, in other words, is a habit; that is, a complex of practices. And practices can always be learned. Practices are simple, deceptively so; even a seven-year-old has no difficulty in understanding a practice. But practices are always exceedingly hard to do well. They have to be acquired, as we all learn the multiplication table; that is, repeated *ad nauseam* until "6×6=36" has become unthinking, conditioned reflex, and firmly ingrained habit. Practices one learns by practicing and practicing and practicing again.

To every practice applies what my old piano teacher said to me in exasperation when I was a small boy. "You will never play Mozart the way Arthur Schnabel does, but there is no reason in the world why you should not play your scales the way he does." What the piano teacher forgot to add—probably because it was so obvious to her—is that even the great pianists could not play Mozart as they do unless they practiced their scales and kept on practicing them.

There is, in other words, no reason why anyone with normal endowment should not acquire competence in any practice. Mastery might well elude him; for this one might need special talents. But what is needed in effectiveness is competence. What is needed are "the scales."

These are essentially five such practices—five such habits of the mind that have to be acquired to be an effective executive:

1. Effective executives know where their time goes. They work

systematically at managing the little of their time that can be brought under their control.

2. Effective executives focus on outward contribution. They gear their efforts to results rather than to work. They start out with the question, "What results are expected of me? " rather than with the work to be done, let alone with its techniques and tools.

3. Effective executives build on strengths—their own strengths, the strengths of their superiors, colleagues, and subordinates; and on the strengths in the situation, that is, on what they can do. They do not build on weakness. They do not start out with the things they cannot do.

4. Effective executives concentrate on the few major areas where superior performance will produce outstanding results. They force themselves to set priorities and stay with their priority decisions. They know that they have no choice but to do first things first—and second things not at all. The alternative is to get nothing done.

5. Effective executives, finally, make effective decisions. They know that this is, above all, a matter of system—of the right steps in the right sequence. They know that an effective decision is always a judgment based on "dissenting opinions" rather than on "consensus on the facts." And they know that to make many decisions fast means to make the wrong decisions. What is needed are few, but fundamental, decisions. What is needed is the right strategy rather than razzle-dazzle tactics.

These are the elements of executive effectiveness—and these are the subjects of this book.

CHAPTER 2

# Know Thy Time

Most discussions of the executive's task start with the advice to plan one's work. This sounds eminently plausible. The only thing wrong with it is that it rarely works. The plans always remain on paper, always remain good intentions. They seldom turn into achievement.

Effective executives, in my observation, do not start with their tasks. They start with their time. And they do not start out with planning. They start by finding out where their time actually goes. Then they attempt to manage their time and to cut back unproductive demands on their time. Finally they consolidate their "discretionary" time into the largest possible continuing units. This three-step process:

- recording time.
- managing time, and
- consolidating time

is the foundation of executive effectiveness.

Effective executives know that time is the limiting factor. The output limits of any process are set by the scarcest resource. In the process we call "accomplishment," this is time.

Time is also a unique resource. Of the other major resources, money is actually quite plentiful. We long ago should have learned that it is the demand for capital, rather than the supply thereof, which sets the limit to economic growth and activity. People—the third limiting resource—one can hire, though one can rarely hire enough good people. But one cannot rent, hire, buy, or otherwise obtain more time.

The supply of time is totally inelastic. No matter how high the demand, the supply will not go up. There is no price for it and no marginal utility curve for it. Moreover, time is totally perishable and cannot be stored. Yesterday's time is gone forever and will never come back. Time is, therefore, always in exceedingly short supply.

Time is totally irreplaceable. Within limits we can substitute one resource for another, copper for aluminum, for instance. We can substitute capital for human labor. We can use more knowledge or more brawn. But there is no substitute for time.

Everything requires time. It is the one truly universal condition. All work takes place in time and uses up time. Yet most people take for granted this unique, irreplaceable, and necessary resource. Nothing else, perhaps, distinguishes effective executives as much as their tender loving care of time.

Man is ill-equipped to manage his time.

Though man, like all living beings, has a "biological clock" —as anyone discovers who crosses the Atlantic by jet—he lacks a reliable time sense, as psychological experiments have shown. People kept in a room in which they cannot see light and darkness outside rapidly lose all sense of time. Even in total darkness, most people retain their sense of space. But even with the lights on, a few hours in a sealed room make most people incapable of estimating how much time has elapsed. They are as likely to underrate grossly the time spent in the room as to overrate it grossly.

If we rely on our memory, therefore, we do not know how time has been spent.

I sometimes ask executives who pride themselves on their memory to put down their guess as to how they spend their own time. Then I lock these guesses away for a few weeks or months. In the meantime, the executives run an actual time record on themselves. There is never much resemblance between the way these men thought they used their time and their actual records.

One company chairman was absolutely certain that he divided his time roughly into three parts. One third he thought he was spending with his senior men. One third he thought he spent with his important customers. And one third he thought was devoted to community activities. The actual record of his activities over six weeks brought out clearly that he spent almost no time in any of these areas. These were the tasks on which he knew he *should* spend time—and therefore memory, obliging as usual, told him that these were the tasks on which he actually had spent his time. The record showed, however, that he spent most of his hours as a kind of dispatcher, keeping track of orders from customers he personally knew, and bothering the plant with telephone calls about them. Most of these orders were going through all right anyhow and his intervention could only delay them. But when his secretary first came in with the time record, he did not believe her. It took two or three more time logs to convince him that record, rather than memory, has to be trusted when it comes to the use of time.

The effective executive therefore knows that to manage his time, he first has to know where it actually goes.

## THE TIME DEMANDS ON THE EXECUTIVE

There are constant pressures toward unproductive and wasteful time-use. Any executive, whether he is a manager or not, has to spend a great deal of his time on things that do not contribute at all. Much is inevitably wasted. The higher up in the organization he is, the more demands on his time will the organization make.

The head of a large company once told me that in two years as chief executive officer he had "eaten out" every evening except on Christmas Day and New Year's Day. All the other dinners were "official" functions, each of which wasted several hours. Yet he saw no possible alternative. Whether the dinner honored an employee retiring after fifty years of service, or the governor of one of the states in which the company did business, the chief executive officer had to be there. Ceremony is one of his tasks. My friend had no illusions that these dinners contributed anything either to the company or to his own entertainment or self-development. Yet he had to be there and dine graciously.

Similar time-wasters abound in the life of every executive. When a company's best customer calls up, the sales manager cannot say "I am busy." He has to listen, even though all the customer wants to talk about may be a bridge game the preceding Saturday or the chances of his daughter's getting into the right college. The hospital administrator has to attend the meetings of every one of his staff committees, or else the physicians, the nurses, the technicians, and so on feel that they are being slighted. The government administrator had better pay attention when a congressman calls and wants some information he could, in less time, get out of the telephone book or the *World Almanac*. And so it goes all day long.

Nonmanagers are no better off. They too are bombarded with demands on their time which add little, if anything, to their productivity, and yet cannot be disregarded.

In every executive job, a large part of the time must therefore be wasted on things which, though they apparently have to be done, contribute nothing or little.

Yet most of the tasks of the executive require, for minimum effectiveness, a fairly large quantum of time. To spend in one stretch less than this minimum is sheer waste. One accomplishes nothing and has to begin all over again.

To write a report may, for instance, require six or eight hours, at least for the first draft. It is pointless to give seven hours to the task by spending fifteen minutes twice a day for three weeks. All one has at the end is blank paper with some doodles on it. But if one can lock the door, disconnect the telephone, and sit down to wrestle with the report for five or six hours without interruption, one has a good chance to come up with what I call a "zero draft" —the one before the first draft. From then on, one can indeed work in fairly small installments, can rewrite, correct and edit section by section, paragraph by paragraph, sentence by sentence.

The same goes for an experiment. One simply has to have five to twelve hours in a single stretch to set up the apparatus and to do at least one completed run. Or one has to start all over again after an interruption.

To be effective, every knowledge worker, and especially every executive, therefore needs to be able to dispose of time in fairly large chunks. To have small dribs and drabs of time at his disposal will not be sufficient even if the total is an impressive number of hours.

This is particularly true with respect to time spent working with people, which is, of course, a central task in the work of the executive. People are time-consumers. And most people are time-wasters.

To spend a few minutes with people is simply not productive. If one wants to get anything across, one has to spend a fairly large minimum quantum of time. The manager who thinks that he can discuss the plans, direction, and performance of one of his subordinates in fifteen minutes—and many managers believe this—is just deceiving himself. If one wants to get to the point of having an impact, one needs probably at least an hour and usually much more. And if one has to establish a human relationship, one needs infinitely more time.

Relations with other knowledge workers are especially time-consuming. Whatever the reason—whether it is the absence of or the barrier of class and authority between superior and subordinate in knowledge work, or whether he simply takes himself more seriously—the knowledge worker makes much greater time demands than the manual worker on his superior as well as on his associates. Moreover, because knowledge work cannot be measured the way manual work can, one cannot tell a knowledge worker in a few simple words whether he is doing the right job and how well he is doing it. One can say to a manual worker, "our work standard calls for fifty pieces an hour, and you are only turning out forty-two." One has to sit down with a knowledge worker and think through with him what should be done and why, before one can even know whether he is doing a satisfactory job or not. And this is time-consuming.

Since the knowledge worker directs himself, he must understand what achievement is expected of him and why. He must also understand the work of the people who have to use his knowledge output. For this, he needs a good deal of information, discussion, instruction—all things that take time. And contrary to common belief, this time demand is made not only on his superior but equally on his colleagues.

The knowledge worker must be focused on the results and performance goals of the entire organization to have any results and performance at all. This means that he has to set aside time to direct his vision from his work to results, and from his specialty to the outside in which alone performance lies.

Wherever knowledge workers perform well in large organizations, senior executives take time out, on a regular schedule, to sit down with them, sometimes all the way down to green juniors, and ask: "What should we at the head of this organization know about your work? What do you want to tell me regarding this organization? Where do you see opportunities we do not exploit? Where do you see dangers to which we are still blind? And, all together, what do you want to know from me about the organization?"

This leisurely exchange is needed equally in a government agency and in a business, in a research lab and in an army staff. Without it, the knowledge people either lose enthusiasm and become time-servers, or they direct their energies toward their specialty and away from the opportunities and needs of the organization. But such a session takes a great deal of time, especially as it should be unhurried and relaxed. People must feel that "we have all the time in the world." This actually means that one gets a great deal done fast. But it means also that one has to make available a good deal of time in one chunk and without too much interruption.

Mixing personal relations and work relations is time-consuming. If hurried, it turns into friction. Yet any organization rests on this mixture. The more people are together, the more time will their sheer interaction take, the less time will be available to them for work, accomplishment, and results.

Management literature has long known the theorem of "the span of control," which asserts that one man can manage only a few people if these people have to come together in their own work (that is, for instance, an accountant, a sales manager, and a manufacturing man, all three of whom have to work with each other to get any results). On the other hand, managers of chain stores in different cities do not have to work with each other, so that any number could conceivably report to one regional vice-president without violating the principle of the "span of control." Whether this theorem is valid or not, there is little doubt that the more people have to work together, the more time will be spent on "interacting" rather than on work and accomplishment. Large organization creates strength by lavishly using the executive's time.

The larger the organization, therefore, the less actual time will the executive have. The more important will it be for him to know where his time goes and to manage the little time at his disposal.

The more people there are in an organization, the more often does a decision on people arise. But fast personnel decisions are likely to be wrong decisions. The time quantum of the good personnel decision is amazingly large. What the decision involves often becomes clear only when one has gone around the same track several times.

Among the effective executives I have had occasion to observe, there have been people who make decisions fast, and people who make them rather slowly. But without exception, they make personnel decisions slowly and they make them several times before they really commit themselves.

Alfred P. Sloan, Jr., former head of General Motors, the world's largest manufacturing company, was reported never to make a personnel decision the first time it came up. He made a tentative judgment, and even that took several hours as a rule. Then, a few days or weeks later, he tackled the question again, as if he had never worked on it before. Only when he came up with the same name two or three times in a row was he willing to go ahead. Sloan had a deserved reputation for the "winners" he picked. But when asked about his secret, he is reported to have said: "No secret—I have simply accepted that the first name I come up with is likely to be the wrong name—and I therefore retrace the whole process of thought and analysis a few times before I act." Yet Sloan was far from a patient man.

Few executives make personnel decisions of such impact. But all effective executives I have had occasion to observe have learned that they have to give several hours of continuous and uninterrupted thought to decisions on people if they hope to come up with the right answer.

The director of a medium-sized government research institute found this out when one of his senior administrators had to be removed from his job. The man was in his fifties and had been with the institute all his working life. After years of good work, the man suddenly began to deteriorate. He clearly could no longer handle his job. But even if civil service rules had permitted it, the man could not be fired. He could of course have been demoted. But this, the director felt, would destroy the man—and the institute owed him consideration and loyalty for years of productive, loyal service. Yet he could not be kept in an administrative position; his shortcomings were much too obvious and were, indeed, weakening the whole institute.

The director and his deputy had been over this situation many times without seeing a way out. But when they sat down for a quiet evening where they could give three or four hours uninterruptedly to the problem, the "obvious" solution finally emerged. It was indeed so simple that neither could explain why he had not seen it before. It got the man out of the wrong job into a job which needed being done and which yet did not require the administrative performance he was no longer able to give.

Time in large, continuous, and uninterrupted units is needed for such decisions as whom to put on a task force set up to study a specific problem; what responsibilities to entrust to the manager of a new organizational unit or to the new manager of an old organizational unit; whether to promote into a vacancy a man who has the marketing knowledge needed for the job but lacks technical training, or whether to put in a first-rate technical man without much marketing background, and so on.

People-decisions are time-consuming, for the simple reason that the Lord did not create people as "resources" for organization. They do not come in the proper size and shape for the tasks that have to be done in organization—and they cannot be machined down or recast for these tasks. People are always "almost fits" at best. To get the work done with people (and no other resource is available) therefore requires lots of time, thought, and judgment.

The Slavic peasant of Eastern Europe used to have a proverb: "What one does not have in one's feet, one's got to have in one's head." This may be considered a fanciful version of the law of the conservation of energy. But it is above all something like a "law of the conservation of time." The more time we take out of the task of the "legs" —that is, of physical, manual work—the more will we have to spend on the work of the "head" —that is, on knowledge work. The easier we make it for rank-and-file workers, machine tenders as well as clerks, the more will have to be done by the knowledge worker. One cannot "take knowledge out of the work." It has to be put back somewhere—and in much larger and cohesive amounts.

Time demands on the knowledge workers are not going down. Machine tenders now work only forty hours a week—and soon may work only thirty-five and live better than anybody ever lived before, no matter how much he worked or how rich he was. But the machine tender's leisure is inescapably being paid for by the knowledge worker's longer hours. It is not the executives who have a problem of spending their leisure time in the industrial countries of the world today. On the contrary, they are working everywhere longer hours and have greater demands on their time to satisfy. And the executive time scarcity is bound to become worse rather than better.

One important reason for this is that a high standard of living presupposes an economy of innovation and change. But innovation and change make inordinate time demands on the executive. All one can think and do in a short time is to think what one already knows and to do as one has always done.

> There has been an enormous amount of discussion lately to explain why the British economy has lagged so badly since World War II. One of the reasons is surely that the British businessman of the older generation tried to have it as easy as his workers and to work the same short hours. But this is possible only if the business or the industry clings to the old established routine and shuns innovation and change.

For all these reasons, the demands of the organization, the demands of people, the time demands of change and innovation, it will become increasingly important for executives to be able to manage their time. But one cannot even think of managing one's time unless one first knows where it goes.

## TIME-DIAGNOSIS

That one has to record time before one can know where it goes and before, in turn, one can attempt to manage it we have realized for the best part of a century. That is, we have known this in respect to manual work, skilled and unskilled, since Scientific Management around 1900 began to record the time it takes for a specific piece of manual work to be done. Hardly any country is today so far behind in industrial methods as not to time systematically the operations of manual workers.

We have applied this knowledge to the work where time does not greatly matter; that is, where the difference between time-use and time-waste is primarily efficiency and costs. But we have not applied it to the work that matters increasingly, and that particularly has to cope with time: the work of the knowledge worker and especially of the executive. Here the difference between time-use and time-waste is effectiveness and results.

The first step toward executive effectiveness is therefore to record actual time-use.

> The specific method in which the record is put together need not concern us here. There are executives who keep such a time log themselves. Others, such as the company chairman just mentioned, have their secretaries do it for them. The important thing is that it gets done,

and that the record is made in "real" time, that is at the time of the event itself, rather than later on from memory.

A good many effective executives keep such a log continuously and look at it regularly every month. At a minimum, effective executives have the log run on themselves for three to four weeks at a stretch twice a year or so, on a regular schedule. After each such sample, they rethink and rework their schedule. But six months later, they invariably find that they have "drifted" into wasting their time on trivia. Time-use does improve with practice. But only constant efforts at managing time can prevent drifting.

Systematic time management is therefore the next step. One has to find the nonproductive, time-wasting activities and get rid of them if one possibly can. This requires asking oneself a number of diagnostic questions.

1. First one tries to identify and eliminate the things that need not be done at all, the things that are purely waste of time without any results whatever. To find these time-wastes, one asks of *all* activities in the time records: "What would happen if this were not done at all? " And if the answer is, "Nothing would happen," then obviously the conclusion is to stop doing it.

It is amazing how many things busy people are doing that never will be missed. There are, for instance, the countless speeches, dinners, committee memberships, and directorships which take an unconscionable toll of the time of busy people, which are rarely enjoyed by them or done well by them, but which are endured, year in and year out, as an Egyptian plague ordained from on high. Actually, all one has to do is to learn to say "no" if an activity contributes nothing to one's own organization, to oneself, or to the organization for which it is to be performed.

The chief executive mentioned above who had to dine out every night found, when he analyzed these dinners, that at least one third would proceed just as well without anyone from the company's senior management. In fact, he found (somewhat to his chagrin) that his acceptance of a good many of these invitations was by no means welcome to his hosts. They had invited him as a polite gesture. But they had fully expected to be turned down and did not quite know what to do with him when he accepted.

I have yet to see an executive, regardless of rank or station, who could not consign something like a quarter of the demands on his time to the wastepaper basket without anybody's noticing their disappearance.

2. The next question is: "Which of the activities on my time log could be done by somebody else just as well, if not better?"

The dinner-eating company chairman found that any senior executive of the company would do for another third of the formal dinners—all the occasion demanded was the company's name on the guest list.

There has been for years a great deal of talk about "delegation" in management. Every manager whatever the organization—business, government, university, or armed service—has been exhorted to be a better "delegator." In fact, most managers in large organizations have themselves given this sermon and more than once. I have yet to see any results from all this preaching. The reason why no one listens is simple: As usually presented, delegation makes little sense. If it means that somebody else ought to do part of *"my* work," it is wrong. One is paid for doing one's own work. And if it implies, as the usual sermon does, that the laziest manager is the best manager, it is not only nonsense; it is immoral.

But I have never seen an executive confronted with his time record who did not rapidly acquire the habit of pushing at other people everything that he need not do personally. The first look at the time record makes it abundantly clear that there just is not time enough to do the things the executive himself considers important, himself wants to do, and is himself committed to doing. The only way he can get to the important things is by pushing on others anything that can be done by them at all.

A good example is executive travel. Professor C. Northcote Parkinson has pointed out in one of his delightful satires that the quickest way to get rid of an inconvenient superior is to make a world traveler out of him. The jet plane is indeed overrated as a management tool. A great many trips have to be made; but a junior can make most of them. Travel is still a novelty for him. He is still young enough to get a good night's rest in hotel beds. The junior can take the fatigue—and he will therefore also do a better job than the more experienced, perhaps better trained, but tired superior.

There are also the meetings one attends, even though nothing is going to happen that someone else could not handle. There are the hours spent discussing a document before there is even a first draft that can be discussed. There is, in the research lab, the time spent by a senior physicist to write a "popular" news release on some of his work. Yet there are plenty of people around with enough science to understand what the physicist is trying to say, who can write readable English, where the physicist only speaks higher mathematics. Altogether, an enormous amount of the work being done by executives is work that can easily be done by others, and therefore should be done by others.

"Delegation" as the term is customarily used, is a misunderstanding—is indeed misdirection. But getting rid of anything that can be done by somebody else so that one does not have to delegate but can really get to one's own work—that is a major improvement in effectiveness.

3. A common cause of time-waste is largely under the executive's control and can be eliminated by him. That is the time of others he himself wastes.

There is no one symptom for this. But there is still a simple way to find out. That is to ask other people. Effective executives have learned to ask systematically and without coyness: "What do I do that wastes your time without contributing to your effectiveness? " To ask this question, and to ask it without being afraid of the truth, is a mark of the effective executive.

The manner in which an executive does productive work may still be a major waste of somebody's else's time.

> The senior financial executive of a large organization knew perfectly well that the meetings in his office wasted a lot of time. This man asked all his direct subordinates to every meeting, whatever the topic. As a result the meetings were far too large. And because every participant felt that he had to show interest, everybody asked at least one question—most of them irrelevant. As a result the meetings stretched on endlessly. But the senior executive had not known, until he asked, that his

subordinates too considered the meetings a waste of their time. Aware of the great importance everyone in the organization placed on status and on being "in the know," he had feared that the uninvited men would feel slighted and left out.

Now, however, he satisfies the status needs of his subordinates in a different manner. He sends out a printed form which reads: "I have asked (Messrs Smith, Jones, and Robinson) to meet with me (Wednesday at 3) in (the fourth floor conference room) to discuss (next year's capital appropriations budget). Please come if you think that you need the information or want to take part in the discussion. But you will in any event receive right away a full summary of the discussion and of any decisions reached, together with a request for your comments."

Where formerly a dozen people came and stayed all afternoon, three men and a secretary to take the notes now get the matter over with within an hour or so. And no one feels left out.

Many executives know all about these unproductive and unnecessary time demands; yet they are afraid to prune them. They are afraid to cut out something important by mistake. But this mistake, if made, can be speedily corrected. If one prunes too harshly, one usually finds out fast enough.

Every new President of the United States accepts too many invitations at first. Then it dawns on him that he has other work to do and that most of these invitations do not add to his effectiveness. Thereupon, he usually cuts back too sharply and becomes inaccessible. A few weeks or months later, however, he is being told by the press and the radio that he is "losing touch." Then he usually finds the right balance between being exploited without effectiveness and using public appearances as his national pulpit.

In fact, there is not much risk that an executive will cut back too much. We usually tend to overrate rather than underrate our importance and to conclude that far too many things can only be done by ourselves. Even very effective executives still do a great many unnecessary, unproductive things.

But the best proof that the danger of overpruning is a bugaboo is the extraordinary effectiveness so often attained by severely ill or severely handicapped people.

A good example was Harry Hopkins, President Roosevelt's confidential adviser in World War II. A dying, indeed almost a dead man for whom every step was torment, he could only work a few hours every other day or so. This forced him to cut out everything but truly vital matters. He did not lose effectiveness thereby; on the contrary, he became, as Churchill called him once, "Lord Heart of the Matter" and accomplished more than anyone else in wartime Washington.

This is an extreme, of course. But it illustrates both how much control one can exercise over one's time if one really tries, and how much of the time-wasters one can cut out without loss of effectiveness.

## PRUNING THE TIME WASTERS

These three diagnostic questions deal with unproductive and time-consuming activities over which every executive has some control. Every knowledge worker and every executive should ask them. Managers, however, need to be equally concerned with time-loss that results from poor management and deficient organization. Poor management wastes everybody's time—but above all, it wastes the manager's time.

1. The first task here is to identify the time-wasters which follow from lack of system or foresight. The symptom to look for is the recurrent "crisis," the crisis that comes back year after year. A crisis that recurs a second time is a crisis that must not occur again.

> The annual inventory crisis belongs here. That with the computer we now can meet it even more "heroically" and at greater expense than we could in the past is hardly a great improvement.

A recurrent crisis should always have been foreseen. It can therefore either be prevented or reduced to a routine which clerks can manage. The definition of a "routine" is that it makes unskilled people without judgment capable of doing what it took near-genius to do before; for a routine puts down in systematic, step-by-step form what a very able man learned in surmounting yesterday's crisis.

The recurrent crisis is not confined to the lower levels of an organization. It afflicts everyone.

> For years, a fairly large company ran into one of these crises annually around the first of December. In a highly seasonal business, with the last quarter usually the year's low, fourth-quarter sales and profits were not easily predictable. Every year, however, management made an earnings prediction when it issued its interim report at the end

of the second quarter. Three months later, in the fourth quarter, there was tremendous scurrying and companywide emergency action to live up to top management's forecast. For three to five weeks, nobody in the management group got any work done. It took only one stroke of the pen to solve this crisis; instead of predicting a definite year-end figure, top management is now predicting results within a range. This fully satisfies directors, stockholders, and the financial community. And what used to be a crisis a few years ago, now is no longer even noticed in the company—yet fourthquarter results are quite a bit better than they used to be, since executive time is no longer being wasted on making results fit the forecast.

Prior to Mr. McNamara's appointment as Secretary of Defense, a similar last-minute crisis shook the entire American defense establishment every spring, toward the end of the fiscal year on June 30. Every manager in the defense establishment, military or civilian, tried desperately in May and June to find expenditures for the money appropriated by Congress for the fiscal year. Otherwise, he was afraid he would have to give back the money. (This last-minute spending spree has also been a chronic disease in Russian planning.) And yet, this crisis was totally unnecessary as Mr. McNamara immediately saw. The law had always permitted the placing of unspent, but needed, sums into an interim account.

**The recurrent crisis is simply a symptom of slovenliness and laziness.**

Years ago when I first started out as a consultant, I had to learn how to tell a well-managed industrial plant from a poorly managed one—

without any pretense to production knowledge. A well-managed plant, I soon learned, is a quiet place. A factory that is "dramatic," a factory in which the "epic of industry" is unfolded before the visitor's eyes, is poorly managed. A well-managed factory is boring. Nothing exciting happens in it because the crises have been anticipated and have been converted into routine.

Similarly a well-managed organization is a "dull" organization. The "dramatic" things in such an organization are basic decisions that make the future, rather than heroics in mopping up yesterday.

2. Time-wastes often result from overstaffing.

My first-grade arithmetic primer asked: "If it takes two ditch-diggers two days to dig a ditch, how long would it take four ditch-diggers?" In first grade, the correct answer is, of course, "one day." In the kind of work, however, with which executives are concerned, the right answer is probably "four days" if not "forever."

A work force may, indeed, be too small for the task. And the work then suffers, if it gets done at all. But this is not the rule. Much more common is the work force that is too big for effectiveness, the work force that spends, therefore, an increasing amount of its time "interacting" rather than working.

There is a fairly reliable symptom of overstaffing. If the senior people in the group—and of course the manager in particular—spend more than a small fraction of their time, maybe one tenth, on "problems of human relations," on feuds and frictions, on jurisdictional disputes and questions of cooperation, and so on, then the work force is almost certainly too large. People get into each other's way. People have become an impediment to performance, rather than the means there to. In a lean organization people have room to move without colliding with one another and can do their work without having to explain it all the time.

> The excuse for overstaffing is always "but we have to have a thermodynamicist (or a patent lawyer, or an economist) on the staff." This specialist is not being used much; he may not be used at all; but "we have to have him around just in case we need him." (And he always "has to be familiar with our problem" and "be part of the group from the start" !)One should only have on a team the knowledges and skills that are needed day in and day out for the bulk of the work. Specialists that may be needed once in a while, or that may have to be consulted on this or on that, should always remain outside. It is infinitely cheaper to go to them and consult them against a fee than to have them in the group to say nothing of the impact an underemployed but overskilled man has on the effectiveness of the entire group. All he can do is mischief.

3. Another common time-waster is malorganization. Its symptom is an excess of meetings.

Meetings are by definition a concession to deficient organization For one either meets or one works. One cannot do both at the same time. In an ideally designed structure (which in a changing world is of course only a dream) there would be no meetings. Everybody would know what he needs to know to do his job. Everyone would have the resources available to him to do his job. We meet because people holding different jobs have to cooperate to get a specific task done. We meet because the knowledge and experience needed in a specific situation are not available in one head, but have to be pieced together out of the experience and knowledge of several people.

There will always be more than enough meetings. Organization will always require so much working together that the attempts of well-meaning behavioral scientists to create opportunities for "cooperation" may be somewhat redundant. But if executives in an organization spend more than a fairly small part of their time in meeting, it is a sure sign of malorganization.

Every meeting generates a host of little follow-up meetings —some formal, some informal, but both stretching out for hours. Meetings, therefore, need to be purposefully directed. An undirected meeting is not just a nuisance; it is a danger. But above all, meetings have to be the exception rather than the rule. An organization in which everybody meets all the time is an organization in which no one gets anything done. Wherever a time log shows the fatty degeneration of meetings—whenever, for instance, people in an organization find them-selves in meetings a quarter of their time or more—there is time-wasting malorganization.

There are exceptions, special organs whose purpose it is to meet—the boards of directors, for instance, of such companies as Du Pont and Standard Oil of New Jersey which are the final organs of deliberation and appeal but which do not operate anything. But as these two companies realized a long time ago, the people who sit on these boards cannot be permitted to do anything else; for the same reason, by the way, that judges cannot be permitted to be also advocates in their spare time.

As a rule, meetings should never be allowed to become the main demand on an executive's time. Too many meetings always bespeak poor structure of jobs and the wrong organizational components. Too many meetings signify that work that should be in one job or in one component is spread over several jobs or several components. They signify that responsibility is diffused and that information is not addressed to the people who need it.

In one large company, the root cause of an epidemic of meetings was a traditional but obsolescent organization of the energy business. Large steam turbines, the company's traditional business since before 1900, were one division under their own management and with their own staff. During World War II, however, the company also went into aircraft engines and, as a result, had organized in another division concerned with aircraft and defense production a large jet engine capacity. Finally, there was an atomic energy division, really an offspring of the research labs and still organizationally more or less tied to them.

But today these three power sources are no longer separate, each with its own market. Increasingly, they are becoming substitutes for, as well as complements to, each other. Each of the three is the most economical and most advantageous generating equipment for electric power under certain conditions. In this sense the three are competitive. But by putting two of them together, one can also obtain performance capacities which no one type of equipment by itself possesses.

What the company needed, clearly, was an energy strategy. It needed a decision whether to push all three types of generating equipment, in competition with each other; whether to make one of the three the main business and consider the other two supplementary; or finally, whether to develop two of the three—and which two—as one "energy package." It needed a decision how to divide available capital among the three. Above all, however, the energy business needed an organization which expressed the reality of one energy market, producing the same end product, electric power, for the same customers. Instead there were three components, each carefully shielded from the others by layers of organization, each having its own special folkways, rituals, and its own career ladders—and each blithely confident that it would get by itself 75 percent of the total energy business of the next decade.

As a result, the three were engaged in a nonstop meeting for years. Since each reported to a different member of management, these meetings sucked in the entire top group. Finally, the three were cut loose from their original groups and put together into one organizational component under one manager. There is still a good deal of infighting going on; and the big strategy decisions still have to be made. But at least there is understanding now as to what these decisions are. At least top management no longer has to chair and referee every meeting. And total meeting-time is a fraction of what it used to be.

4. The last major time-waster is malfunction in information.

The administrator of a large hospital was plagued for years by telephone calls from doctors asking him to find a bed for one of their patients who should be hospitalized. The admissions people "knew" that there was no empty bed. Yet the administrator almost invariably found a few. The admissions people simply were not informed immediately when a patient was discharged. The floor nurse knew, of course, and so did the people in the front office who presented the bill to the departing patient. The admissions people, however, got a "bed count" made every morning at 5: 00 A. M. —while the great majority of patients were being sent home in midmorning after the doctors had made the rounds. It did not take genius to put this right; all it needed was an extra carbon copy of the chit that goes from the floor nurse to the front office.

**Even worse, but equally common, is information in the wrong form.**

Manufacturing businesses typically suffer from production figures that have to be "translated" before operating people can use them. They report "averages"; that is, they report what the accountants need. Operating people, however, usually need not the averages but the range and the extremes—product mix and production fluctuations, length of runs, and so on. To get what they need, they must either spend hours each day adapting the averages or build their own "secret" accounting organization. The accountant has all the information, but no one, as a rule, has thought of telling him what is needed.

Time-wasting management defects such as overstaffing, malorganization, or malfunctioning information can sometimes be remedied fast. At other times, it takes long, patient work to correct them. The results of such work are, however, great—and especially in terms of time gained.

## CONSOLIDATING DISCRETIONARY TIME

The executive who records and analyzes his time and then attempts to manage it can determine how much he has for his important tasks. How much time is there that is "discretionary," that is, available for the big tasks that will really make a contribution?

It is not going to be a great deal, no matter how ruthlessly the executive prunes time-wasters.

One of the most accomplished time managers I have ever met was the president of a big bank with whom I worked for two years on top-management structure. I saw him once a month for two years. My appointment was always for an hour and a half. The president was always prepared for the sessions—and I soon learned to do my homework too. There was never more than one item on the agenda. But when I had been in there for an hour and twenty minutes, the president would turn to me and say, "Mr. Drucker, I believe you'd better sum up now and outline what we should do next." And an hour and thirty minutes after I had been ushered into his office, he was at the door shaking my hand and saying good-by.

After this had been going on for about one year, I finally asked him, "Why always an hour and a half?" He answered, "That's easy. I have found out that my attention span is about an hour and a half. If I work on any one topic longer than this, I begin to repeat myself. At the same time, I have learned that nothing of importance can really be tackled in much less time. One does not get to the point where one understands what one is talking about."

During the hour and a half I was in his office every month, there was never a telephone call, and his secretary never stuck her head in the door to announce that an important man wanted to see him urgently. One day I asked him about this. He said, "My secretary has strict instructions not to put anyone through except the President of the United States and my wife. The President rarely calls—and my wife knows better. Everything else the secretary holds till I have finished. Then I have half an hour in which I return every call and make sure I get every message. I have yet to come across a crisis which could not wait ninety minutes."

Needless to say, this president accomplished more in this one monthly session than many other and equally able executives get done in a month of meetings.

But even this disciplined man had to resign himself to having at least half his time taken up by things of minor importance and dubious value, things that nonetheless had to be done—the seeing of important customers who just "dropped in," attendance at meetings which could just as well have proceeded without him; specific decisions on daily problems that should not have reached him but invariably did.

Whenever I see a senior executive asserting that more than half his time is under his control and is really discretionary time which he invests and spends according to his own judgment, I am reasonably certain that he has no idea where his time goes. Senior executives rarely have as much as one quarter of their time truly at their disposal and available for the important matters, the matters that contribute, the matters they are being paid for. This is true in any organization—except that in the government agency the unproductive time demands on the top people tend to be even higher than they are in other large organizations.

The higher up an executive, the larger will be the proportion of time that is not under his control and yet not spent on contribution. The larger the organization, the more time will be needed just to keep the organization together and running, rather than to make it function and produce.

The effective executive therefore knows that he has to consolidate his discretionary time. He knows that he needs large chunks of time and that small driblets are no time at all. Even one quarter of the working day, if consolidated in large time units, is usually enough to get the important things done. But even three quarters of the working day are useless if they are only available as fifteen minutes here or half an hour there.

The final step in time management is therefore to consolidate the time that record and analysis show as normally available and under the executive's control.

There are a good many ways of doing this. Some people, usually senior men, work at home one day a week; this is a particularly common method of time-consolidation for editors or research scientists.

Other men schedule all the operating work—the meetings, reviews, problem-sessions, and so on—for two days a week, for example, Monday and Friday, and set aside the mornings of the remaining days for consistent, continuing work on major issues.

This was how the bank president handled his time. Monday and Friday he had his operating meetings, saw senior executives on current matters, was available to important customers, and so on. Tuesday, Wednesday, and Thursday afternoons were left unscheduled—for whatever might come up; and something of course always did, whether urgent personnel problems, a surprise visit by one of the bank's representatives from abroad or by an important customer, or a trip to Washington. But in the mornings of these three days he scheduled the work on the major matters—in chunks of ninety minutes each.

Another fairly common method is to schedule a daily work period at home in the morning.

One of the most effective executives in Professor Sune Carlson's study, mentioned above, spent ninety minutes each morning before going to work in a study without telephone at home. Even if this means working very early so as to get to the office on time, it is preferable to the most popular way of getting to the important work: taking it home in the evening and spending three hours after dinner on it. By that time, most executives are too tired to do a good job. Certainly those of middle age or older are better off going to bed earlier and getting up earlier. And the reason why working home nights is so popular is actually its worst feature: It enables an executive to avoid tackling his time and its management during the day.

But the method by which one consolidates one's discretionary time is far less important than the approach. Most people tackle the job by trying to push the secondary, the less productive matters together, thus clearing, so to speak, a free space between them. This does not lead very far, however. One still gives priority in one's mind and in one's schedule to the less important things, the things that have to be done even though they contribute little. As a result, any new time pressure is likely to be satisfied at the expense of the discretionary time and of the work that should be done in it. Within a few days or weeks, the entire discretionary time will then be gone again, nibbled away by new crises, new immediacies, new trivia.

Effective executives start out by estimating how much discretionary time they can realistically call their own. Then they set aside continuous time in the appropriate amount. And if they find later that other matters encroach on this reserve, they scrutinize their record again and get rid of some more time demands from less than fully productive activities. They know that, as has been said before, one rarely overprunes.

And all effective executives control their time management perpetually. They not only keep a continuing log and analyze it periodically. They set themselves deadlines for the important activities, based on their judgment of their discretionary time.

> One highly effective man I know keeps two such lists—one of the urgent and one of the unpleasant things that have to be done—each with a deadline. When he finds his deadlines slipping, he knows his time is again getting away from him.

Time is the scarcest resource, and unless it is managed, nothing else can be managed. The analysis of one's time, moreover, is the one easily accessible and yet systematic way to analyze one's work and to think through what really matters in it.

"Know Thyself," the old prescription for wisdom, is almost impossibly difficult for mortal men. But everyone can follow the injunction "Know Thy Time" if he wants to, and be well on the road toward contribution and effectiveness.

CHAPTER 3

# What Can I Contribute?

The effective executive focuses on contribution. He looks up from his work and outward toward goals. He asks: "What can I contribute that will significantly affect the performance and the results of the institution I serve?" His stress is on responsibility.

The focus on contribution is the key to effectiveness: in a man's own work—its content, its level, its standards, and its impacts; in his relations with others—his superiors his associates, his subordinates; in his use of the tools of the executive such as meetings or reports.

The great majority of executives tend to focus downward. They are occupied with efforts rather than with results. They worry over what the organization and their superiors "owe" them and should do for them. And they are conscious above all of the authority they "should have." As a result, they render themselves ineffectual.

The head of one of the large management consulting firms always starts an assignment with a new client by spending a few days visiting the senior executives of the client organization one by one. After he has chatted with them about the assignment and the client organization, its history and its people, he asks (though rarely, of course, in these words): "And what do *you* do that justifies your being on the payroll?" The great majority, he reports, answer: "I run the accounting department," or "I am in charge of the sales force." Indeed, not uncommonly the answer is, "I have 850 people working under me." Only a few say, "It's my job to give our managers the information they need to make the right decisions," or "I am responsible for finding out what products the customer will want tomorrow," or "I have to think through and prepare the decisions the president will have to face tomorrow."

The man who focuses on efforts and who stresses his downward authority is a subordinate no matter how exalted his title and rank. But the man who focuses on contribution and who takes responsibility for results, no matter how junior, is in the most literal sense of the phrase, "top management." He holds himself accountable for the performance of the whole.

## THE EXECUTIVE'S OWN COMMITMENT

The focus on contribution turns the executive's attention away from his own specialty, his own narrow skills, his own department, and toward the performance of the whole. It turns his attention to the outside, the only place where there are results. He is likely to have to think through what relationships his skills, his specialty, his function, or his department have to the entire organization and *its* purpose. He therefore will also come to think in terms of the customer, the client, or the patient, who is the ultimate reason for whatever the organization produces, whether it be economic goods, governmental policies, or health services. As a result, what he does and how he does it will be materially different.

A large scientific agency of the U. S. government found this out a few years ago. The old director of publications retired. He had been with the agency since its inception in the thirties and was neither scientist nor trained writer. The publications which he turned out were often criticized for lacking professional polish. He was replaced by an accomplished science writer. The publications immediately took on a highly professional look. But the scientific community for whom these publications were intended stopped reading them. A highly respected university scientist, who had for many years worked closely with the agency, finally told the administrator: "The former director was writing *for* us; your new man writes *at* us."

The old director had asked the question, "What can I contribute to the results of this agency? " His answer was, "I can interest the young scientists on the outside in our work, can make them want to come to work for us." He therefore stressed major problems, major decisions, and even major controversies inside the agency. This had brought him more than once into head-on collision with the administrator. But the old man had stood by his guns. "The test of our publications is not whether we like them; the test is how many young scientists apply to us for jobs and how good they are," he said.

To ask, "What can I contribute? " is to look for the unused potential in the job. And what is considered excellent performance in a good many positions is often but a pale shadow of the job's full potential of contribution.

The Agency department in a large American commercial bank is usually considered a profitable but humdrum activity. This department acts, for a fee, as the registrar and stocktransfer agent for the securities of corporations. It keeps the names of stockholders on record, issues and mails their dividend checks, and does a host of similar clerical chores—all demanding precision and high efficiency but rarely great imagination.

Or so it seemed until a new Agency vice-president in a large New York bank asked the question, "What could Agency contribute? " He then realized that the work brought him into direct contact with the senior financial executives of the bank's customers who make the "buying decisions" on all banking services—deposits, loans, investments, pension-fund management, and so on. Of course, the Agency department by itself has to be run efficiently. But as this new vice-president realized, its greatest potential was as a sales force for all the other services of the bank. Under its new head, Agency, formerly an efficient paper-pusher, became a highly successful marketing force for the entire bank.

Executives who do not ask themselves, "What can I contribute? " are not only likely to aim too low, they are likely to aim at the wrong things. Above all, they may define their contribution too narrowly.

"Contribution," as the two illustrations just given show, may mean different things. For every organization needs performance in three major areas: It needs direct results; building of values and their reaffirmation; and building and developing people for tomorrow. If deprived of performance in any one of these areas, it will decay and die. All three therefore have to be built into the contribution of every executive. But their relative importance varies greatly with the personality and the position of the executive as well as with the needs of the organization.

The direct results of an organization are clearly visible, as a rule. In a business, they are economic results such as sales and profits. In a hospital, they are patient care, and so on. But even direct results are not totally unambiguous, as the example of the Agency vice-president in the bank illustrates. And when there is confusion as to what they should be, there are no results.

> One example is the performance (or rather lack of performance) of the nationalized airlines of Great Britain. They are supposed to be run as a business. They are also supposed to be run as an instrument of British national policy and Commonwealth cohesion. But they have been run largely to keep alive the British aircraft industry. Whipsawed between three different concepts of direct results, they have done poorly in respect to all three.

Direct results always come first. In the care and feeding of an organization, they play the role calories play in the nutrition of the human body. But any organization also needs a commitment to values and their constant reaffirmation, as a human body needs vitamins and minerals. There has to be something "this organization stands for," or else it degenerates into disorganization, confusion, and paralysis. In a business, the value commitment may be to technical leadership or (as in Sears Roebuck) to finding the right goods and services for the American family and to procuring them at the lowest price and the best quality.

Value commitments, like results, are not unambiguous.

> The U. S. Department of Agriculture has for many years been torn between two fundamentally incompatible value commitments—one to agricultural productivity and one to the "family farm" as the "backbone of the nation." The former has been pushing the country toward industrial agriculture, highly mechanical, highly industrialized, and essentially a large-scale commercial business. The latter has called for nostalgia supporting a nonproducing rural proletariat. But because farm policy—at least until very recently—has wavered between two different value commitments, all it has really succeeded in doing has been to spend prodigious amounts of money.

Finally, organization is, to a large extent, a means of overcoming the limitations mortality sets to what any one man can contribute. An organization that is not capable of perpetuating itself has failed. An organization therefore has to provide today the men who can run it tomorrow. It has to renew its human capital. It should steadily upgrade its human resources. The next generation should take for granted what the hard work and dedication of this generation has accomplished. They should then, standing on the shoulders of their predecessors, establish a new "high" as the baseline for the generation after them.

An organization which just perpetuates today's level of vision, excellence, and accomplishment has lost the capacity to adapt. And since the one and only thing certain in human affairs is change, it will not be capable of survival in a changed tomorrow.

An executive's focus on contribution by itself is a powerful force in developing people. People adjust to the level of the demands made on them. The executive who sets his sights on contribution, raises the sights and standards of everyone with whom he works.

A new hospital administrator, holding his first staff meeting, thought that a rather difficult matter had been settled to everyone's satisfaction, when one of the participants suddenly asked: "Would this have satisfied Nurse Bryan? " At once the argument started all over and did not subside until a new and much more ambitious solution to the problem had been hammered out.

Nurse Bryan, the administrator learned, had been a long-serving nurse at the hospital. She was not particularly distinguished, had not in fact ever been a supervisor. But whenever a decision on patient care came up on her floor, Nurse Bryan would ask, "Are we doing the best we can do to help this patient? " Patients on Nurse Bryan's floor did better and recovered faster. Gradually over the years, the whole hospital had learned to adopt what came to be known as "Nurse Bryan's Rule" ; had learned, in other words, to ask: "Are we really making the best contribution to the purpose of this hospital? "

Though Nurse Bryan herself had retired almost ten years earlier, the standards she had set still made demands on people who in terms of training and position were her superiors.

Commitment to contribution is commitment to responsible effective-ness. Without it, a man shortchanges himself, deprives his organization, and cheats the people he works with.

The most common cause of executive failure is inability or unwillingness to change with the demands of a new position. The executive who keeps on doing what he has done successfully before he moved is almost bound to fail. Not only do the results change to which his contribution ought to direct itself. The relative importance between the three dimensions of performance changes. The executive who fails to understand this will suddenly do the wrong things the wrong way—even though he does exactly what in his old job had been the right things done the right way.

This was the main reason for the failure of so many able men as executives in World War II Washington. That Washington was "political" or that men who had always been on their own suddenly found themselves "cogs in a big machine" were at most contributing factors. Plenty of men proved themselves highly effective Washington executives even though they had no political sense or had never worked in anything bigger than a two-man law practice. Robert E. Sherwood, a most effective administrator in the large Office of War Information (and the author of one of the most perceptive books on effectiveness in power⊖) had been a playwright whose earlier "organization" had consisted of his own desk and typewriter.

---

⊖ *Roosevelt and Hopkins* (New York, Harper & Row, 1948).

The men who succeeded in wartime Washington focused on contribution. As a result, they changed both what they did and the relative weight they gave to each of the value dimensions in their work. The failures worked much harder in a good many cases. But they did not challenge themselves, and they failed to see the need for redirecting their efforts.

An outstanding example of success was the man who, already sixty, became chief executive officer of a large nationwide chain of retail stores. This man had been in the second spot in the company for twenty years or more. He served contentedly under an outgoing and aggressive chief executive officer who was actually several years younger. He never expected to be president himself. But his boss died suddenly while still in his fifties, and the faithful lieutenant had to take over.

The new head had come up as a financial man and was at home with figures—the costing system, purchasing and inventory, the financing of new stores, traffic studies, and so on. People were by and large a shadowy abstraction to him. But when he suddenly found himself president, he asked himself: "What can I and no one else do which, if done really well, would make a real difference to this company?" The one, truly significant contribution, he concluded, would be the development of tomorrow's managers. The company had prided itself for many years on its executive development policies. "But," the new chief executive argued, "a policy does nothing by itself. My contribution is to make sure that this actually gets done."

From then on for the rest of his tenure, he walked through the personnel department three times a week on his way back from lunch and picked up at random eight or ten file folders of young men in the supervisory group. Back in his office, he opened the first man's folder, scanned it rapidly, and put through a telephone call to the man's superior. "Mr. Robertson, this is the president in New York. You have on your staff a young man, Joe Jones. Didn't you recommend six months ago that he be put in a job where he could acquire some merchandising experience? You did. Why haven't you done anything about it? " And down would go the receiver.

The next folder opened, he would call another manager in another city: "Mr. Smith, this is the president in New York. I understand that you recommended a young man on your staff, Dick Roe, for a job in which he can learn something about store accounting. I just noticed that you have followed through with this recommendation, and I want to tell you how pleased I am to see you working at the development of our young people."

This man was in the president's chair only a few years before he himself retired. But today, ten or fifteen years later, executives who never met him attribute to him, and with considerable justice, the tremendous growth and success of the company since his time.

That he asked himself, "What can I contribute? " also seems to explain in large part the extraordinary effectiveness of Robert McNamara as U. S. Secretary of Defense—a position for which he was completely unprepared when President Kennedy, in the fall of 1960, plucked him out of the Ford Motor Company and put him into the toughest Cabinet job.

McNamara, who at Ford had been the perfect "inside" man, was for instance totally innocent of politics and tried to leave congressional liaison to subordinates. But after a few weeks, he realized that the Secretary of Defense depends on congressional understanding and support. As a result, he forced himself to do what for so publicity-shy and nonpolitical a man must have been both difficult and distasteful: to cultivate Congress, to get to know the influential men on the congressional committees, and to acquire a mastery of the strange art of congressional infighting. He has surely not been completely successful in his dealings with Congress, but he has done better than any earlier Secretary.

The McNamara story shows that the higher the position an executive holds, the larger will the outside loom in his contribution. No one else in the organization can as a rule move as freely on the outside.

Perhaps the greatest shortcoming of the present generation of university presidents in the United States is their inside focus on administration, on money-raising, and so on. Yet no other administrator in the large university is free to establish contact with the students who are the university's "customers." Alienation of the students from the administration is certainly a major factor in the student unhappiness and unrest that underlay, for instance, the Berkeley riots at the University of California in 1965.

## HOW TO MAKE THE SPECIALIST EFFECTIVE

For the knowledge worker to focus on contribution is particularly important. This alone can enable him to contribute at all.

Knowledge workers do not produce a "thing." They produce ideas, information, concepts. The knowledge worker, moreover, is usually a specialist. In fact, he can, as a rule, be effective only if he has learned to do one thing very well; that is, if he has specialized. By itself, however, a specialty is a fragment and sterile. Its output has to be put together with the output of other specialists before it can produce results.

The task is not to breed generalists. It is to enable the specialist to make himself and his specialty effective. This means that he must think through who is to use his output and what the user needs to know and to understand to be able to make productive the fragment the specialist produces.

It is popular today to believe that our society is divided into "scientists" and "laymen." It is then easy to demand that the laymen learn a little bit of the scientists' knowledge, his terminology, his tools, and so on. But if society was ever divided that way, it was a hundred years ago. Today almost everybody in modern organization is an expert with a high degree of specialized knowledge, each with its own tools, its own concerns, and its own jargon. And the sciences, in turn, have all become splintered to the point where one kind of physicist finds it difficult to comprehend what another kind of physicist is concerned with.

The cost accountant is as much a "scientist" as the biochemist, in the sense that he has his own special area of knowledge with its own assumptions, its own concerns, and its own language. And so is the market researcher and the computer logician, the budget officer of the government agency and the psychiatric case worker in the hospital. Each of these has to be understood by others before he can be effective.

The man of knowledge has always been expected to take responsibility for being understood. It is barbarian arrogance to assume that the layman can or should make the effort to understand him, and that it is enough if the man of knowledge talks to a handful of fellow experts who are his peers. Even in the university or in the research laboratory, this attitude—alas, only too common today—condemns the expert to uselessness and converts his knowledge from learning into pedantry. If a man wants to be an executive—that is, if he wants to be considered responsible for his contribution—he has to concern himself with the usability of his "product" —that is, his knowledge.

Effective executives know this. For they are almost imperceptibly led by their upward orientation into finding out what the other fellow needs, what the other fellow sees, and what the other fellow understands. Effective executives find them selves asking other people in the organization, their superiors, their subordinates, but above all, their colleagues in other areas: "What contribution from me do you require to make *your* contribution to the organization? When do you need this, how do you need it, and in what form? "

> If cost accountants, for example, asked these questions, they would soon find out which of their assumptions—obvious to them—are totally unfamiliar to the managers who are to use the figures. They would soon find out which of the figures that to them are important are irrelevant to the operating people and which figures, barely seen by them and rarely reported, are the ones the operating people really need every day.
>
> The biochemist who asks this question in a pharmaceutical company will soon find out that the clinicians can use the findings of the biochemist only if presented in the clinicians' language rather than

in biochemical terms. The clinicians, however, in making the decision whether to put a new compound into clinical testing or not decide whether the biochemist's research product will even have a chance to become a new drug.

The scientist in government who focuses on contribution soon realizes that he must explain to the policy-maker where a scientific development *might* lead to; he must do something forbidden to scientists as a rule—that is, speculate about the outcome of a line of scientific inquiry.

The only meaningful definition of a "generalist" is a specialist who can relate his own small area to the universe of knowledge. Maybe a few people have knowledge in more than a few small areas. But that does not make them generalists; it makes them specialists in several areas. And one can be just as bigoted in three areas as in one. The man, however, who takes responsibility for his contribution will relate his narrow area to a genuine whole. He may never himself be able to integrate a number of knowledge areas into one. But he soon realizes that he has to learn enough of the needs, the directions, the limitations, and the perceptions of others to enable them to use his own work. Even if this does not make him appreciate the richness and the excitement of diversity, it will give him immunity against the arrogance of the learned—that degenerative disease which destroys knowledge and deprives it of beauty and effectiveness.

## THE RIGHT HUMAN RELATIONS

Executives in an organization do not have good human relations because they have a "talent for people." They have good human relations because they focus on contribution in their own work and in their relationships with others. As a result, their relationships are productive—and this is the only valid definition of "good human relations." Warm feelings and pleasant words are meaningless, are indeed a false front for wretched attitudes, if there is no achievement in what is, after all, a work-focused and task-focused relationship. On the other hand, an occasional rough word will not disturb a relationship that produces results and accomplishments for all concerned.

If I were asked to name the men who, in my own experience, had the best human relations, I would name three: General George C. Marshall, Chief of Staff of the U. S. Army in World War II; Alfred P. Sloan, Jr., the head of General Motors from the early nineteen-twenties into the mid-fifties; and one of Sloan's senior associates, Nicholas Dreystadt, the man who built Cadillac into the successful luxury car in the midst of the depression (and might well have been chief executive of General Motors sometime in the nineteen-fifties but for his early death right after World War II ).

These men were as different as men can be: Marshall, the "professional soldier," sparse, austere, dedicated, but with great, shy charm; Sloan, the "administrator," reserved, polite and very distant; and Dreystadt, warm, bubbling and, superficially, a typical German craftman of the "Old Heidelberg" tradition. Every one of them inspired deep devotion, indeed, true affection in all who worked for them. All three, in their different ways, built their relationship to people—their superiors, their colleagues, and their subordinates—around contribution. All three men, of necessity, worked closely with people and thought a good deal about people. All three had to make crucial "people" decisions. But not one of the three worried about "human relations." They took them for granted.

The focus on contribution by itself supplies the four basic requirements of effective human relations.

- communications;
- teamwork;
- self-development; and.
- development of others.

1. Communications have been in the center of managerial attention these last twenty years or more. In business, in public administration, in armed services, in hospitals, in other words in all the major institutions of modern society, there has been great concern with communications.

Results to date have been meager. Communications are by and large just as poor today as they were twenty or thirty years ago when we first became aware of the need for, and lack of, adequate communications in the modern organization. But we are beginning to understand why this massive communications effort cannot produce results.

We have been working at communications downward from management to the employees, from the superior to the subordinate. But communications are practically impossible if they are based on the downward relationship. This much we have learned from our work in perception and communications theory. The harder the superior tries to say something to his subordinate, the more likely is it that the subordinate will *mis*-hear. He will hear what he expects to hear rather than what is being said.

But executives who take responsibility for contribution in their own work will as a rule demand that their subordinates take responsibility too. They will tend to ask their men: "What are the contributions for which this organization and I, your superior, should hold you accountable? What should we expect of you? What is the best utilization of your knowledge and your ability? " And then communication becomes possible, becomes indeed easy.

Once the subordinate has thought through what contribution should be expected of him, the superior has, of course, both the fight and the responsibility to judge the validity of the proposed contribution.

> According to all our experience, the objectives set by subordinates for themselves are almost never what the superior thought they should be. The subordinates or juniors, in other words, do see reality quite differently. And the more capable they are, the more willing to take responsibility, the more will their perception of reality and of its objective opportunities and needs differ from the view of their superior or of the organization. But any discrepancy between their conclusions and what their superior expected will stand out strongly.

Who is right in such a difference is not as a rule important. For effective communication in meaningful terms has already been established.

2. The focus on contribution leads to communications sideways and thereby makes teamwork possible.

The question, "Who has to use my output for it to become effective? " immediately shows up the importance of people who are not in line of authority, either upward or downward, from and to the individual executive. It underlines what is the reality of a knowledge organization: The effective work is actually done in and by teams of people of diverse knowledges and skills. These people have to work together voluntarily and according to the logic of the situation and the demands of the task, rather than according to a formal jurisdictional structure.

In a hospital, for instance—perhaps the most complex of the modern knowledge organizations—nurses, dieticians, physical therapists, medical and X-ray technicians, pharmacologists, pathologists, and a host of other health-service professionals, have to work on and with the same patient, with a minimum of conscious command or control by anyone. And yet, they have to work together for a common end and in line with a general plan of action: the doctor's prescription for treatment. In terms of organizational structure, each of these health-service professionals reports to his own chief. Each operates in terms of his own highly specialized field of knowledge; that is, as a "professional." But each has to keep all the others informed according to the specific situation, the condition, and the need of an individual patient. Otherwise, their efforts are more likely to do harm than good.

In a hospital in which the focus on contribution has become ingrained habit, there is almost no difficulty in achieving such team work. In other hospitals this sideways communication, this spontaneous self-organization into the right task-focused teams, does not occur despite frantic efforts to obtain communications and coordination through all kinds of committees, staff conferences, bulletins, sermons, and the like.

The typical institution of today has an organization problem for which traditional concepts and theories are totally inadequate. Knowledge workers must be professionals in their attitude toward their own field of knowledge. They must consider themselves responsible for their own competence and for the standards of their work. In terms of formal organization, they will see themselves as "belonging" to a functional specialty—whether this is biochemistry or, as in the hospitals, nursing, for example. In terms of their personnel management—their training, their records, but also their appraisal and promotion—they will be governed by this knowledge-oriented function. But in their work they increasingly have to act as responsible members of a team with people from entirely different knowledge areas, organized around the specific task on hand.

Focus on upward contribution will not, by itself, provide the organizational solution. It will, however, contribute understanding of the task and communications to make imperfect organization perform.

> Communications within the knowledge work force is becoming critical as a result of the computer revolution in information. Throughout the ages the problem has always been how to get "communication" out of "information." Because information had to be handled and transmitted by people, it was always distorted by communications; that is, by opinion, impression, comment, judgment, bias, and so on. Now suddenly we are in a situation in which information is largely impersonal and, therefore, without any communications content. It is pure information.
>
> But now we have the problem of establishing the necessary

minimum of communications so that we understand each other and can know each other's needs, goals, perceptions, and ways of doing things. Information does not supply this. Only direct contact, whether by voice or by written word, can communicate.

The more we automate information-handling, the more we will have to create opportunities for effective communication.

3. Individual self-development in large measure depends on the focus on contributions.

The man who asks of himself, "What is the most important contribution I can make to the performance of this organization?" asks in effect, "What self-development do I need? What knowledge and skill do I have to acquire to make the contribution I should be making? What strengths do I have to put to work? What standards do I have to set myself?"

4. The executive who focuses on contribution also stimulates others to develop themselves, whether they are subordinates, colleagues, or superiors. He sets standards which are not personal but grounded in the requirements of the task. At the same time, they are demands for excellence. For they are demands for high aspiration, for ambitious goals, and for work of great impact.

We know very little about self-development. But we do know one thing: People in general, and knowledge workers in particular, grow according to the demands they make on themselves. They grow according to what they consider to be achievement and attainment. If they demand little of themselves, they will remain stunted. If they demand a good deal of themselves, they will grow to giant stature—without any more effort than is expended by the nonachievers.

## THE EFFECTIVE MEETING

The meeting, the report, or the presentation are the typical work situation of the executive. They are his specific, everyday tools. They also make great demands on his time—even if he succeeds in analyzing his time and in controlling whatever can be controlled.

Effective executives know what they expect to get out of a meeting, a report, or a presentation and what the purpose of the occasion is or should be. They ask themselves: "Why are we having this meeting? Do we want a decision, do We want to inform, or do we want to make clear to ourselves what we should be doing?" They insist that the purpose be thought through and spelled out before a meeting is called, a report asked for, or a presentation organized. They insist that the meeting serve the contribution to which they have committed themselves.

The effective man always states at the outset of a meeting the specific purpose and contribution it is to achieve. He makes sure that the meeting addresses itself to this purpose. He does not allow a meeting called to inform to degenerate into a "bull session" in which everyone has bright ideas. But a meeting called by him to stimulate thinking and ideas also does not become simply a presentation on the part of one of the members, but is run to challenge and stimulate everybody in the room. He always, at the end of his meetings, goes back to the opening statement and relates the final conclusions to the original intent.

There are other rules for making a meeting productive (for instance, the obvious but usually disregarded rule that one can either direct a meeting and listen for the important things being said, or one can take part and talk; one cannot do both). But the cardinal rule is to focus it from the start on contribution.

The focus on contribution counteracts one of the basic problems of the executive: the confusion and chaos of events and their failure to indicate by themselves which is meaningful and which is merely "noise." The focus on contribution imposes an organizing principle. It imposes relevance on events.

Focusing on contribution turns one of the inherent weaknesses of the executive's situation—his dependence on other people, his being within the organization—into a source of strength. It creates a team.

Finally, focusing on contribution fights the temptation to stay within the organization. It leads the executive—especially the top-level man—to lift his eyes from the inside of efforts, work, and relationships, to the outside; that is, to the results of the organization. It makes him try hard to have direct contact with the outside—whether markets and customers, patients in a community, or the various "publics" which are the outside of a government agency.

To focus on contribution is to focus on effectiveness.

CHAPTER 4

# Making Strength Productive

The effective executive makes strength productive. He knows that one cannot build on weakness. To achieve results, one has to use all the available strengths—the strengths of associates, the strengths of the superior, and one's own strengths. These strengths are the true opportunities. To make strength productive is the unique purpose of organization. It cannot, of course, overcome the weaknesses with which each of us is abundantly endowed. But it can make them irrelevant. Its task is to use the strength of each man as a building block for joint performance.

## STAFFING FROM STRENGTH

The area in which the executive first encounters the challenge of strength is in staffing. The effective executive fills positions and promotes on the basis of what a man can do. He does not make staffing decisions to minimize weaknesses but to maximize strength.

President Lincoln when told that General Grant, his new commander-in-chief, was fond of the bottle said: "If I knew his brand, I'd send a barrel or so to some other generals." After a childhood on the Kentucky and Illinois frontier, Lincoln assuredly knew all about the bottle and its dangers. But of all the Union generals, Grant alone had proven consistently capable of planning and leading winning campaigns. Grant's appointment was the turning point of the Civil War. It was an effective appointment because Lincoln chose his general for his tested ability to win battles and not for his sobriety, that is, for the absence of a weakness.

Lincoln learned this the hard way however. Before he chose Grant, he had appointed in succession three or four Generals whose main qualifications were their lack of major weaknesses. As a result, the North, despite its tremendous superiority in men and matériel, had not made any headway for three long years from 1861 to 1864. In sharp contrast, Lee, in command of the Confederate forces, had staffed from strength. Every one of Lee's generals, from Stonewall Jackson on, was a man of obvious and monumental weaknesses. But these failings Lee considered—rightly—to be irrelevant. Each of them had, however, one area of real strength—and it was this strength, and only this strength, that Lee utilized and made effective. As a result, the "well-rounded" men Lincoln had appointed were beaten time and again by Lee's "single-purpose tools," the men of narrow but very great strength.

Whoever tries to place a man or staff an organization to avoid weakness will end up at best with mediocrity. The idea that there are "well-rounded" people,

people who have only strengths and no weaknesses (whether the term used is the "whole man," the "mature personality," the "well-adjusted personality," or the "generalist" ) is a prescription for mediocrity if not for incompetence. Strong people always have strong weaknesses too. Where there are peaks, there are valleys. And no one is strong in many areas. Measured against the universe of human knowledge, experience, and abilities, even the greatest genius would have to be rated a total failure. There is no such thing as a "good man." Good for what? is the question.

The executive who is concerned with what a man cannot do rather than with what he can do, and who therefore tries to avoid weakness rather than make strength effective is a weak man himself. He probably sees strength in others as a threat to himself. But no executive has ever suffered because his subordinates were strong and effective. There is no prouder boast, but also no better prescription, for executive effectiveness than the words Andrew Carnegie, the father of the U. S. steel industry, chose for his own tombstone: "Here lies a man who knew how to bring into his service men better than he was himself." But of course every one of these men was "better" because Carnegie looked for his strength and put it to work. Each of these steel executives was a "better man" in one specific area and for one specific job. Carnegie, however, was the effective executive among them.

> Another story about General Robert E. Lee illustrates the meaning of making strength productive. One of his generals, the story goes, had disregarded orders and had thereby completely upset Lee's plans—and not for the first time either. Lee, who normally controlled his temper, blew up in a towering rage. When he had simmered down, one of his

aides asked respectfully, "Why don't you relieve him of his command? " Lee, it is said, turned around in complete amazement, looked at the aide, and said, "What an absurd question—he performs."

Effective executives know that their subordinates are paid to perform and not to please their superiors. They know that it does not matter how many tantrums a prima donna throws as long as she brings in the customers. The opera manager is paid after all for putting up with the prima donna's tantrums if that is her way to achieve excellence in performance. It does not matter whether a first-rate teacher or a brilliant scholar is pleasant to the dean or amiable in the faculty meeting. The dean is paid for enabling the first-rate teacher or the first-rate scholar to do his work effectively—and if this involves unpleasantness in the administrative routine, it is still cheap at the price.

Effective executives never ask "How does he get along with me? " Their question is "What does he contribute? " Their question is never "What can a man not do? " Their question is always "What can he do uncommonly well? " In staffing they look for excellence in one major area, and not for performance that gets by all around.

To look for one area of strength and to attempt to put it to work is dictated by the nature of man. In fact, all the talk of "the whole man" or the "mature personality" hides a profound contempt for man's most specific gift: his ability to put all his resources behind one activity, one field of endeavor, one area of accomplishment. It is, in other words, contempt for excellence. Human excellence can only be achieved in one area, or at the most in very few.

People with many interests do exist—and this is usually what we mean when we talk of a "universal genius." People with outstanding accomplishments in many areas are unknown. Even Leonardo performed only in the area of design despite his manifold interests; if Goethe's poetry had been lost and all that were known of his work were his dabblings in optics and philosophy, he would not even rate a footnote in the most learned encyclopedia. What is true for the giants holds doubly for the rest of us. Unless, therefore, an executive looks for strength and works at making strength productive, he will only get the impact of what a man cannot do, of his lacks, his weaknesses, his impediments to performance and effectiveness. To staff from what there is not and to focus on weakness is wasteful—a misuse, if not abuse, of the human resource.

To focus on strength is to make demands for performance. The man who does not first ask, "What can a man do?" is bound to accept far less than the associate can really contribute. He excuses the associate's nonperformance in advance. He is destructive but not critical, let alone realistic. The really "demanding boss" —and one way or another all makers of men are demanding bosses—always starts out with what a man should be able to do well—and then demands that he really do it.

To try to build against weakness frustrates the purpose of organization. Organization is the specific instrument to make human strengths redound to performance while human weakness is neutralized and largely rendered harmless. The very strong neither need nor desire organization. They are much better off working on their own. The rest of us, however, the great majority, do not have so much strength that by itself it would become effective despite our limitations. "One cannot hire a hand—the whole man always comes with it," says a proverb of the human relations people. Similarly, one cannot by oneself be only strong; the weaknesses are always with us.

But we can so structure an organization that the weaknesses become a personal blemish outside of, or at least beside, the work and accomplishment. We can so structure as to make the strength relevant. A good tax accountant in private practice might be greatly hampered by his inability to get along with people. But in an organization such a man can be set up in an office of his own and shielded from direct contact with other people. In an organization one can make his strength effective and his weakness irrelevant. The small businessman who is good at finance but poor at production or marketing is likely to get into trouble. In a somewhat larger business one can easily make productive a man who has true strength in finance alone.

Effective executives are not blind to weakness. The executive who understands that it is his job to enable John Jones to do his tax accounting has no illusions about Jones's ability to get along with people. He would never appoint Jones a manager.

But there are others who get along with people. First-rate tax accountants are a good deal rarer. Therefore, what this man—and many others like him—can do is pertinent in an organization. What he cannot do is a limitation and nothing else.

All this is obvious, one might say. Why then, is it not done all the time? Why are executives rare who make strength productive—especially the strength of their associates? Why did even a Lincoln staff from weakness three times before he picked strength.

The main reason is that the immediate task of the executive is not to place a man; it is to fill a job. The tendency is therefore to start out with the job as being a part of the order of nature. Then one looks for a man to fill the job. It is only too easy to be misled this way into looking for the "least misfit"—the one man who leaves least to be desired. And this is invariably the mediocrity.

The widely advertised "cure" for this is to structure jobs to fit the personalities available. But this cure is worse than the disease—except perhaps in a very small and simple organization. Jobs have to be objective; that is, determined by task rather than by personality.

One reason for this is that every change in the definition, structure, and position of a job within an organization sets off a chain reaction of changes throughout the entire institution. Jobs in an organization are interdependent and interlocked. One cannot change everybody's work and responsibility just because one has to replace a single man in a single job. To structure a job to a person is almost certain to result in the end in greater discrepancy between the demands of the job and the available talent. It results in a dozen people being uprooted and pushed around in order to accommodate one.

> This is by no means true only of bureaucratic organizations such as a government agency or a large business corporation. Somebody has to teach the introductory course in biochemistry in the university. It had better be a good man. Such a man will be a specialist. Yet the course has to be general and has to include the foundation materials of the discipline, regardless of the interests and inclinations of the teacher. What is to be taught is determined by what the students need—that is, by an objective requirement—which the individual instructor has to accept. When the orchestra conductor has to fill the job of first cellist, he will not even consider a poor cellist who is a first-rate oboe player, even though the oboist might be a greater musician than any of the available cellists. The conductor will not rewrite the score to accommodate a man. The opera manager who knows that he is being paid for putting up with

the tantrums of the prima donna still expects her to sing "Tosca" when the playbill announces *Tosca*.

But there is a subtler reason for insistence on impersonal, objective jobs. It is the only way to provide the organization with the human diversity it needs. It is the only way to tolerate—indeed to encourage—differences in temperament and personality in an organization. To tolerate diversity, relationships must be task-focused rather than personality-focused. Achievement must be measured against objective criteria of contribution and performance. This is possible, however, only if jobs are defined and structured impersonally. Otherwise the accent will be on "Who is fight? " rather than on "What is right? " In no time, personnel decisions will be made on "Do I like this fellow? " or "Will he be acceptable? " rather than by asking "Is he the man most likely to do an outstanding job? "

Structuring jobs to fit personality is almost certain to lead to favoritism and conformity. And no organization can afford either. It needs equity and impersonal fairness in its personnel decisions. Or else it will either lose its good people or destroy their incentive. And it needs diversity. Or else it will lack the ability to change and the ability for dissent which (as Chapter 7 will discuss) the right decision demands.

One implication is that the men who build first-class executive teams are not usually close to their immediate colleagues and subordinates. Picking people for what they can do rather than on personal likes or dislikes, they seek performance, not conformance. To insure this outcome, they keep a distance between themselves and their close colleagues.

Lincoln, it has often been remarked, only became an effective chief executive after he had changed from close personal relations—for example, with Stanton, his Secretary of War—to aloofness and distance. Franklin D. Roosevelt had no "friend" in the Cabinet—not even Henry Morgenthau, his Secretary of the Treasury, and a close friend on all nongovernmental matters. General Marshall and Alfred P. Sloan were similarly remote. These were all warm men, in need of close human relationships, endowed with the gift of making and keeping friends. They knew however that their friendships had to be "off the job." They knew that whether they liked a man or approved of him was irrelevant, if not a distraction. And by staying aloof they were able to build teams of great diversity but also of strength.

Of course there are always exceptions where the job should be fitted to the man. Even Sloan, despite his insistence on impersonal structure, consciously designed the early engineering organization of General Motors around a man, Charles F. Kettering, the great inventor. Roosevelt broke every rule in the book to enable the dying Harry Hopkins to make his unique contribution. But these exceptions should be rare. And they should only be made for a man who has proven exceptional capacity to do the unusual with excellence.

How then do effective executives staff for strength without stumbling into the opposite trap of building jobs to suit personality.

By and large they follow four rules.

1. They do not start out with the assumption that jobs are created by nature or by God. They know that they have been designed by highly fallible men. And

they are therefore forever on guard against the "impossible" job, the job that simply is not for normal human beings.

Such jobs are common. They usually look exceedingly logical on paper. But they cannot be filled. One man of proven performance capacity after the other is tried—and none does well. Six months or a year later, the job has defeated them.

Almost always such a job was first created to accommodate an unusual man and tailored to his idiosyncrasies. It usually calls for a mixture of temperaments that is rarely found in one person. Individuals can acquire very divergent kinds of knowledge and highly disparate skills. But they cannot change their temperaments. A job that calls for disparate temperaments becomes an "undoable" job, a man-killer.

The rule is simple: Any job that has defeated two or three men in succession, even though each had performed well in his previous assignments, must be assumed unfit for human beings. It must be redesigned.

Every text on marketing concludes, for instance, that sales management belongs together with advertising and promotion and under the same marketing executive. The experience of large, national manufacturers of branded and massmarketed consumer goods has been, however, that this overall marketing job is impossible. Such a business needs both high effectiveness in field selling—that is, in moving goods—and high effectiveness in advertising and promotion—that is, in moving people. These appeal to different personalities which rarely can be found in one man.

The presidency of a large university in the United States is also such an impossible job. At least our experience has been that only a small minority of the appointments to this position work out—even though the men chosen have almost always a long history of substantial achievement in earlier assignments.

Another example is probably the international vicepresident of today's large multinational business. As soon as production and sales outside the parent company's territory become significant—as soon as they exceed one fifth of the total or so—putting everything that is "not parent company" in one organizational component creates an impossible, a man-killing, job. The work either has to be reorganized by worldwide product groups (as Philips in Holland has done, for instance) or according to common social and economic characteristics of major markets. For instance, it might be split into three jobs: one managing the business in the industrialized countries (the United States, Canada, Western Europe, Japan); one the business in the developing countries (most of Latin America, Australia, India, the near East); one the business in the remaining underdeveloped ones. Several major chemical companies are going this route.

The ambassador of a major power today is in a similar predicament. His embassy has become so huge, unwieldy, and diffuse in its activities that a man who can administer it has no time for, and almost certainly no interest in, his first job: getting to know the country of his assignment, its government, its policies, its people, and to get known and trusted by them. And despite Mr. McNamara's lion-taming act at the Pentagon, I am not yet convinced that the job of Secretary of Defense of the United States is really possible (though I admit I cannot conceive of an alternative).

The effective executive therefore first makes sure that the job is well-designed. And if experience tells him otherwise, he does not hunt for genius to do the impossible. He redesigns the job. He knows that the test of organization is not genius. It is its capacity to make common people achieve uncommon performance.

2. The second rule for staffing from strength is to make each job demanding and big. It should have challenge to bring out whatever strength a man may have. It should have scope so that any strength that is relevant to the task can produce significant results.

This, however, is not the policy of most large organizations. They tend to make the job small—which would make sense only if people were designed and machined for specific performance at a given moment. Yet not only do we have to fill jobs with people as they come. The demands of any job above the simplest are also bound to change, and often abruptly. The "perfect fit" then rapidly becomes the misfit. Only if the job is big and demanding to begin with, will it enable a man to rise to the new demands of a changed situation.

This rule applies to the job of the beginning knowledge worker in particular. Whatever his strength it should have a chance to find full play. In his first job the standards are set by which a knowledge worker will guide himself the rest of his career and by which he will measure himself and his contribution. Till he enters the first adult job, the knowledge worker never has had a chance to perform. All one can do in school is to show promise. Performance is possible only in real work, whether in a research lab, in a teaching job, in a business or in a government agency. Both for the beginner in knowledge work and for the rest of the organization, his colleagues and his superiors, the most important thing to find out is what he really can do.

It is equally important for him to find out as early as possible whether he is indeed in the right place, or even in the right kind of work. There are fairly reliable tests for the aptitudes and skills needed in manual work. One can test in advance whether a man is likely to do well as a carpenter or as a machinist. There is no such test appropriate to knowledge work. What is needed in knowledge work is not this or that particular skill, but a configuration, and this will be revealed only by the test of performance.

A carpenter's or a machinist's job is defined by the craft and varies little from one shop to another. But for the ability of a knowledge worker to contribute in an organization, the values and the goals of the organization are at least as important as his own professional knowledge and skills. A young man who has the right strength for one organization may be a total misfit in another, which from the outside looks just the same. The first job should, therefore, enable him to test both himself and the organization.

> This not only holds for different kinds of organization, such as government agencies, universities, or businesses. It is equally true between organizations of the same kind. I have yet to see two large businesses which have the same values and stress the same contributions. That a man who was happy and productive as a member of the faculty of one university may find himself lost, unhappy, and frustrated when he moves to another one every academic administrator has learned. And no matter how much the Civil Service Commission tries to make all government departments observe the same rules and use the same yardsticks, government agencies, once they have been in existence for a few years, have a distinct personality. Each requires a different behavior

from its staff members, especially from those in the professional grades, to be effective and to make a contribution.

It is easy to move while young—at least in the Western countries where mobility is accepted. Once one has been in an organization for ten years or more, however, it becomes increasingly difficult, especially for those who have not been too effective. The young knowledge worker should, therefore, ask himself early: "Am I in the right work and in the right place for my strengths to tell?"

But he cannot ask this question, let alone answer it, if the beginning job is too small, too easy, and designed to offset his lack of experience rather than to bring out what he can do.

Every survey of young knowledge workers—physicians in the Army Medical Corps, chemists in the research lab, accountants or engineers in the plant, nurses in the hospital—produces the same results. The ones who are enthusiastic and who, in turn, have results to show for their work, are the ones whose abilities are being challenged and used. Those that are deeply frustrated all say, in one way or another: "My abilities are not being put to use."

The young knowledge worker whose job is too small to challenge and test his abilities either leaves or declines rapidly into premature middle-age, soured, cynical, unproductive. Executives everywhere complain that many young men with fire in their bellies turn so soon into burned-out sticks. They have only themselves to blame: They quenched the fire by making the young man's job too small.

3. Effective executives know that they have to start with what a man can do rather than with what a job requires. This, however, means that they do their

thinking about people long before the decision on filling a job has to be made, and independently of it.

This is the reason for the wide adoption of appraisal procedures today, in which people, especially those in knowledge work, are regularly judged. The purpose is to arrive at an appraisal of a man *before* one has to decide whether he is the right person to fill a bigger position.

However, while almost every large organization has an appraisal procedure, few of them actually use it. Again and again the same executives who say that of course they appraise every one of their subordinates at least once a year, report that, to the best of their knowledge, they themselves have never been appraised by their own superiors. Again and again the appraisal forms remain in the files, and nobody looks at them when a personnel decision has to be made. Everybody dismisses them as so much useless paper. Above all, almost without exception, the "appraisal interview" in which the superior is to sit down with the subordinate and discuss the findings never takes place. Yet the appraisal interview is the crux of the whole system. One clue to what is wrong was contained in an advertisement of a new book on management which talked of the appraisal interview as "the most distasteful job" of the superior.

Appraisals, as they are now being used in the great majority of organizations, were designed originally by the clinical and abnormal psychologists for their own purposes. The clinician is a therapist trained to heal the sick. He is legitimately concerned with what is wrong, rather than with what is right with the patient. He assumes as a matter of course that nobody comes to him unless he is in trouble. The clinical psychologist or the abnormal psychologist, therefore, very properly looks upon appraisals as a process of diagnosing the weaknesses of a man.

I became aware of this in my first exposure to Japanese management. Running a seminar on executive development, I found to my surprise that none of the Japanese participants—all top men in large organizations—used appraisals. When I asked why not, one of them said: "Your appraisals are concerned only with bringing out a man's faults and weaknesses. Since we can neither fire a man nor deny him advancement and promotion, this is of no interest to us. On the contrary, the less we know about his weaknesses, the better. What we do need to know are the strengths of a man and what he can do. Your appraisals are not even interested in this." Western psychologists—especially those that design appraisals—might well disagree. But this is how every executive, whether Japanese, American, or German, sees the traditional appraisals.

Altogether the West might well ponder the lessons of the Japanese achievement. As everyone has heard, there is "lifetime employment" in Japan. Once a man is on the payroll, he will advance in his category—as a worker, a whitecollar employee, or a professional and executive employee—according to his age and length of service, with his salary doubling about once every fifteen years. He cannot leave, neither can he be fired. Only at the top and after age fortyfive is there differentiation, with a very small group selected by ability and merit into the senior executive positions. How can such a system be squared with the tremendous capacity for results and achievement Japan has shown? The answer is that their system forces the Japanese to play down weaknesses. Precisely because they cannot move people, Japanese executives always look for the man in the group who can do the job. They always look for strength.

I do not recommend the Japanese system. It is far from ideal. A very small number of people who have proven their capacity to perform do, in effect, everything of any importance whatever. The rest are carried by the organization. But if we in the West expect to get the benefit of the much greater mobility that both individual and organization enjoy in our tradition, we had better adopt the Japanese custom of looking for strength and using strength.

For a superior to focus on weakness, as our appraisals require him to do, destroys the integrity of his relationship with his subordinates. The many executives who in effect sabotage the appraisals their policy manuals impose on them follow sound instinct. It is also perfectly understandable that they consider an appraisal interview that focuses on a search for faults, defects, and weaknesses distasteful. To discuss a man's defects when he comes in as a patient seeking help is the responsibility of the healer. But, as has been known since Hippocrates, this presupposes a professional and privileged relationship between healer and patient which is incompatible with the authority relationship between superior and subordinate. It is a relationship that makes continued working together almost impossible, That so few executives use the official appraisal is thus hardly surprising. It is the wrong tool, in the wrong situation, for the wrong purpose.

Appraisals—and the philosophy behind them—are also far too much concerned with "potential." But experienced people have learned that one cannot appraise potential for any length of time ahead or for anything very different from what a man is already doing. "Potential" is simply another word for "promise." And even if the promise is there, it may well go unfulfilled, while people who have not shown such promise (if only because they may not have had the opportunity) actually produce the performance.

All one can measure is performance. And all one should measure is performance. This is another reason for making jobs big and challenging. It is also a reason for thinking through the contribution a man should make to the results and the performance of his organization. For one can measure the performance of a man only against specific performance expectations.

Still one needs some form of appraisal procedure—or else one makes the personnel evaluation at the wrong time, that is when a job has to be filled. Effective executives, therefore, usually work out their own radically different form. It starts out with a statement of the major contributions expected from a man in his past and present positions and a record of his performance against these goals. Then it asks four questions.

(a) "What has he (or she) done well?"

(b) "What, therefore, is he likely to be able to do well?"

(c) "What does he have to learn or to acquire to be able to get the full benefit from his strength?"

(d) "If I had a son or daughter, would I be willing to have him or her work under this person?"

(i) "If yes, why?"

(ii) "If no, why?"

This appraisal actually takes a much more critical look at a man than the usual procedure does. But it focuses on strengths. It begins with what a man can do. Weaknesses are seen as limitations to the full use of his strengths and to his own achievement, effectiveness, and accomplishment.

The last question(ii)is the only one which is not primarily concerned with strengths. Subordinates, especially bright, young, and ambitious ones, tend to mold themselves after a forceful boss. There is, therefore, nothing more corrupting and more destructive in an organization than a forceful but basically corrupt executive. Such a man might well operate effectively on his own; even within an organization, he might be tolerable if denied all power over others. But in a position of power within an organization, he destroys. Here, therefore, is the one area in which weakness in itself is of importance and relevance.

By themselves, character and integrity do not accomplish anything. But their absence faults everything else. Here, therefore, is the one area where weakness is a disqualification by itself rather than a limitation on performance capacity and strength.

4. The effective executive knows that to get strength one has to put up with weaknesses.

> There have been few great commanders in history who were not self-centered, conceited, and full of admiration for what they saw in the mirror. (The reverse does not, of course, hold: There have been plenty of generals who were convinced of their own greatness, but who have not gone down in history as great commanders. ) Similarly, the politician who does not with every fiber in his body want to be President or Prime Minister is not likely to be remembered as a statesman. He will at best be a useful—perhaps a highly useful—journeyman. To be more requires a man who is conceited enough to believe that the world—or at least the nation—really needs him and depends on his getting into power. (Again the reverse does not hold true. ) If the need is for the ability to command in a perilous situation, one has to accept a Disraeli or a Franklin D.

Roosevelt and not worry too much about their lack of humility. There are indeed no great men to their valets. But the laugh is on the valet. He sees, inevitably, all the traits that are not relevant, all the traits that have nothing to do with the specific task for which a man has been called on the stage of history.

The effective executive will therefore ask: "Does this man have strength in *one* major area? And is this strength relevant to the task? If he achieves excellence in this one area, will it make a significant difference? " And if the answer is "yes," he will go ahead and appoint the man.

Effective executives rarely suffer from the delusion that two mediocrities achieve as much as one good man. They have learned that, as a rule, two mediocrities achieve even less than one mediocrity—they just get in each other's way. They accept that abilities must be specific to produce performance. They never talk of a "good man" but always about a man who is "good" for some one task. But in this one task, they search for strength and staff for excellence.

This also implies that they focus on opportunity in their staffing—not on problems.

They are above all intolerant of the argument: "I can't spare this man; I'd be in trouble without him." They have learned that there are only three explanations for an "indispensable man" : He is actually incompetent and can only survive if carefully shielded from demands; his strength is misused to bolster a weak superior who cannot stand on his own two feet; or his strength is misused to delay tackling a serious problem if not to conceal its existence.

In every one of these situations, the "indispensable man" should be moved anyhow—and soon. Otherwise one only destroys whatever strengths he may have.

The chief executive who was mentioned in Chapter 3 for his unconventional methods of making effective the manager-development policies of a large retail chain also decided to move automatically anyone whose boss described him as indispensable. "This either means," he said, "that I have a weak superior or a weak subordinate—or both. Whichever of these, the sooner we find out, the better."

Altogether it must be an unbreakable rule to promote the man who by the test of performance is best qualified for the job to be filled. All arguments to the contrary— "He is indispensable" . . . "He won't be acceptable to the people there" . . . "He is too young" . . . or "We never put a man in there without field experience"—should be given short shrift. Not only does the job deserve the best man. The man of proven performance has earned the opportunity. Staffing the opportunities instead of the problems not only creates the most effective organization, it also creates enthusiasm and dedication.

Conversely, it is the duty of the executive to remove ruthlessly anyone—and especially any manager—who consistently fails to perform with high distinction. To let such a man stay on corrupts the others. It is grossly unfair to the whole organization. It is grossly unfair to his subordinates who are deprived by their superior's inadequacy of opportunities for achievement and recognition. Above all, it is senseless cruelty to the man himself. He knows that he is inadequate whether he admits it to himself or not. Indeed, I have never seen anyone in a job for which he was inadequate who was not slowly being destroyed by the pressure and the strains, and who did not secretly pray for deliverance. That neither the Japanese "lifetime employment" nor the various civil service systems of the West consider proven incompetence ground for removal is a serious weakness—and an unnecessary one.

General Marshall during World War II insisted that a general officer be immediately relieved if found less than outstanding. To keep him in command, he reasoned, was incompatible with the responsibility the army and the nation owed the men under an officer's command. Marshall flatly refused to listen to the argument: "But we have no replacement." "All that matters," he pointed out, "is that you know that this man is not equal to the task. Where his replacement comes from is the next question."

But Marshall also insisted that to relieve a man from command was less a judgment on the man than on the commander who had appointed him. "The only thing we know is that this spot was the wrong one for the man," he argued. "This does not mean that he is not the ideal man for some other job. Appointing him was my mistake, now it's up to me to find what he can do."

Altogether General Marshall offers a good example how one makes strength productive. When he first reached a position of influence in the mid-thirties, there was no general officer in the U. S. Army still young enough for active duty. (Marshall himself only beat the deadline by four months. His sixtieth birthday when he would have been too old to take office as Chief of Staff, was on December 31, 1939. He was appointed on September 1 of the same year.) The future generals of World War II were still junior officers with few hopes for promotion when Marshall began to select and train them. Eisenhower was one of the older ones and even he, in the mid-thirties, was only a major. Yet by

1942, Marshall had developed the largest and clearly the ablest group of general officers in American history. There were almost no failures in it and not many second-raters.

This—one of the greatest educational feats in military history—was done by a man who lacked all the normal trappings of "leadership," such as the personal magnetism or the towering self-confidence of a Montgomery, a de Gaulle or a MacArthur. What Marshall had were principles. "What can this man do?" was his constant question. And if a man could do something, his lacks became secondary.

Marshall, for instance, again and again came to George Patton's rescue and made sure that this ambitious, vain, but powerful wartime commander would not be penalized for the absence of the qualities that make a good staff officer and a successful career soldier in peacetime. Yet Marshall himself personally loathed the dashing *beau sabreur* of Patton's type.

Marshall was only concerned with weaknesses when they limited the full development of a man's strength. These he tried to overcome through work and career opportunities.

The young Major Eisenhower, for instance, was quite deliberately put by Marshall into war-planning in the mid-thirties to help him acquire the systematic strategic understanding which he apparently lacked. Eisenhower did not himself become a strategist as a result. But he acquired respect for strategy and an understanding of its importance and thereby removed a serious limitation on his great strength as a team-builder and tactical planner.

Marshall always appointed the best qualified man no matter how badly he was needed where he was. "We owe this move to the job. . . we owe it to the man and we owe it to the troops," was his reply when someone—usually someone high up—pleaded with him not to pull out an "indispensable" man.

He made but one exception: When President Roosevelt pleaded that Marshall was indispensable to him, Marshall stayed in Washington, yielded supreme command in Europe to Eisenhower, and thus gave up his life's dream.

Finally Marshall knew—and everyone can learn it from him—that every people-decision is a gamble. By basing it on what a man can do, it becomes at least a rational gamble.

A superior has responsibility for the work of others. He also has power over the careers of others. Making strengths productive is therefore much more than an essential of effectiveness. It is a moral imperative, a responsibility of authority and position. To focus on weakness is not only foolish; it is irresponsible. A superior owes it to his organization to make the strength of every one of his subordinates as productive as it can be. But even more does he owe it to the human beings over whom he exercises authority to help them get the most out of whatever strength they may have. Organization must serve the individual to achieve through his strengths and regardless of his limitations and weaknesses.

This is becoming increasingly important, indeed critical. Only a short generation ago the number of knowledge jobs and the range of knowledge employments were small. To be a civil servant in the German or in the Scandinavian governments; one had to have a law degree. A mathematician need not apply. Conversely, a young man wanting to make a living by putting his knowledge to work had only three or four choices of fields and employment. Today there is a bewildering variety of knowledge work and an equally bewildering variety of employment choices for men of knowledge. Around 1900, the only knowledge fields for all practical purposes were still the traditional professions—the law, medicine, teaching, and preaching. There are now literally hundreds of different disciplines. Moreover, practically every knowledge area is being put to productive use in and by organization, especially, of course, by business and government.

On the one hand, therefore, one can today try to find the knowledge area and the kind of work to which one's abilities are best fitted. One need no longer, as one had to do even in the recent past, fit oneself to the available knowledge areas and employments. On the other hand, it is increasingly difficult for a young man to make his choice. He does not have enough information, either about himself or about the opportunities.

This makes it much more important for the individual that he be directed toward making his strengths productive. It also makes it important for the organization that its executives focus on strengths and work on making strengths productive in their own group and with their own subordinates.

Staffing for strength is thus essential to the executive's own effectiveness and to that of his organization but equally to individual and society in a world of knowledge work.

## HOW DO I MANAGE MY BOSS?

Above all, the effective executive tries to make fully productive the strengths of his own superior.

I have yet to find a manager, whether in business, in government, or in any other institution, who did not say: "I have no great trouble managing my subordinates. But how do I manage my boss?" It is actually remarkably easy—but only effective executives know that. The secret is that effective executives make the strengths of the boss productive.

This should be elementary prudence. Contrary to popular legend, subordinates do not, as a rule, rise to position and prominence over the prostrate bodies of incompetent bosses. If their boss is not promoted, they will tend to be bottled up behind him. And if their boss is relieved for incompetence or failure, the successor is rarely the bright, young man next in line. He usually is brought in from the outside and brings with him his own bright, young men. Conversely, there is nothing quite as conducive to success, as a successful and rapidly promoted superior.

But way beyond prudence, making the strength of the boss productive is a key to the subordinate's own effectiveness. It enables him to focus his own contribution in such a way that it finds receptivity upstairs and will be put to use. It enables him to achieve and accomplish the things he himself believes in.

One does not make the strengths of the boss productive by toadying to him. One does it by starting out with what is right and presenting it in a form which is accessible to the superior.

The effective executive accepts that the boss is human (something that intelligent young subordinates often find hard). Because the superior is human, he has his strengths; but he also has limitations. To build on his strengths, that is, to enable him to do what he can do, will make him effective—and will make the subordinate effective. To try to build on his weaknesses will be as frustrating and as stultifying as to try to build on the weaknesses of a subordinate. The effective executive, therefore, asks: "What can my boss do really well? " "What has he done really well? " "What does he need to know to use his strength? " "What does he need to get from me to perform? " He does not worry too much over what the boss cannot do.

Subordinates typically want to "reform" the boss. The able senior civil servant is inclined to see himself as the tutor to the newly appointed political head of his agency. He tries to get his boss to overcome his limitations. The effective ones ask instead: "What can the new boss do? " And if the answer is: "He is good at relationships with Congress, the White House, and the public," then the civil servant works at making it possible for his minister to use these abilities. For the best administration and the best policy decisions are futile unless there is also political skill in representing them. Once the politician knows that the civil servant supports him, he will soon enough listen to him on policy and on administration.

The effective executive also knows that the boss, being human, has his own ways of being effective. He looks for these ways. They may be only manners and habits, but they are facts.

It is, I submit, fairly obvious to anyone who has ever looked that people are either "readers" or "listeners" (excepting only the very small group who get their information through talking, and by watching with a form of psychic radar the reactions of the people they talk to; both President Franklin Roosevelt and President Lyndon Johnson belong in this category, as apparently did Winston Churchill). People who are both readers and listeners—trial lawyers have to be both, as a rule—are exceptions. It is generally a waste of time to talk to a reader. He only listens after he has read. It is equally a waste of time to submit a voluminous report to a listener. He can only grasp what it is all about through the spoken word.

Some people need to have things summed up for them in one page. (President Eisenhower needed this to be able to act. ) Others need to be able to follow the thought processes of the man who makes the recommendation and therefore require a big report before anything becomes meaningful to them. Some superiors want to see sixty pages of figures on everything. Some want to be in at the early stages so that they can prepare themselves for the eventual decision. Others do not want even to hear about the matter until it is "ripe," and so on.

The adaptation needed to think through the strengths of the boss and to try to make them productive always affects the "how" rather than the "what." It concerns the order in which different areas, all of them relevant, are presented, rather than what is important or right. If the superior's strength lies in his political ability in a job in which political ability is truly relevant, then one presents to him first the political aspect of a situation. This enables him to grasp what the issue is all about and to put his strength effectively behind a new policy.

All of us are "experts" on other people and see them much more clearly than they see themselves. To make the boss effective is therefore usually fairly easy. But it requires focus on his strengths and on what he can do. It requires building on strength to make weaknesses irrelevant. Few things make an executive as effective as building on the strengths of his superior.

## MAKING YOURSELF EFFECTIVE

Effective executives lead from strength in their own work. They make productive what they can do.

Most executives I know in government, in the hospital, in a business, know all the things they cannot do. They are only too conscious of what the boss won't let them do, of what company policy won't let them do, of what the government won't let them do. As a result, they waste their time and their strengths complaining about the things they cannot do anything about.

Effective executives are of course also concerned with limitations. But it is amazing how many things they find that can be done and are worth while doing. While the others complain about their inability to do anything, the effective executives go ahead and do. As a result, the limitations that weigh so heavily on their brethren often melt away.

> Everyone in the management of one of the major railroads knew that the government would not let the company do anything. But then a new financial vice-president came in who had not yet learned that "lesson." Instead he went to Washington, called on the Interstate Commerce Commission and asked for permission to do a few rather

radical things. "Most of these things," the commissioners said, "are none of our concern to begin with. The others you have to try and test out and then we will be glad to give you the go-ahead."

The assertion that "somebody else will not let me do anything" should always be suspected as a cover-up for inertia. But even where the situation does set limitations—and everyone lives and works within rather stringent limitations—there are usually important, meaningful, pertinent things that can be done. The effective executive looks for them. If he starts out with the question: "What can I do? " he is almost certain to find that he can actually do much more than he has time and resources for.

Making strengths productive is equally important in respect to one's own abilities and work habits.

It is not very difficult to know *how* we achieve results. By the time one has reached adulthood, one has a pretty good idea as to whether one works better in the morning or at night. One usually knows whether one writes best by making a great many drafts fast, or by working meticulously on every sentence until it is right. One knows whether one speaks well in public from a prepared text, from notes, without any prop, or not at all. One knows whether one works well as a member of a committee or better alone—or whether one is altogether unproductive as a committee member.

Some people work best if they have a detailed outline in front of them; that is, if they have thought through the job before they start it. Others work best with nothing more than a few rough notes. Some work best under pressure. Others work better if they have a good deal of time and can finish the job long before the deadline. Some are "readers," others "listeners." All this one knows, about oneself—just as one knows whether one is right-handed or left-handed.

These, it will be said, are superficial. This is not necessarily correct—a good many of these traits and habits mirror fundamentals of a man's personality such as his perception of the world and of himself in it. But even if superficial, these work habits are a source of effectiveness. And most of them are compatible with any kind of work. The effective executive knows this and acts accordingly.

All in all, the effective executive tries to be himself; he does not pretend to be someone else. He looks at his own performance and at his own results and tries to discern a pattern. "What are the things," he asks, "that I seem to be able to do with relative ease, while they come rather hard to other people? " One man, for instance, finds it easy to write up the final report while many others find it a frightening chore. At the same time, however, he finds it rather difficult and unrewarding to think through the report and face up to the hard decisions. He is, in other words, more effective as a staff thinker who organizes and lays out the problems than as the decision-maker who takes command responsibility.

One can know about oneself that one usually does a good job working alone on a project from start to finish. One can know that one does, as a rule, quite well in negotiations, particularly emotional ones such as negotiating a union contract. But at the same time, one also knows whether one's predictions what the union will ask for have usually been correct or not.

These are not the things most people have in mind when they talk about the strengths or weaknesses of a man. They usually mean knowledge of a discipline or talent in an art. But temperament is also a factor in accomplishment and a big one. An adult usually knows quite a bit about his own temperament. To be effective he builds on what he knows he can do and does it the way he has found out he works best.

Unlike everything else discussed in this book so far, making strength productive is as much an attitude as it is a practice. But it can be improved with practice. If one disciplines oneself to ask about one's associates—subordinates as well as superiors— "What can this man do? " rather than "What can he not do? " one soon will acquire the attitude of looking for strength and of using strength. And eventually one will learn to ask this question of oneself.

In every area of effectiveness within an organization, *one feeds the opportunities and starves the problems*. Nowhere is this more important than in respect to people. The effective executive looks upon people including himself as an opportunity. He knows that only strength produces results. Weakness only produces headaches—and the absence of weakness produces nothing.

He knows, moreover, that the standard of any human group is set by the performance of the leaders. And he, therefore, never allows leadership performance to be based on anything but true strength.

> In sports we have long learned that the moment a new record is set every athlete all over the world acquires a new dimension of accomplishment. For years no one could run the mile in less than four minutes. Suddenly Roger Bannister broke through the old record. And soon the average sprinters in every athletic club in the world were approaching yesterday's record, while new leaders began to break through the four-minute barrier.

In human affairs, the distance between the leaders and the average is a constant. If leadership performance is high, the average will go up. The effective executive knows that it is easier to raise the performance of one leader than it is to raise the performance of a whole mass. He therefore makes sure that he puts into the leadership position, into the standard-setting, the performance-making position, the man who has the strength to do the outstanding, the pace-setting job. This always requires focus on the one strength of a man and dismissal of weaknesses as irrelevant unless they hamper the full deployment of the available strength.

The task of an executive is not to change human beings. Rather, as the Bible tells us in the parable of the Talents, the task is to multiply performance capacity of the whole by putting to use whatever strength, whatever health, whatever aspiration there is in individuals.

CHAPTER 5

# First Things First

If there is any one "secret" of effectiveness, it is concentration. Effective executives do first things first and they do one thing at a time.

The need to concentrate is grounded both in the nature of the executive job and in the nature of man. Several reasons for this should already be apparent: There are always more important contributions to be made than there is time available to make them. Any analysis of executive contributions comes up with an embarrassing richness of important tasks; any analysis of executives' time discloses an embarrassing scarcity of time available for the work that really contributes. No matter how well an executive manages his time, the greater part of it will still not be his own. Therefore, there is always a time deficit.

The more an executive focuses on upward contribution, the more will he require fairly big continuous chunks of time. The more he switches from being busy to achieving results, the more will he shift to sustained efforts—efforts which require a fairly big quantum of time to bear fruit. Yet to get even that half-day or those two weeks of really productive time requires self-discipline and an iron determination to say "No."

Similarly, the more an executive works at making strengths productive, the more will he become conscious of the need to concentrate the human strengths available to him on major opportunities. This is the only way to get results.

But concentration is dictated also by the fact that most of us find it hard enough to do well even one thing at a time, let alone two. Mankind is indeed capable of doing an amazingly wide diversity of things; humanity is a "multipurpose tool." But the way to apply productively mankind's great range is to bring to bear a large number of individual capabilities on one task. It is concentration in which all faculties are focused on one achievement.

> We rightly consider keeping many balls in the air a circus stunt. Yet even the juggler does it only for ten minutes or so. If he were to try doing it longer, he would soon drop all the balls.

People do, of course, differ. Some do their best work when doing two tasks in parallel at the same time, thus providing a change of pace. This presupposes however that they give each of the two tasks the minimum quantum needed to get anything done. But few people, I think, can perform with excellence three major tasks simultaneously.

> There was Mozart, of course. He could, it seems, work on several compositions at the same time, all of them masterpieces. But he is the only known exception. The other prolific composers of the first rank—Bach, for instance, Handel, or Haydn, or Verdi—composed one work at

a time. They did not begin the next until they had finished the preceding one, or until they had stopped work on it for the time being and put it away in the drawer. Executives can hardly assume that they are "executive Mozarts."

Concentration is necessary precisely because the executive faces so many tasks clamoring to be done. For doing one thing at a time means doing it fast. The more one can concentrate time, effort, and resources, the greater the number and diversity of tasks one can actually perform.

No chief executive of any business I have ever known accomplished as much as the recently retired head of a pharmaceutical firm. When he took over, the company was small and operated in one country only. When he retired eleven years later, the company had become a worldwide leader.

This man worked for the first years exclusively on research direction, research program, and research personnel. The organization had never been a leader in research and had usually been tardy even as a follower. The new chief executive was not a scientist. But he realized that the company had to stop doing five years later what the leaders had pioneered five years before. It had to decide on its own direction. As a result, it moved within five years into a leadership position in two new important fields.

The chief executive then turned to building an international company—years after the leaders, such as the old Swiss pharmaceutical houses, had established themselves as leaders all over the world. Carefully analyzing drug consumption, he concluded that health insurance and government health services act as the main stimuli to drug demand. By timing his entry into a new country to coincide with a major expansion of its health services he managed to start big in countries where his company had never been before, and without having to take away markets from the well-entrenched international drug firms.

The last five years of his tenure he concentrated on working out the strategy appropriate to the nature of modern health care, which is fast becoming a "public utility" in which public bodies such as governments, nonprofit hospitals, and semipublic agencies (such as Blue Cross in the United States) pay the bills, although an individual, the physician, decides on the actual purchase. Whether his strategy will work out, it is too early to say—it was only perfected in 1965, shortly before he retired. But his is the only one of the major drug companies that, to my knowledge, has even thought about strategy, pricing, marketing, and the relationships of the industry worldwide.

It is unusual for any one chief executive to do one task of such magnitude during his entire tenure. Yet this man did three—in addition to building a strong, well-staffed, world-wide organization. He did this by single-minded concentration on one task at a time.

This is the "secret" of those people who "do so many things" and apparently so many difficult things. They do only one at a time. As a result, they need much less time in the end than the rest of us.

The people who get nothing done often work a great deal harder. In the first place, they underestimate the time for any one task. They always expect that everything will go right. Yet, as every executive knows, nothing ever goes right. The unexpected always happens—the unexpected is indeed the only thing one can confidently expect. And almost never is it a pleasant surprise. Effective executives therefore allow a fair margin of time beyond what is actually needed. In the second place, the typical (that is, the more or less ineffectual) executive tries to hurry—and that only puts him further behind. Effective executives do not race. They set an easy pace but keep going steadily. Finally, the typical executive tries to do several things at once. Therefore, he never has the minimum time quantum for any of the tasks in his program. If any one of them runs into trouble, his entire program collapses.

Effective executives know that they have to get many things done—and done effectively. Therefore, they concentrate—their own time and energy as well as that of their organization—on doing one thing at a time, and on doing first things first.

## SLOUGHING OFF YESTERDAY

The first rule for the concentration of executive efforts is to slough off the past that has ceased to be productive. Effective executives periodically review their work programs—and those of their associates—and ask: "If we did not already do this, would we go into it *now*? " And unless the answer is an unconditional "Yes," they drop the activity or curtail it sharply. At the least, they make sure that no more resources are being invested in the no-longer-productive past. And those first-class resources, especially those scarce resources of human strength which are engaged in these tasks of yesterday, are immediately pulled out and put to work on the opportunities of tomorrow.

Executives, whether they like it or not, are forever bailing out the past. This is inevitable. Today is always the result of actions and decisions taken yesterday. Man, however, whatever his title or rank, cannot foresee the future. Yesterday's actions and decisions, no matter how courageous or wise they may have been, inevitably become today's problems, crises, and stupidities. Yet it is the executive's specific job—whether he works in government, in a business, or in any other institution—to commit today's resources to the future. This means that every executive forever has to spend time, energy, and ingenuity on patching up or bailing out the actions and decisions of yesterday, whether his own or those of his predecessors. In fact this always takes up more hours of his day than any other task.

But one can at least try to limit one's servitude to the past by cutting out those inherited activities and tasks that have ceased to promise results.

No one has much difficulty getting rid of the total failures. They liquidate themselves. Yesterday's successes, however, always linger on long beyond their productive life. Even more dangerous are the activities which should do well and which, for some reason or other, do not produce. These tend to become, as I have explained elsewhere "investments in managerial ego" and sacred.<sup>⊖</sup> Yet unless they are pruned, and pruned ruthlessly, they drain the lifeblood from an organization. It is always the most capable people who are wasted in the futile attempt to obtain for the investment in managerial ego the "success it deserves."

Every organization is highly susceptible to these twin diseases. But they are particularly prevalent in government. Government programs

---

⊖ See *Managing for Results*.

and activities age just as fast as the programs and activities of other institutions. Yet they are not only conceived as eternal; they are welded into the structure through civil service rules and immediately become vested interests, with their own spokesmen in the legislature.

This was not too dangerous when government was small and played a minor role in social life as it did up until 1914. Today's government however cannot afford the diversion of its energies and resources into yesterday. Yet, at a guess, at least half the bureaus and agencies of the federal government of the United States either regulate what no longer needs regulation—for example, the Interstate Commerce Commission whose main efforts are still directed toward protecting the public from a monopoly of the railroads that disappeared thirty years ago. Or they are directed, as is most of the farm program, toward investment in politicians' egos and toward efforts that should have had results but never achieved them.

There is serious need for a new principle of effective administration under which every act, every agency, and every program of government is conceived as temporary and as expiring automatically after a fixed number of years—maybe ten—unless specifically prolonged by new legislation following careful outside study of the program, its results and its contributions.

President Johnson in 1965-1966 ordered such a study for all government agencies and their programs, adapting the "program review" which Secretary McNamara had developed to rid the Defense department of the barnacles of obsolete and unproductive work. This is a good first step, and badly needed. But it will not produce results as long as we maintain the traditional assumption that all programs last forever unless proven to have outlived their usefulness. The assumption should rather be that all programs outlive their usefulness fast and should be scrapped unless proven productive and necessary. Otherwise, modern government, while increasingly smothering society under rules, regulations, and forms, will itself be smothered in its own fat.

But while government is particularly endangered by organizational obesity, no organization is immune to the disease. The businessman in the large corporation who complains the loudest about bureaucracy in government may encourage in his own company the growth of "controls" which do not control anything, the proliferation of studies that are only a cover-up for his own unwillingness to face up to a decision, the inflation of all kinds of staffs for all kinds of research or "relations." And he himself may waste his own time and that of his key people on the obsolescent product of yesterday while starving tomorrow's successful product. The academician who is loudest in his denunciation of the horrible wastefulness of big business may fight the hardest in the faculty meeting to prolong the life of an obsolescent subject by making it a required course.

The executive who wants to be effective and who wants his organization to be effective polices all programs, all activities, all tasks. He always asks: "Is this still worth doing?" And if it isn't, he gets rid of it so as to be able to concentrate on the few tasks that, if done with excellence, will really make a difference in the results of his own job and in the performance of his organization.

Above all, the effective executive will slough off an old activity before he starts on a new one. This is necessary in order to keep organizational "weight control." Without it, the organization soon loses shape, cohesion, and manageability. Social organizations need to stay lean and muscular as much as biological organisms.

But also, as every executive has learned, nothing new is easy. It always gets into trouble. Unless one has therefore built into the new endeavor the means for bailing it out when it runs into heavy weather, one condemns it to failure from the start. The only effective means for bailing out the new are people who have proven their capacity to perform. Such people are always already busier than they should be. Unless one relieves one of them of his present burden, one cannot expect him to take on the new task.

The alternative—to "hire in" new people for new tasks—is too risky. One hires new people to expand on already established and smoothly running activity. But one starts something new with people of tested and proven strength, that is, with veterans. Every new task is such a gamble—even if other people have done the same job many times before—that an experienced and effective executive will not, if humanly possible, add to it the additional gamble of hiring an outsider to take charge. He has learned the hard way how many men who looked like geniuses when they worked elsewhere show up as miserable failures six months after they have started working "for us."

An organization needs to bring in fresh people with fresh points of view fairly often. If it only promotes from within it soon becomes inbred and eventually sterile. But if at all possible, one does not bring in the newcomers where the risk is exorbitant—that is, into the top executive positions or into leadership of an important new activity. One brings them in just below the top and into an activity that is already defined and reasonably well understood.

Systematic sloughing off of the old is the one and only way to force the new. There is no lack of ideas in any organization I know. "Creativity" is not our problem. But few organizations ever get going on their own good ideas. Everybody is much too busy on the tasks of yesterday. Putting all programs and activities regularly on trial for their lives and getting rid of those that cannot prove their productivity work wonders in stimulating creativity even in the most hidebound bureaucracy.

Du Pont has been doing so much better than any other of the world's large chemical companies largely because it abandons a product or a process *before* it begins to decline. Du Pont does not invest scarce resources of people and money into defending yesterday. Most other businesses, however, inside and outside the chemical industry, are run on different principles; namely, "There'll always be a market for an efficient buggy-whip plant," and, "This product built this company and it's our duty to maintain for it the market it deserves."

It's those other companies, however, which send their executives to seminars on creativity and which complain about the absence of new products. Du Pont is much too busy making and selling new products to do either.

The need to slough off the outworn old to make possible the productive new is universal. It is reasonably certain that we would still have stagecoaches—nationalized, to be sure, heavily subsidized, and with a fantastic research program to "retrain the horse" —had there been ministries of transportation around 1825.

## PRIORITIES AND POSTERIORITIES

There are always more productive tasks for tomorrow than there is time to do them and more opportunities than there are capable people to take care of them—not to mention the always abundant problems and crises.

A decision therefore has to be made as to which tasks deserve priority and which are of less importance. The only question is which will make the decision—the executive or the pressures. But somehow the tasks will be adjusted to the available time and the opportunities will become available only to the extent to which capable people are around to take charge of them.

If the pressures rather than the executive are allowed to make the decision, the important tasks will predictably be sacrificed. Typically, there will then be no time for the most timeconsuming part of any task, the conversion of decision into action. No task is completed until it has become part of organizational action and behavior. This almost always means that no task is completed unless other people have taken it on as their own, have accepted new ways of doing old things or the necessity for doing something new, and have otherwise made the executive's "completed" project their own daily routine. If this is slighted because there is no time, then all the work and effort have been for nothing. Yet this is the invariable result of the executive's failure to concentrate and to impose priorities.

Another predictable result of leaving control of priorities to the pressures is that the work of top management does not get done at all. That is always postponable work, for it does not try to solve yesterday's crises but to make a different tomorrow. And the pressures always favor yesterday. In particular, a top group which lets itself be controlled by the pressures will slight the one job no one else can do. It will not pay attention to the outside of the organization. It will therefore lose touch with the only reality, the only area in which there are results. For the pressures always favor what goes on inside. They always favor what has happened over the future, the crisis over the opportunity, the immediate and visible over the real, and the urgent over the relevant.

The job is, however, not to set priorities. That is easy. Everybody can do it. The reason why so few executives concentrate is the difficulty of setting "posteriorities" —that is, deciding what tasks not to tackle—and of sticking to the decision.

Most executives have learned that what one postpones, one actually abandons. A good many of them suspect that there is nothing less desirable than to take up later a project one has postponed when it first came up. The timing is almost bound to be wrong, and timing is a most important element in the success of any effort. To do five years later what it would have been smart to do five years earlier is almost a sure recipe for frustration and failure.

> Outside of Victorian novels, happiness does not come to the marriage of two people who almost got married at age 21 and who then, at age 38, both widowed, find each other again. If married at age 21, these people might have had an opportunity to grow up together. But in seventeen years both have changed, grown apart, and developed their own ways.
>
> The man who wanted to become a doctor as a youth but was forced to go into business instead, and who now, at age fifty and successful, goes back to his first love and enrolls in medical school is not likely to finish, let alone to become a successful physician. He may succeed if he

has extraordinary motivation, such as a strong religious drive to become a medical missionary. But otherwise he will find the discipline and rote learning of medical school irksome beyond endurance, and medical practice itself humdrum and a bore.

The merger which looked so right six or seven years earlier, but had to be postponed because one company's president refused to serve under the other, is rarely still the right "marriage" for either side when the stiff-necked executive has finally retired.

That one actually abandons what one postpones makes executives, however, shy from postponing anything altogether. They know that this or that task is not a first priority, but giving it a posteriority is risky. What one has relegated may turn out to be the competitor's triumph. There is no guarantee that the policy area a politician or an administrator has decided to slight may not explode into the hottest and most dangerous political issue.

Neither President Eisenhower nor President Kennedy, for instance, wanted to give high priority to civil rights. And President Johnson most definitely considered Vietnam—and foreign affairs altogether—a posteriority when he came to power. (This, in large measure, explains the violent reaction against him on the part of the liberals who had supported his original priority choice of the War on Poverty, when events forced him to change his priority schedule.)

Setting a posteriority is also unpleasant. Every posteriority is somebody else's top priority. It is much easier to draw up a nice list of top priorities and then to hedge by trying to do "just a little bit" of everything else as well. This makes everybody happy. The only drawback is, of course, that nothing whatever gets done.

A great deal could be said about the analysis of priorities. The most important thing about priorities and posteriorities is, however, not intelligent analysis but courage.

Courage rather than analysis dictates the truly important rules for identifying priorities.

- Pick the future as against the past;
- Focus on opportunity rather than on problem;
- Choose your own direction—rather than climb on the bandwagon; and
- Aim high, aim for something that will make a difference, rather than for something that is "safe" and easy to do.

A good many studies of research scientists have shown that achievement (at least below the genius level of an Einstein, a Niels Bohr, or a Max Planck) depends less on ability in doing research than on the courage to go after opportunity. Those research scientists who pick their projects according to the greatest likelihood of quick success rather than according to the challenge of the problem are unlikely to achieve distinction. They may turn out a great many footnotes, but neither a law of physics nor a new concept is likely to be named after them. Achievement goes to the people who pick their research priorities by the opportunity and who consider other criteria only as qualifiers rather than as determinants.

Similarly, in business the successful companies are not those that work at developing new products for their existing line but those that aim at innovating new technologies or new businesses. As a rule it is just as risky, just as arduous, and just as uncertain to do something small that is new as it is to do something big that is new. It is more productive to convert an opportunity into results than to solve a problem—which only restores the equilibrium of yesterday.

Priorities and posteriorities always have to be reconsidered and revised in the light of realities No American president, for instance, has been allowed by events to stick to his original list of priority tasks. In fact accomplishing one's priority tasks always changes the priorities and posteriorities themselves.

The effective executive does not, in other words, truly commit himself beyond the *one* task he concentrates on right now. Then he reviews the situation and picks the next one task that now comes first.

Concentration——that is, the courage to impose on time and events his own decision as to what really matters and comes first—is the executive's only hope of becoming the master of time and events instead of their whipping boy.

CHAPTER 6

# The Elements of Decision-making

Decision-making is only one of the tasks of an executive. It usually takes but a small fraction of his time. But to make decisions is the *specific* executive task. Decision-making therefore deserves special treatment in a discussion of the effective executive.

Only executives make decisions. Indeed, to be expected—by virtue of position or knowledge—to make decisions that have significant impact on the entire organization, its performance, and results defines the executive.

Effective executives, therefore, make effective decisions.

They make these decisions as a systematic process with clearly defined elements and in a distinct sequence of steps. But this process bears amazingly little resemblance to what so many books today present as "decision-making."

Effective executives do not make a great many decisions. They concentrate on the important ones. They try to think through what is strategic and generic, rather than "solve problems." They try to make the few important decisions on the highest level of conceptual understanding. They try to find the constants in a situation. They are, therefore, not overly impressed by speed in decision-making. Rather they consider virtuosity in manipulating a great many variables a symptom of sloppy thinking. They want to know what the decision is all about and what the underlying realities are which it has to satisfy. They want impact rather than technique, they want to be sound rather than clever.

Effective executives know when a decision has to be based on principle and when it should be made on the merits of the case and pragmatically. They know that the trickiest decision is that between the right and the wrong compromise and have learned to tell one from the other. They know that the most time-consuming step in the process is not making the decision but putting it into effect. Unless a decision has "degenerated into work" it is not a decision; it is at best a good intention. This means that, while the effective decision itself is based on the highest level of conceptual understanding, the action to carry it out should be as close as possible to the working level and as simple as possible.

## TWO CASE STUDIES IN DECISION MAKING

The least-known of the great American business builders, Theodore Vail, was perhaps the most effective decision-maker in U. S. business history. As president of the Bell Telephone System from just before 1910 till the mid-twenties, Vail built the organization into the largest private business in the world and into one of the most prosperous growth companies.

That the telephone system is privately owned is taken for granted in the United States. But the part of the North American continent that the Bell System serves (the United States and the two most populous Canadian provinces, Quebec and Ontario) is the only developed area in the world in which telecommunications are not owned by government. The Bell System is also the only public utility that has shown itself capable of risk-taking leadership and rapid growth, even though it has a monopoly in a vital area and has achieved saturation of its original market.

The explanation is not luck, or "American conservatism." The explanation lies in four strategic decisions Vail made in the course of almost twenty years.

Vail saw early that a telephone system had to do something distinct and different to remain in private ownership and under autonomous management. All over Europe governments were running the telephone without much trouble or risk. To attempt to keep Bell private by defending it against government takeovers would be a delaying action only. Moreover, a purely defensive posture could only be self-defeating. It would paralyze management's imagination and energies. A policy was needed which would make Bell, as a private company, stand for the interest of the public more forcefully than any government agency could. This led to Vail's early decision that the business of the Bell Telephone Company must be anticipation and satisfaction of the service requirements of the public.

"Our business is service" became the Bell commitment as soon as Vail took over. At the time, shortly after the turn of the century, this was heresy. But Vail was not content to preach that it was the business of the company to give service, and that it was the job of management to make service possible and profitable. He saw to it that the yardsticks throughout the system by which managers and their operations were judged, measured service fulfillment rather than profit performance. Managers are responsible for service results. It is then the job of top management to organize and finance the company so as to make the best service also result in optimal financial rewards.

Vail, at about the same time, realized that a nationwide communications monopoly could not be a free enterprise in the traditional sense—that is, unfettered private business. He recognized public regulation as the only alternative to government ownership. Effective, honest, and principled public regulation was, therefore, in the interest of the Bell System and vital to its preservation.

Public regulation, while by no means unknown in the United States, was by and large impotent when Vail reached this conclusion. Business opposition, powerfully aided by the courts, had drawn the teeth of the laws on the statute books. The commissions themselves were understaffed and underfinanced and had become sinecures for third-rate and often venal political hacks.

Vail set the Bell Telephone Sytem the objective of making regulation effective. He gave this as their main task to the heads of each of the affiliated regional telephone companies. It was their job to rejuvenate the regulatory bodies and to innovate concepts of regulation and of rate-making that would be fair and equitable and would protect the public, while at the same time permitting the Bell System to do its job. The affiliated company presidents were the group from which Bell's top management was recruited. This ensured that positive attitudes toward regulation permeated the entire company.

Vail's third decision led to the establishment of one of the most successful scientific laboratories in industry, the Bell Laboratories. Again, Vail started out with the need to make a private monopoly viable. Only this time he asked: "How can one make such a monopoly truly competitive? " Obviously it was not subject to the normal competition from another supplier who offers the purchaser the same product or one supplying the same want. And yet without competition such a mon opoly would rapidly become rigid and incapable of growth and change.

But even in a monopoly, Vail concluded, one can organize the future to compete with the present. In a technical industry such as telecommunications, the future lies in better and different technologies. The Bell Laboratories which grew out of this insight were by no means the first industrial laboratory, not even in the United States. But it was the first industrial research institution that was deliberately designed to make the present obsolete, no matter how profitable and efficient.

When Bell Labs took its final form, during the World War I period, this was a breath-taking innovation in industry. Even today few businessmen understand that research, to be productive, has to be the "disorganizer," the creator of a different future and the enemy of today. In most industrial laboratories, "defensive research" aimed at perpetuating today, predominates. But from the very beginning, the Bell Labs shunned defensive research.

> The last ten or fifteen years have proven how sound Vail's concept was. Bell Labs first extended telephone technology so that the entire North American continent became one automated switchboard. It then extended the Bell System's reach into areas never dreamed of by Vail and his generation, e. g. , the transmission of television programs, the transmission of computer data—in the last few years the most rapidly growing communications area—and the communications satellites. The scientific and technical developments that make possible these new transmission systems originated largely in the Bell Labs, whether they were scientific theory such as mathematical information theory, new products and processes such as the transistor, or computer logic and design.

Finally, toward the end of his career, in the early twenties, Vail invented the mass capital market—again to ensure survival of the Bell System as a private business.

Industries are more commonly taken over by government because they fail to attract the capital they need than because of socialism. Failure to attract the needed capital was a main reason why the European railroads were taken over by government between 1860 and 1920. Inability to attract the needed capital to modernize certainly played a big part in the nationalization of the coal mines and of the electric power industry in Great Britain. It was one of the major reasons for the nationalization of the electric power industry on the European continent in the inflationary period after World War I. The electric power companies, unable to raise their rates to offset currency depreciation, could no longer attract capital for modernization and expansion.

Whether Vail saw the problem in its full breadth, the record does not show. But he clearly saw that the Bell Telephone System needed tremendous sums of capital in a dependable, steady supply which could not be obtained from the then existing capital markets. The other public utilities, especially the electric power companies, tried to make investment in their securities attractive to the one and only mass participant visible in the twenties: the speculator. They built holding companies that gave the common shares of the parent company speculative leverage and appeal, while the needs of the operating businesses were satisfied primarily by debt money raised from traditional sources such as insurance companies. Vail realized that this was not a sound capital foundation.

The AT&T common stock, which he designed to solve his problem in the early twenties, had nothing in common with the speculative shares except legal form. It was to be a security for the general public, the "Aunt Sally's" of the emerging middle class, who could put something aside for investment, but had not enough capital to take much risk. Vail's AT&T common, with its almost-guaranteed dividend, was close enough to a fixed interest-bearing obligation for widows and orphans to buy it. At the same time, it was a common share so that it held out the promise of capital appreciation and of protection in inflation.

When Vail designed this financial instrument, the "Aunt Sally" type of investor did not, in effect, exist. The middle class that had enough money to buy any kind of common share had only recently emerged. It was still following older habits of investment in savings banks, insurance policies, and mortgages. Those who ventured further went into the speculative stock market of the twenties—where they had no business to be at all. Vail did not, of course, invent the "Aunt Sally's." But he made them into investors and mobilized their savings for their benefit as well as for that of the Bell System. This alone has enabled the Bell System to raise the hundreds of billions of dollars it has had to invest over the last half-century. All this time AT&T common has remained the foundation of investment planning for the middle classes in the United States and Canada.

Vail again provided this idea with its own means of execution. Rather than depend on Wall Street, the Bell System has all these years been its own banker and underwriter. And Vail's principal assistant on financial design, Walter Gifford, was made chief officer of the Bell System and became Vail's successor.

The decisions Vail reached were, of course, peculiar to his problems and those of his company. But the basic thinking behind them characterizes the truly effective decision.

The example of Alfred P. Sloan, Jr., shows this clearly. [⊖] Sloan, who in General Motors designed and built the world's largest manufacturing enterprise, took over as head of a big business in 1922, when Vail's career was drawing to its close. He was a very different man, as his was a very different time. And yet the decision for which Sloan is best remembered, the decentralized organization structure of General Motors, is of the same kind as the major decisions Theodore Vail had made somewhat earlier for the Bell Telephone System.

As Sloan has recounted in his recent book, *My Years with General Motors*, [⊖] the company he took over in 1922 was a loose federation of almost independent chieftains. Each of these men ran a unit which a few short years before had still been his own company—and each ran it as if it were still his own company.

There were two traditional ways of handling such a situation. One was to get rid of the strong independent men after they had sold out their business. This was the way in which John D. Rockefeller had put together the Standard Oil Trust, and J. P. Morgan, only a few years before Sloan, had put together U. S. Steel. The alternative was to leave the former owners in their commands with a minimum of interference from the new

---

⊖ Business examples are chosen here because they are still taken in a small enough compass to be easily comprehended—whereas most decisions in government policy require far too much explanation of background, history, and politics. At the same time, these are large enough examples to show structure. But decisions in government, the military, the hospital, or the university exemplify the same concepts as the next sections in this and the following chapter will demonstrate.

⊖ New York, Doubleday, 1964.

central office. It was "anarchy tempered by stock options" in which, it was hoped, their own financial interest would make the chieftains act for the best interests of the entire business. Durant, the founder of General Motors, and Sloan's predecessor, Pierre du Pont, had followed this route. When Sloan took over, however, the refusal of these strong and self-willed men to work together had all but destroyed the company.

Sloan realized that this was not the peculiar and short-term problem of the company just created through merger, but a generic problem of big business. The big business, Sloan saw, needs unity of direction and central control. It needs its own top management with real powers. But it equally needs energy, enthusiasm, and strength in operations. The operating managers have to have the freedom to do things their own way. They have to have responsibility and the authority that goes with it. They have to have scope to show what they can do, and they have to get recognition for performance. This, Sloan apparently saw right away, becomes even more important as a company gets older and as it has to depend on developing strong, independent performing executives from within.

Everyone before Sloan had seen the problem as one of personalities, to be solved through a struggle for power from which one man would emerge victorious. Sloan saw it as a constitutional problem to be solved through a new structure; decentralization which balances local autonomy in operations with central control of direction and policy.

How effective this solution has been shows perhaps best by contrast; that is, in the one area where General Motors has not had extraordinary results. General Motors, at least since the mid-thirties, has done poorly in anticipating and understanding the political temper of the American people and the direction and policies of American government. This is the one area, however, where there has been no "decentralization" in General Motors. Since 1935 or so it has been practically unthinkable for any senior GM executive to be anything but a conservative Republican.

These specific decisions—Vail's as well as Sloan's—have major features in common, even though they dealt with entirely different problems and led to highly specific solutions. They all tackled a problem at the highest conceptual level of understanding. They tried to think through what the decision was all about, and then tried to develop a principle for dealing with it. Their decisions were, in other words, strategic, rather than adaptations to the apparent needs of the moment. They all innovated. They were all highly controversial. Indeed, all five decisions went directly counter to what "everybody knew" at the time.

Vail had actually been fired earlier by the board of the Bell System when he first was president. His concept of service as the business of the company seemed almost insane to people who "knew" that the only purpose of a business is to make a profit. It was only years later, after 1900, when they had become alarmed—and with good reason—by the rising tide of demand for the nationalization of the telephone, that the board called Vail back. But his decision to spend money on obsoleting current processes and techniques just when they made the greatest profits for the company and to build a large research laboratory designed to this end, as well as his refusal to follow the fashion in finance and build a speculative capital structure, were equally resisted by his board as worse than eccentricity.

Similarly, Alfred Sloan's decentralization was completely unacceptable at the time and seemed to fly in the face of everything everybody "knew."

The acknowledged radical among American business leaders of those days was Henry Ford. But Vail's and Sloan's decisions were much too "wild" for Ford. He was certain that the Model T, once it had been designed, was the right car for all time to come. Vail's insistence on organized self-obsolescence would have struck him as lunacy. He was equally convinced that only the tightest centralized control could produce efficiency and results. Sloan's decentralization appeared to him self-destructive weakness.

## THE ELEMENTS OF THE DECISION PROCESS

The truly important features of the decisions Vail and Sloan made are neither their novelty nor their controversial nature. They are:

1. The clear realization that the problem was generic and could only be solved through a decision which established a rule, a principle;

2. The definition of the specifications which the answer to the problem had to satisfy, that is, of the "boundary conditions";

3. The thinking through what is "right," that is, the solution which will fully satisfy the specifications *before* attention is given to the compromises, adaptations, and concessions needed to make the decision acceptable;

4. The building into the decision of the action to carry it out;

5. The "feedback" which tests the validity and effectiveness of the decision

against the actual course of events.

These are the *elements* of the effective decision process.

1. The first question the effective decision-maker asks is: "Is this a generic situation or an exception? " "Is this something that underlies a great many occurrences? Or is the occurrence a unique event that needs to be dealt with as such? " The generic always has to be answered through a rule, a principle. The exceptional can only be handled as such and as it comes.

Strictly speaking, one might distinguish between four, rather than between two, different types of occurrences.

There is first the truly generic of which the individual occurrence is only a symptom.

Most of the problems that come up in the course of the executive's work are of this nature. Inventory decisions in a business, for instance, are not "decisions." They are adaptations. The problem is generic. This is even more likely to be true of events within production.

Typically, a product control and engineering group will handle many hundreds of problems in the course of a month. Yet, whenever these are analyzed, the great majority prove to be just symptoms—that is, manifestations of underlying basic situations. The individual process control engineer or production engineer who works in one part of the plant usually cannot see this. He might have a few problems each month with the couplings in the pipes that carry steam or hot liquids. But only when the total workload of the group over several months is analyzed does the generic problem appear. Then one sees that temperatures or pressures have become too great for the existing equipment and that the couplings, holding different lines together, need to be redesigned for greater loads. Until this is done, process control will spend a tremendous amount of time fixing leaks without ever getting control of the situation.

Then there is the problem which, while a unique event for the individual institution, is actually generic.

The company that receives an offer to merge from another, larger one, will never receive such an offer again if it accepts. This is a nonrecurrent situation as far as the individual company, its board of directors, and its management are concerned. But it is, of course, a generic situation which occurs all the time. To think through whether to accept or to reject the offer requires some general rules. For these, however, one has to look to the experience of others.

Next there is the truly exceptional, the truly unique event.

The power failure that plunged into darkness the whole of northeastern North America from the St. Lawrence to Washington in November 1965 was, according to the first explanations, a truly exceptional situation. So was the thalidomide tragedy which led to the birth of so many deformed babies in the early sixties. The probability of these events, we were told, was one in ten million or one in a hundred million. Such concatenation of malfunctions is as unlikely ever to recur again as it is unlikely, for instance, for the chair on which I sit to disintegrate into its constituent atoms.

Truly unique events are rare, however. Whenever one appears, one has to ask: Is this a true exception or only the first manifestation of a new genus?

And this, the early manifestation of a new generic problem, is the fourth and last category of events with which the decision process deals.

> We know now, for instance, that both the northeastern power failure and the thalidomide tragedy were only the first occurrences of what, under conditions of modern power technology or of modern pharmacology, are likely to become fairly frequent malfunctions unless generic solutions are found.

All events but the truly unique require a generic solution. They require a rule, a policy, a principle. Once the right principle has been developed all manifestations of the same generic situation can be handled pragmatically; that is, by adaptation of the rule to the concrete circumstances of the case. Truly unique events, however, must be treated individually. One cannot develop rules for the exceptional.

The effective decision-maker spends time to determine with which of these four situations he is dealing. He knows that he will make the wrong decision if he classifies the situation wrongly.

By far the most common mistake is to treat a generic situation as if it were a series of unique events; that is, to be pragmatic when one lacks the generic understanding and principle. This inevitably leads to frustration and futility.

> This was clearly shown, I think, by the failure of most of the policies, whether domestic or foreign, of the Kennedy administration.

For all the brilliance of its members, the administration achieved fundamentally only one success, in the Cuban missile crisis. Otherwise, it achieved practically nothing. The main reason was surely what its members called "pragmatism" ; that is, its refusal to develop rules and principles, and its insistence on treating everything "on its merits." Yet it was clear to everyone, including the members of the administration, that the basic assumptions on which its policies rested, the basic assumptions of the postwar years, had become increasingly unrealistic in international as well as in domestic affairs.

Equally common is the mistake of treating a new event as if it were just another example of the old problem to which, therefore, the old rules should be applied.

This was the error that snowballed a local power failure on the New York-Ontario border into the great northeastern blackout. The power engineers, especially in New York City, applied the right rule for a normal overload. Yet their own instruments had signaled that something quite extraordinary was going on which called for exceptional, rather than for standard, countermeasures.

By contrast, the one great triumph of President Kennedy, in the Cuban missile crisis, rested on acceptance of the challenge to think through an extraordinary, exceptional occurrence. As soon as Mr. Kennedy accepted this, his own tremendous resources of intelligence and courage effectively came into play.

Almost as common is the plausible but erroneous definition of the fundamental problem. Here is one example.

Since the end of World War II the American military services have been plagued by their inability to keep highly trained medical people in uniform. There have been dozens of studies and dozens of proposed remedies. However, all of the studies start out with the plausible hypothesis that pay is the problem—whereas the real problem lies in the traditional structure of military medicine. With its emphasis on the general practitioner, it is out of alignment with today's medical profession, which stresses the specialist. The career ladder in military medicine leads from specialization to medical and hospital administration and away from research and specialized practice. Today's young, well-trained physicians, therefore, feel that they waste their time and skill in the military service where they either have to work as general practitioners or become chairbound administrators. They want the opportunity to develop the skills and apply the practice of today's highly scientific, specialized doctor.

So far the military has not faced up to the basic decision. Are the armed services willing to settle for a second-rate medical organization staffed with people who cannot make the grade in the highly scientific, research-oriented, and highly specialized civilian profession of medicine? Or are they willing and able to organize the practice of medicine within the services in ways that differ fundamentally from the organization and structure of a military service? Until the military accepts this as the real decision, its young doctors will keep on leaving as soon as they can.

Or the definition of the problem may be incomplete.

This largely explains why the American automobile industry found itself in 1966 suddenly under sharp attack for its unsafe cars—and also why the industry itself was so totally bewildered by the attack. It is simply not true that the industry has paid no attention to safety. On the contrary, it has worked hard at safer highway engineering and at driver training. That accidents are caused by unsafe roads and unsafe drivers is plausible enough. Indeed, all other agencies concerned with automotive safety, from the highway patrol to the schools, picked the same targets for their campaigns. These campaigns have produced results. Highways built for safety have many fewer accidents; and so have safety-trained drivers. But though the ratio of accidents per thousand cars or per thousand miles driven has been going down, the total number of accidents and their severity has kept creeping up.

Long ago it should have been clear that a small percentage of drivers—drunken drivers, for instance, or the 5 per cent who are "accident-prone" and cause three quarters or so of all accidents—are beyond the reach of driver training and can cause accidents on the safest road. Long ago it should have become clear that we have to do something about a small but significant probability of accidents that will occur despite safety laws and safety training. And this means that safe-highway and safe-driving campaigns have to be supplemented by engineering to make accidents themselves less dangerous. Where we engineered to make cars safe when used right, we also have to engineer to make cars safe when used wrong. This, however, the automobile industry failed to see.

This example shows why the incomplete explanation is often more dangerous than the totally wrong explanation. Everyone connected with safe-driving campaigns—the automobile industry, but also state highway commissioners, automobile clubs, and insurance companies—felt that to accept a probability of accidents was to condone, if not to encourage, dangerous driving—just as my grandmother's generation believed that the doctor who treated venereal diseases abetted immorality. It is this common human tendency to confuse plausibility with morality which makes the incomplete hypothesis so dangerous a mistake and so hard to correct.

The effective decision-maker, therefore, always assumes initially that the problem is generic.

He always assumes that the event that clamors for his attention is in reality a symptom. He looks for the true problem. He is not content with doctoring the symptom alone.

And if the event is truly unique, the experienced decision-maker suspects that this heralds a new underlying problem and that what appears as unique will turn out to have been simply the first manifestation of a new generic situation.

This also explains why the effective decision-maker always tries to put his solution on the highest possible conceptual level. He does not solve the immediate financing problem by issuing whatever security would be easiest to sell at the best price for the next few years. If he expects to need the capital market for the foreseeable future, he invents a new kind of investor and designs the appropriate security for a mass-capital market that does not yet exist. If he has to bring into line a flock of undisciplined but capable divisional presidents, he does not get rid of the most obstreperous ones and buy off the rest. He develops a constitutional concept of large-scale organization.

One of the most obvious facts of social and political life is the longevity of the temporary. British licensing hours for taverns, for instance, French rent controls, or Washington "temporary" government buildings, all three hastily developed in World War I to last "a few months of temporary emergency" are still with us fifty years later. The effective decision-maker knows this. He too improvises, of course. But he asks himself every time, "If I had to live with this for a long time, would I be willing to? " And if the answer is "No," he keeps on working to find a more general, a more conceptual, a more comprehensive solution—one which establishes the right principle.

As a result, the effective executive does not make many decisions. But the reason is not that he takes too long in making one—in fact, a decision on principle does not, as a rule, take longer than a decision on symptoms and expediency. The effective executive does not need to make many decisions. Because he solves generic situations through a rule and policy, he can handle most events as cases under the rule; that is, by adaptation. "A country with many laws is a country of incompetent lawyers," says an old legal proverb. It is a country which attempts to solve every problem as a unique phenomenon, rather than as a special case under general rules of law. Similarly, an executive who makes many decisions is both lazy and ineffectual.

The decision-maker also always tests for signs that something atypical, something unusual, is happening; he always asks: "Does the explanation explain the observed events and does it explain all of them? ; he always writes out what the solution is expected to make happen—make automobile accidents disappear, for instance—and then tests regularly to see if this really happens; and finally, he goes back and thinks the problem through again when he sees something atypical, when he finds phenomena his explanation does not really explain, or when the course of events deviates, even in details, from his expectations.

These are in essence the rules Hippocrates laid down for medical diagnosis well over 2, 000 years ago. They are the rules for scientific observation first formulated by Aristotle and then reaffirmed by Galileo three hundred years ago. These, in other words, are old, well-known, time-tested rules, rules one can learn and can systematically apply.

2. The second major element in the decision process is clear specifications as to what the decision has to accomplish. What are the objectives the decision has to reach? What are the minimum goals it has to attain? What are the conditions it has to satisfy? In science these are known as "boundary conditions." A decision, to be effective, needs to satisfy the boundary conditions. It needs to be adequate to its purpose.

The more concisely and clearly boundary conditions are stated, the greater the likelihood that the decision will indeed be an effective one and will accomplish what it set out to do. Conversely, any serious shortfall in defining these boundary conditions is almost certain to make a decision ineffectual, no matter how brilliant it may seem.

"What is the minimum needed to resolve this problem? " is the form in which the boundary conditions are usually probed. "Can our needs be satisfied," Alfred P. Sloan presumably asked himself when he took command of General Motors in 1922, "by removing the autonomy of the division heads? " His answer was clearly in the negative. The boundary conditions of his problem demanded strength and responsibility in the chief operating positions. This was needed as much as unity and control at the center. The boundary conditions demanded a solution to a problem of structure, rather than an accommodation among personalities. And this in turn made his solution last.

It is not always easy to find the appropriate boundary conditions. And intelligent people do not necessarily agree on them.

On the morning after the power blackout one New York newspaper managed to appear: *The New York Times*. It had shifted its printing operations immediately across the Hudson to Newark, New Jersey, where the power plants were functioning and where a local paper, *The Newark Evening News*, had a substantial printing plant. But instead of the million copies the *Times* management had ordered, fewer than half this number actually reached the readers. Just as the *Times* went to press (so at least goes a widely told anecdote) the executive editor and three of his assistants started arguing how to hyphenate *one* word. This took them forty-eight minutes (so it is said)—or half of the available press time. The *Times*, the editor argued, sets a standard for written English in the United States and therefore cannot afford a grammatical mistake.

Assuming the tale to be true—and I do not vouch for it —one wonders what the management thought about the decision. But there is no doubt that, given the fundamental assumptions and objectives of the executive editor, it was the right decision. His boundary conditions quite clearly were not the number of copies sold at any one morning, but the infallibility of the *Times* as a grammarian and as *Magister Americae*.

The effective executive knows that a decision that does not satisfy the boundary conditions is ineffectual and inappropriate. It may be worse indeed than a decision that satisfies the wrong boundary conditions. Both will be wrong, of course. But one can salvage the appropriate decision for the incorrect boundary conditions. It is still an effective decision. One cannot get anything but trouble from the decision that is inadequate to its specifications.

In fact, clear thinking about the boundary conditions is needed so that one knows when a decision has to be abandoned. There are two famous illustrations for this—one of a decision where the boundary conditions had become confused and one of a decision where they were kept so clear as to make possible immediate replacement of the outflanked decision by a new and appropriate policy.

The first example is the famous Schlieffen Plan of the German General Staff at the outbreak of World War I. This plan was meant to enable Germany to fight a war on both the eastern and the western fronts simultaneously without having to splinter her forces between East and West. To accomplish this, the Schlieffen Plan proposed to offer only token opposition to the weaker enemy, that is, to Russia, and to concentrate all forces first on a quick knockout blow against France, after which Russia would be dealt with. This, of course, implied willingness to let the Russian armies move fairly deeply into German territory at the outbreak of the war and until the decisive victory over France. But in August 1914, it became clear that the speed of the Russian armies had been underrated. The Junkers in East Prussia whose estates were overrun by the Russians set up a howl for protection.

Schlieffen himself had kept the boundary conditions clearly in his mind. But his successors were technicians rather than decision-makers and strategists. They jettisoned the basic commitment underlying the Schlieffen Plan, the commitment not to splinter the German forces. They should have dropped the plan. Instead they kept it but made its attainment impossible. They weakened the armies in the West sufficiently to deprive their initial victories of full impact, yet did not strengthen the armies in the East sufficiently to knock out the Russians. They thereby brought about the one thing the Schlieffen Plan had been designed to prevent: a stalemate with its ensuing war of attrition in which superiority of manpower, rather than superiority of strategy, eventually had to win. Instead of a strategy, all they had from there on was confused improvisation, impassioned rhetoric, and hopes for miracles.

Contrast with this the second example: the action of Franklin D. Roosevelt when becoming president in 1933. All through his campaign Roosevelt had worked on a plan for *economic recovery*. Such a plan, in 1933, could only be built on financial conservatism and a balanced budget. Then, immediately before FDR's inauguration, the economy collapsed in the Bank Holiday. Economic policy might still have done the work economically. But it had become clear that the patient would not survive politically.

Roosevelt immediately substituted a political objective for his former economic one. He switched from recovery to reform. The new specifications called for political dynamics. This, almost automatically, meant a complete change of economic policy from one of conservatism to one of radical innovation. The boundary conditions had changed—and Roosevelt was enough of a decision-maker to know almost intuitively that this meant abandoning his original plan altogether if he wanted to have any effectiveness.

**But clear thinking about the boundary conditions is needed also to identify**

the most dangerous of all possible decisions: the one that might—just might—work if nothing whatever goes wrong. These decisions always seem to make sense. But when one thinks through the specifications they have to satisfy, one always finds that they are essentially incompatible with each other. That such a decision might succeed is not impossible—it is merely grossly improbable. The trouble with miracles is not, after all, that they happen rarely; it is that one cannot rely on them.

Yet, defining the specifications and setting the boundary conditions cannot be done on the "facts" in any decision of importance. It always has to be done on interpretation. It is risk-taking judgment.

Everyone can make the wrong decision—in fact, everyone will sometimes make a wrong decision. But no one needs to make a decision which, on its face, falls short of satisfying the boundary conditions.

3. One has to start out with what is right rather than what is acceptable(let alone who is right)precisely because one always has to compromise in the end. But if one does not know what is right to satisfy the specifications and boundary conditions, one cannot distinguish between the right compromise and the wrong compromise—and will end up by making the wrong compromise.

> I was taught this when I started in 1944 on my first big consulting assignment, a study of the management structure and management policies of the General Motors Corporation. Alfred P. Sloan, Jr., who was then chairman and chief executive officer of the company, called me to his office at the start of my study and said: "I shall not tell you what to study, what to write, or what conclusions to come to. This is your task. My only instruction to you is to put down what you think is right as

you see it. Don't you worry about our reaction. Don't you worry about whether we will like this or dislike that. And don't you, above all, concern yourself with the compromises that might be needed to make your recommendations acceptable. There is not one executive in this company who does not know how to make every single conceivable compromise without any help from you. But he can't make the *right* compromise unless you first tell him what 'right' is." The executive thinking through a decision might put this in front of himself in neon lights.

For there are two different kinds of compromise. One kind is expressed in the old proverb: "Half a loaf is better than no bread." The other kind is expressed in the story of the Judgment of Solomon, which was clearly based on the realization that "half a baby is worse than no baby at all." In the first instance, the boundary conditions are still being satisfied. The purpose of bread is to provide food, and half a loaf is still food. Half a baby, however, does not satisfy the boundary conditions. For half a baby is not half of a living and growing child. It is a corpse in two pieces.

It is fruitless and a waste of time to worry about what is acceptable and what one had better not say so as not to evoke resistance. The things one worries about never happen. And objections and difficulties no one thought about suddenly turn out to be almost insurmountable obstacles. One gains nothing in other words by starting out with the question: "What is acceptable?" And in the process of answering it, one gives away the important things, as a rule, and loses any chance to come up with an effective, let alone with the right, answer.

4. Converting the decision into action is the fourth major element in the decision process. While thinking through the boundary conditions is the most

difficult step in decision-making, converting the decision into effective action is usually the most time-consuming one. Yet a decision will not become effective unless the action commitments have been built into the decision from the start.

In fact, no decision has been made unless carrying it out in specific steps has become someone's work assignment and responsibility. Until then, there are only good intentions.

This is the trouble with so many policy statements, especially of business: They contain no action commitment. To carry them out is no one's specific work and responsibility. No wonder that the people in the organization tend to view these statements cynically if not as declarations of what top management is really not going to do.

Converting a decision into action requires answering several distinct questions: Who has to know of this decision? What action has to be taken? Who is to take it? And what does the action have to be so that the people who have to do it *can* do it? The first and the last of these are too often overlooked—with dire results.

A story that has become a legend among operations researchers illustrates the importance of the question "Who has to know?" A major manufacturer of industrial equipment decided several years ago to discontinue one model. For years it had been standard equipment on a line of machine tools, many of which were still in use. It was decided, therefore, to sell the model to present owners of the old equipment for another three years as a replacement, and then to stop making and selling it. Orders for this particular model had been going down for a good many years. But they shot up as former customers reordered against the day when the model would no longer be available. No one had, however, asked, "Who needs to know of this decision?" Therefore nobody informed the clerk in the purchasing department who was in charge of buying the parts from which the model itself was being assembled. His instructions were to buy parts in a given ratio to current sales—and the instructions remained unchanged. When the time came to discontinue further production of the model, the company had in its warehouse enough parts for another eight to ten years of production, parts that had to be written off at a considerable loss.

**The action must also be appropriate to the capacities of the people who have to carry it out.**

A chemical company found itself, in recent years, with fairly large amounts of blocked currency in two West African countries. It decided that to protect this money, it had to invest it locally in businesses which would contribute to the local economy, would not require imports from abroad, and would, if successful, be the kind that could be sold to local investors if and when currency remittances became possible again. To establish these businesses, the company developed a simple chemical process to preserve a tropical fruit which is a staple crop in both countries and which, up until then, had suffered serious spoilage in transit to its Western markets.

The business was a success in both countries. But in one country the local manager set the business up in such a manner that it required highly skilled and, above all, technically trained management of the kind not easily available in West Africa. In the other country the local manager thought through the capacities of the people who would eventually have to run the business and worked hard at making both process and business simple and at staffing from the start with nationals of the country right up to the top.

A few years later it became possible again to transfer currency from these two countries. But though the business flourished, no buyer could be found for it in the first country. No one available locally had the necessary managerial and technical skills. The business had to be liquidated at a loss. In the other country so many local entrepreneurs were eager to buy the business that the company repatriated its original investment with a substantial profit.

The process and the business built on it were essentially the same in both places. But in the first country no one had asked: "What kind of people do we have available to make this decision effective? And what can they do?" As a result, the decision itself became frustrated.

All this becomes doubly important when people have to change behavior, habits, or attitudes if a decision is to become effective action. Here one has to make sure not only that responsibility for the action is clearly assigned and that the people responsible are capable of doing the needful. One has to make sure that their measurements, their standards for accomplishment, and their incentives are changed simultaneously. Otherwise, the people will get caught in a paralyzing internal emotional conflict.

Theodore Vail's decision that the business of the Bell System was service might have remained dead letter but for the yardsticks of service performance which he designed to measure managerial performance. Bell managers were used to being measured by the profitability of their units, or at the least, by cost. The new yardsticks made them accept rapidly the new objectives.

In sharp contrast is the recent failure of a brilliant chairman and chief executive to make effective a new organization structure and new objectives in an old, large, and proud American company. Everyone agreed that the changes were needed. The company, after many years as leader of its industry, showed definite signs of aging; in almost all major fields newer, smaller, and more aggressive competitors were outflanking it. But to gain acceptance for the new ideas, the chairman promoted the most prominent spokesmen of the old school into the most visible and best-paid positions—especially into three new executive vice-presidencies. This meant only one thing to the people in the company: "They don't really mean it."

If the greatest rewards are given for behavior contrary to that which the new course of action requires, then everyone will conclude that this contrary behavior is what the people at the top really want and are going to reward.

Not everyone can do what Vail did and build the execution of his decisions into the decision itself. But everyone can think what action commitments a specific decision requires, what work assignments follow from it, and what people are available to carry it out.

5. Finally, a feedback has to be built into the decision to provide a continuous testing, against actual events, of the expectations that underlie the

decision.

Decisions are made by men. Men are fallible; at their best their works do not last long. Even the best decision has a high probability of being wrong. Even the most effective one eventually becomes obsolete.

If this needs documentation, the Vail and Sloan decisions supply it. Despite their imagination and daring, only one of Vail's decisions, the decision that service was the business of the Bell System, is still valid today and applicable in the form in which he worked it out. The investment character of the AT&T common share had to be drastically changed in the nineteen-fifties in response to the emergence of the institutional investors—pension trusts and mutual funds—as the new channels through which the middle class invests. While Bell Labs has maintained its dominant position, the new scientific and technological developments—especially in space technology and in such devices as the laser—have made it reasonably clear that no communications company, no matter how large, can any longer hope to provide by its own means all its own technological and scientific needs. At the same time, the development of technology has made it probable—for the first time in seventy-five years—that new processes of telecommunications will seriously compete with the telephone, and that in major communications fields, for example, information and data communication, no single communications medium can maintain dominance, let alone the monopoly which Bell has had for oral communications over distance. And while regulation remains a necessity for the existence of a privately owned telecommunications company, the regulation Vail worked so hard to make effective—that is, regulation by the individual states—is becoming increasingly inappropriate to the realities of a nationwide and indeed international system. But the inevitable—and necessary—regulation by the federal government has not been worked out by the Bell System and has instead been fought by it through the kind of delaying action Vail was so careful not to engage in.

As to Sloan's decentralization of General Motors, it still stands—but it is becoming clear that it will have to be thought through again soon. Not only have basic principles of his design been changed and revised so often that they have become fuzzy beyond recognition—the autonomous automotive divisions, for instance, increasingly are not in full control of their manufacturing and assembly operations and therefore not fully responsible for the results. The individual makes of car, from Chevrolet to Cadillac, have also long ceased to represent major price classes the way Sloan originally designed them. Above all, Sloan designed a U. S. company; and though it soon acquired foreign subsidiaries, it remained a U. S. company in its organization and management structure. But General Motors is clearly an international company today. Its great growth and major opportunities are increasingly outside the United States and especially in Europe. It will survive and prosper only if it finds the right principles and the right organization for the multinational company. The job Sloan did in 1922 will have to be done over again soon—it will predictably become pressing as soon as the industry runs into a period of economic difficulties. And if not done over fairly drastically, Sloan's solution is likely to become a millstone around GM's neck and increasingly a bar to its success.

When General Eisenhower was elected president, his predecessor, Harry S. Truman, said: "Poor Ike; when he was a general, he gave an order and it was carried out. Now he is going to sit in that big office and he'll give an order and not a damn thing is going to happen."

The reason why "not a damn thing is going to happen" is, however, not that generals have more authority than presidents. It is that military organizations learned long ago that futility is the lot of most orders and organized the feedback to check on the execution of the order. They learned long ago that to go oneself and look is the only reliable feedback.⊖ Reports—all a president is normally able to mobilize—are not much help. All military services have long ago learned that the officer who has given an order goes out and sees for himself whether it has been carried out. At the least he sends one of his own aides—he never relies on what he is told by the subordinate to whom the order was given. Not that he distrusts the subordinate; he has learned from experience to distrust communications.

This is the reason why a battalion commander is expected to go out and taste the food served his men. He could, of course, read the menus and order this or that item to be brought in to him. But no; he is expected to go into the mess hall and take his sample of the food from the same kettle that serves the enlisted men.

With the coming of the computer this will become even more important,

---

⊖ This was certainly established military practice in very ancient times—Thucydides and Xenophon both take it for granted, as do the earliest Chinese texts on war we have—and so did Caesar.

for the decision-maker will, in all likelihood, be even further removed from the scene of action. Unless he accepts, as a matter of course, that he had better go out and look at the scene of action, he will be increasingly divorced from reality. All a computer can handle are abstractions. And abstractions can be relied on only if they are constantly checked against the concrete. Otherwise, they are certain to mislead us.

To go and look for oneself is also the best, if not the only, way to test whether the assumptions on which a decision had been made are still valid or whether they are becoming obsolete and need to be thought through again. And one always has to expect the assumptions to become obsolete sooner or later. Reality never stands still very long.

Failure to go out and look is the typical reason for persisting in a course of action long after it has ceased to be appropriate or even rational. This is true for business decisions as well as for governmental policies.

One needs organized information for the feedback. One needs reports and figures. But unless one builds one's feedback around direct exposure to reality—unless one disciplines oneself to go out and look—one condemns oneself to a sterile dogmatism and with it to ineffectiveness.

These are the elements of the decision process. But what about the decision itself?

CHAPTER 7

# Effective Decisions

A decision is a judgment. It is a choice between alternatives. It is rarely a choice between right and wrong. It is at best a choice between "almost right" and "probably wrong" —but much more often a choice between two courses of action neither of which is provably more nearly right than the other.

Most books on decision-making tell the reader: "First find the facts." But executives who make effective decisions know that one does not start with facts. One starts with opinions. These are, of course, nothing but untested hypotheses and, as such, worthless unless tested against reality. To determine what is a fact requires first a decision on the criteria of relevance, especially on the appropriate measurement. This is the hinge of the effective decision, and usually its most controversial aspect.

Finally, the effective decision does not, as so many texts on decision-making proclaim, flow from a consensus on the facts. The understanding that underlies the right decision grows out of the clash and conflict of divergent opinions and out of the serious consideration of competing alternatives.

To get the facts first is impossible. There are no facts unless one has a criterion of relevance. Events by themselves are not facts.

> In physics the taste of a substance is not a fact. Nor, until fairly recently, was its color. In cooking, the taste is a fact of supreme importance, and in painting, the color matters. Physics, cooking, and painting consider different things as relevant and therefore consider different things to be facts.

But the effective executive also knows that people do not start out with the search for facts. They start out with an opinion. There is nothing wrong with this. People experienced in an area should be expected to have an opinion. Not to have an opinion after having been exposed to an area for a good long time would argue an unobservant eye and a sluggish mind.

People inevitably start out with an opinion; to ask them to search for the facts first is even undesirable. They will simply do what everyone is far too prone to do anyhow: look for the facts that fit the conclusion they have already reached. And no one has ever failed to find the facts he is looking for. The good statistician knows this and distrusts all figures—he either knows the fellow who found them or he does not know him; in either case he is suspicious.

The only rigorous method, the only one that enables us to test an opinion against reality, is based on the clear recognition that opinions come first—and that this is the way it should be. Then no one can fail to see that we start out with untested hypotheses—in decision-making as in science the only starting point. We know what to do with hypotheses—one does not argue them; one tests them.

One finds out which hypotheses are tenable, and therefore worthy of serious consideration, and which are eliminated by the first test against observable experience.

The effective executive encourages opinions. But he insists that the people who voice them also think through what it is that the "experiment" —that is, the testing of the opinion against reality—would have to show. The effective executive, therefore, asks: "What do we have to know to test the validity of this hypothesis? " "What would the facts have to be to make this opinion tenable? " And he makes it a habit—in himself and in the people with whom he works—to think through and spell out what needs to be looked at, studied, and tested. He insists that people who voice an opinion also take responsibility for defining what factual findings can be expected and should be looked for.

Perhaps the crucial question here is: "What is the criterion of relevance? " This, more often than not, turns on the measurement appropriate to the matter under discussion and to the decision to be reached. Whenever one analyzes the way a truly effective, a truly right, decision has been reached, one finds that a great deal of work and thought went into finding the appropriate measurement.

> This, of course, is what made Theodore Vail's conclusion that service was the business of the Bell System such an effective decision.

The effective decision-maker assumes that the traditional measurement is not the right measurement. Otherwise, there would generally be no need for a decision; a simple adjustment would do. The traditional measurement reflects yesterday's decision. That there is need for a new one normally indicates that the measurement is no longer relevant.

That the procurement and inventory policies of the U. S. armed services were in bad shape had been known ever since the Korean War. There had been countless studies—but things got worse, rather than better. When Robert McNamara was appointed Secretary of Defense by President Kennedy, however, he challenged the traditional measurements of military inventory—measurements in total dollars and in total number of items in procurement and inventory. Instead, Mr. McNamara identified and separated the very few items—maybe 4 per cent of the items by number—which together account for 90 per cent or more of the total procurement dollars. He similarly identified the very few items—perhaps again 4 per cent—which account for 90 per cent of combat readiness. Since some items belong in both categories, the list of crucial items came to 5 or 6 per cent of the total, whether measured by number or by dollars. Each of these, McNamara insisted, had to be managed separately and with attention to minute detail. The rest, the 95 per cent or so of all items which account neither for the bulk of the dollars nor for essential combat readiness, he changed to management by exception, that is, to management by probability and averages. The new measurement immediately made possible highly effective decisions on procurement and inventory-keeping and on logistics.

The best way to find the appropriate measurement is again to go out and look for the "feedback" discussed earlier—only this is "feedback" before the decision.

In most personnel matters, for instance, events are measured in "averages," such as the average number of lost-time accidents per hundred employees, the average percentage of absenteeism in the whole work force, or the average illness rate per hundred. But the executive who goes out and looks for himself will soon find that he needs a different measurement. The averages serve the purposes of the insurance company, but they are meaningless, indeed misleading, for personel management decisions.

The great majority of all accidents occur in one or two places in the plant. The great bulk of absenteeism is in one department. Even illness resulting in absence from work, we now know, is not distributed as an average, but is concentrated in a very small part of the work force, e. g., young unmarried women. The personnel actions to which dependence on the averages will lead—for instance, the typical plantwide safety campaign—will not produce the desired results, may indeed make things worse.

Similarly, failure to go and look was a major factor in the failure of the automobile industry to realize in time the need for safety engineering of the car. The automobile companies measured only by the conventional averages of number of accidents per passenger mile or per car. Had they gone out and looked, they would have seen the need to measure also the severity of bodily injuries resulting from accidents. And this would soon have highlighted the need to supplement their safety campaigns by measures aimed at making the accident less dangerous; that is, by automotive design.

Finding the appropriate measurement is thus not a mathematical exercise. It is a risk-taking judgment.

Whenever one has to judge, one must have alternatives among which one can choose. A judgment in which one can only say "yes" or "no" is no judgment at all. Only if there are alternatives can one hope to get insight into what is truly at stake.

Effective executives therefore insist on alternatives of measurement—so that they can choose the one appropriate one.

> There are a number of measurements for a proposal on a capital investment. One of these focuses on the length of time it will take before the original investment has been earned back. Another one focuses on the rate of profitability expected from the investment. A third one focuses on the present value of the returns expected to result from the investment, and so on. The effective executive will not be content with any one of these conventional yardsticks, no matter how fervently his accounting department assures him that only one of them is "scientific." He knows, if only from experience, that each of these analyses brings out a different aspect of the same capital investment decision. Until he has looked at each possible dimension of the decision, he cannot really know which of these ways of analyzing and measuring is appropriate to the specific capital decision before him. Much as it annoys the accountants, the effective executive will insist on having the same investment decision calculated in all three ways—so as to be able to say at the end: "This measurement is appropriate to this decision."

Unless one has considered alternatives, one has a closed mind.

This, above all, explains why effective decision-makers deliberately disregard the second major command of the textbooks on decision-making and create dissension and disagreement, rather than consensus.

Decisions of the kind the executive has to make are not made well by acclamation. They are made well only if based on the clash of conflicting views, the dialogue between different points of view, the choice between different judgments. The first rule in decision-making is that one does not make a decision unless there is disagreement.

> Alfred P. Sloan is reported to have said at a meeting of one of his top committees: "Gentlemen, I take it we are all in complete agreement on the decision here." Everyone around the table nodded assent. "Then," continued Mr. Sloan, "I propose we postpone further discussion of this matter until our next meeting to give ourselves time to develop disagreement and perhaps gain some understanding of what the decision is all about."

Sloan was anything but an "intuitive" decision-maker. He always emphasized the need to test opinions against facts and the need to make absolutely sure that one did not start out with the conclusion and then look for the facts that would support it. But he knew that the right decision demands adequate disagreement.

Every one of the effective Presidents in American history had his own method of producing the disagreement he needed in order to make an effective decision. Lincoln, Theodore Roosevelt, Franklin D. Roosevelt, Harry Truman—each had his own ways. But each created the disagreement he needed for "some understanding of what the decision is all about." Washington, we know, hated conflicts and quarrels and wanted a united Cabinet. Yet he made quite sure of the necessary differences of opinion on important matters by asking both Hamilton and Jefferson for their opinions.

The President who understood best the need for organized disagreement was probably Franklin D. Roosevelt. Whenever anything of importance came up, he would take aside one of his aides and say to him, "I want you to work on this for me—but keep it a secret." (This made sure, as Roosevelt knew perfectly well, that everybody in Washington heard about it immediately.) Then Roosevelt would take aside a few other men, known to differ from the first and would give them the same assignment, again "in the strictest confidence." As a result, he could be reasonably certain that all important aspects of every matter were being thought through and presented to him. He could be certain that he would not become the prisoner of somebody's preconceived conclusions.

This practice was severely criticized as execrable administration by the one "professional manager" in Roosevelt's Cabinet, his secretary of the Interior, Harold Ickes, whose diaries are full of diatribes against the President's "sloppiness," "indiscretions," and "treachery." But Roosevelt knew that the main task of an American President is not administration. It is the making of policy, the making of the right decisions. And these are made best on the basis of "adversary proceedings" to use the term of the lawyers for their method of getting at the true facts in a dispute, and of making sure that all relevant aspects of a case are presented to the court.

There are three main reasons for the insistence on disagreement.

It is, first, the only safeguard against the decision-maker's becoming the prisoner of the organization. Everybody always wants something from the decision-maker. Everybody is a special pleader, trying—often in perfectly good faith—to obtain the decision he favors. This is true whether the decisionmaker is the President of the United States or the most junior engineer working on a design modification.

The only way to break out of the prison of special pleading and preconceived notions is to make sure of argued, documented, thought-through disagreements.

Second, disagreement alone can provide alternatives to a decision. And a decision without an alternative is a desperate gambler's throw, no matter how carefully thought through it might be. There is always a high possibility that the decision will prove wrong—either because it was wrong to begin with or because a change in circumstances makes it wrong. If one has thought through alternatives during the decision-making process, one has something to fall back on, something that has already been thought through, that has been studied, that is understood. Without such an alternative, one is likely to flounder dismally when reality proves a decision to be inoperative.

In the last chapter, I referred to both the Schlieffen Plan of the German army in 1914 and President Franklin D. Roosevelt's original economic program. Both were disproven by events at the very moment when they should have taken effect.

The German army never recovered. It never formulated another strategic concept. It went from one ill-conceived improvisation to the next. But this was inevitable. For twenty-five years no alternatives to the

Schlieffen Plan had been considered by the General Staff. All its skills had gone into working out the details of this master plan. When the plan fell to pieces, no one had an alternative to fall back on.

Despite all their careful training in strategic planning, the generals could only improvise; that is, dash off first in one direction and then in another, without any real understanding why they dashed off in the first place.

Another 1914 event also shows the danger of having no alternative. After the Russians had ordered mobilization, the Tsar had second thoughts. He called in his Chief of Staff and asked him to halt the mobilization. "Your Majesty," the general answered, "this is impossible; there is no plan for calling off the mobilization once it has started." I do not believe that World War I would necessarily have been averted had the Russians been able to stop their military machine at the last moment. But there would have been one last chance for sanity.

By contrast, President Roosevelt, who, in the months before he took office, had based his whole campaign on the slogan of economic orthodoxy, had a team of able people, the later "Brains Trust," working on an alternative —a radical policy based on the proposals of the old-time "Progressives," and aimed at economic and social reform on a grand scale. When the collapse of the banking system made it clear that economic orthodoxy had become political suicide, Roosevelt had his alternative ready. He therefore had a policy.

Yet without a prepared alternative, Roosevelt was as totally lost as the German General Staff or the Tsar of the Russians. When he assumed the Presidency, Roosevelt was committed to conventional nineteenth-century theory for the international economy. Between his election in November 1932, however, and his taking office the following March, the bottom fell out of the international economy just as much as it had fallen out of the domestic economy. Roosevelt clearly saw this but, without alternatives, he was reduced to impotent improvisation. And even as able and agile a man as President Roosevelt could only grope around in what suddenly had become total fog, could only swing wildly from one extreme to another—as he did when he torpedoed the London Economic Conference—could only become the prisoner of the economic snake-oil salesmen with their patent nostrums such as dollar devaluation or the remonetization of silver—both totally irrelevant to any of the real problems.

An even clearer example was Roosevelt's plan to "pack" the Supreme Court after his landslide victory in 1936. When this plan ran into strong opposition in a Congress which he thought he controlled completely, Roosevelt had no alternative. As a result, he not only lost his plan for court reform. He lost control of domestic politics—despite his towering popularity and his massive majorities.

Above all, disagreement is needed to stimulate the imagination. One does not, to be sure, need imagination to find the right solution to a problem. But then this is of value only in mathematics. In all matters of true uncertainty such as the executive deals with—whether his sphere is political, economic, social, or military—one needs "creative" solutions which create a new situation. And this means that one needs imagination—a new and different way of perceiving and understanding.

Imagination of the first order is, I admit, not in abundant supply. But neither is it as scarce as is commonly believed. Imagination needs to be challenged and stimulated, however, or else it remains latent and unused. Disagreement, especially if forced to be reasoned, thought through, documented, is the most effective stimulus we know.

Few people have Humpty-Dumpty's ability to imagine a great many impossible things before breakfast. And still fewer have the imagination of Humpty-Dumpty's creator, Lewis Carroll, the author of *Alice in Wonderland*. But even very small children have the imagination to enjoy *Alice*. And as Jerome S. Bruner points out, even an eight-year-old sees in a flash that while "4×6 equals 6×4, 'a blind Venetian' isn't the same thing as 'a Venetian blind'."⊖ This is imaginative sight of a high order. Far too many adult decisions are made on the assumption that a "blind Venetian" must indeed be the same as a "Venetian blind."

An old story tells of a South Sea Islander of Victorian times who, after his return from a visit to the West, told his fellow islanders that the Westerners had no water in their houses and buildings. On his native island water flowed through hollowed logs and was clearly visible. In the Western city it was conducted in pipes and, therefore, flowed only when someone turned a tap. But no one had explained the tap to the visitor.

Whenever I hear this story, I think of imagination. Unless we turn the "tap," imagination will not flow. The tap is argued, disciplined disagreement.

The effective decision-maker, therefore, organizes disagreement. This

---

⊖ See his perceptive book, *Toward a Theory of Instruction* (Cambridge, Harvard, 1966), p. 64.

protects him against being taken in by the plausible but false or incomplete. It gives him the alternatives so that he can choose and make a decision, but also so that he is not lost in the fog when his decision proves deficient or wrong in execution. And it forces the imagination—his own and that of his associates. Disagreement converts the plausible into the right and the right into the good decision.

The effective decision-maker does not start out with the assumption that one proposed course of action is right and that all others must be wrong. Nor does he start out with the assumption, "I am right and he is wrong." He starts out with the commitment to find out why people disagree.

Effective executives know, of course, that there are fools around and that there are mischief-makers. But they do not assume that the man who disagrees with what they themselves see as clear and obvious is, therefore, either a fool or a knave. They know that unless proven otherwise, the dissenter has to be assumed to be reasonably intelligent and reasonably fairminded. Therefore, it has to be assumed that he has reached his so obviously wrong conclusion because he sees a different reality and is concerned with a different problem. The effective executive, therefore, always asks: "What does this fellow have to see if his position were, after all, tenable, rational, intelligent? " The effective executive is concerned first with *understanding*. Only then does he even think about who is right and who is wrong. ⊖

In a good law office, the beginner, fresh out of law school, is first assigned to drafting the strongest possible case for the other lawyer's client.

---

⊖ This, of course, is nothing new. It is indeed only a rephrasing of Mary Parker Follet (see her *Dynamic Administration*, ed. by Henry C. Metcalf and L. Urwick [New York, Harper & Row, 1942]), who in turn only extended Plato's arguments in his great dialogue on rhetoric, the *Phaedrus*.

This is not only the intelligent thing to do before one sits down to work out the case for one's own client. (One has to assume, after all, that the opposition's lawyer knows his business too.) It is also the right training for a young lawyer. It trains him not to start out with, "I know why my case is right," but with thinking through what it is that the other side must know, see, or take as probable to believe that it has a case at all. It tells him to see the two cases as alternatives. And only then is he likely to understand what his own case is all about. Only then can he make out a strong case in court that his alternative is to be preferred over that of the other side.

Needless to say, this is not done by a great many people, whether executives or not. Most people start out with the certainty that what they see is the only way to see at all.

The American steel executives have never missed the question: "Why do these union people get so terribly exercised every time we mention the word 'featherbedding'?" The union people in turn have never asked themselves why steel managements make such a fuss over featherbedding when every single instance thereof they have ever produced has proved to be petty, and irrelevant to boot. Instead, both sides have worked mightily to prove each other wrong. If either side had tried to understand what the other one sees and why, both would be a great deal stronger, and labor relations in the steel industry, if not in U. S. industry, would be a good deal better and healthier.

No matter how high his emotions run, no matter how certain he is that the other side is completely wrong and has no case at all, the executive who wants to make the right decision forces himself to see opposition as *his* means to think through the alternatives. He uses conflict of opinion as his tool to make sure all major aspects of an important matter are looked at carefully.

There is one final question the effective decision-maker asks: "Is a decision really necessary?" *One* alternative is always the alternative of doing nothing.

Every decision is like surgery. It is an intervention into a system and therefore carries with it the risk of shock. One does not make unnecessary decisions any more than a good surgeon does unnecessary surgery. Individual decision-makers, like individual surgeons, differ in their styles. Some are more radical or more conservative than others. But by and large, they agree on the rules.

One has to make a decision when a condition is likely to degenerate if nothing is done. This also applies with respect to opportunity. If the opportunity is important and is likely to vanish unless one acts with dispatch, one acts—and one makes a radical change.

> Theodore Vail's contemporaries agreed with him as to the degenerative danger of government ownership: But they wanted to fight it by fighting symptoms—fighting this or that bill in the legislature, opposing this or that candidate and supporting another, and so on. Vail alone understood that this is the ineffectual way to fight a degenerative condition. Even if one wins every battle, one can never win the war. He saw that drastic action was needed to create a new situation. He alone saw that private business had to make public regulation into an effective alternative to nationalization.

At the opposite end there are those conditions in respect to which one can, without being unduly optimistic, expect that they will take care of themselves even if nothing is done. If the answer to the question "What will happen if we do nothing?" is "It will take care of itself," one does not interfere. Nor does one interfere if the condition, while annoying, is of no importance and unlikely to make any difference anyhow.

It is a rare executive who understands this. The controller who in a desperate financial crisis preaches cost reduction is seldom capable of leaving alone minor blemishes, elimination of which will achieve nothing. He may know, for instance, that the significant costs that are out of control are in the sales organization and in physical distribution. And he will work hard and brilliantly at getting them under control. But then he will discredit himself and the whole effort by making a big fuss about the "unnecessary" employment of two or three old employees in an otherwise efficient and well-run plant. And he will dismiss as immoral the argument that eliminating these few semipensioners will not make any difference anyhow. "Other people are making sacrifices," he will argue, "Why should the plant people get away with inefficiency?"

When it is all over, the organization will forget fast that he saved the business. They will remember, though, his vendetta against the two or three poor devils in the plant— and rightly so. "*De minimis non curat praetor*" [The magistrate does not consider trifles] said the Roman law almost two thousand years ago—but many decision-makers still need to learn it.

The great majority of decisions will lie between these extremes. The problem is not going to take care of itself; but it is unlikely to turn into degenerative malignancy either. The opportunity is only for improvement rather than for real change and innovation; but it is still quite considerable. If we do not act, in other words, we will in all probability survive. But if we do act, we may be better off.

In this situation the effective decision-maker compares effort and risk of action to risk of inaction. There is no formula for the right decision here. But the guidelines are so clear that decision in the concrete case is rarely difficult. They are:

- Act if on balance the benefits greatly outweigh cost and risk; and
- Act or do not act; but do not "hedge" or compromise.

The surgeon who only takes out half the tonsils or half the appendix risks as much infection or shock as if he did the whole job. And he has not cured the condition, has indeed made it worse. He either operates or he doesn't. Similarly, the effective decision-maker either acts or he doesn't act. He does not take half-action. This is the one thing that is always wrong, and the one sure way not to satisfy the minimum specifications, the minimum boundary conditions.

The decision is now ready to be made. The specifications have been thought through, the alternatives explored, the risks and gains weighed. Everything is known. Indeed, it is always reasonably clear by now what course of action must be taken. At this point the decision does indeed almost "make itself."

And it is at this point that most decisions are lost. It becomes suddenly quite obvious that the decision is not going to be pleasant, is not going to be popular, is not going to be easy. It becomes clear that a decision requires courage as much as it requires judgment. There is no inherent reason why medicines should taste horrible—but effective ones usually do. Similarly, there is no inherent reason why decisions should be distasteful—but most effective ones are.

One thing the effective executive will not do at this point. He will not give in to the cry, "Let's make another study." This is the coward's way—and all the coward achieves is to die a thousand deaths where the brave man dies but one. When confronted with the demand for "another study" the effective executive asks: "Is there any reason to believe that additional study will produce anything new? And is there reason to believe that the new is likely to be relevant? " And if the answer is "no" —as it usually is—the effective executive does not permit another study. He does not waste the time of good people to cover up his own indecision.

But at the same time he will not rush into a decision unless he is sure he understands it. Like any reasonably experienced adult, he has learned to pay attention to what Socrates called his "daemon" : the inner voice, somewhere in the bowels, that whispers, "Take care." Just because something is difficult, disagreeable, or frightening is no reason for not doing it if it is right. But one holds back—if only for a moment—if one finds oneself uneasy, perturbed, bothered without quite knowing why. "I always stop when things seem out of focus," is the way one of the best decision-makers of my acquaintance puts it.

Nine times out of ten the uneasiness turns out to be over some silly detail. But the tenth time one suddenly realizes that one has overlooked the most important fact in the problem, has made an elementary blunder, or has misjudged altogether. The tenth time one suddenly wakes up at night and realizes—as Sherlock Holmes did in the famous story—that the "most significant thing is that the hound of Baskerville didn't bark."

But the effective decision-maker does not wait long—a few days, at the most a few weeks. If the "daemon" has not spoken by then, he acts with speed and energy whether he likes to or not.

Executives are not paid for doing things they like to do. They are paid for getting the right things done—most of all in their specific task, the making of effective decisions.

## DECISION MAKING AND THE COMPUTER

Does all this still apply today when we have the computer? The computer, we are being told, will replace the decision-maker, at least in middle management. It will make, in a few years, all the operating decisions—and fairly soon thereafter it will take over the strategic decisions too.

Actually the computer will force executives to make, as true decisions, what are today mostly made as on-the-spot adaptations. It will convert a great many people who traditionally have reacted rather than acted into genuine executives and decision-makers.

The computer is a potent tool of the executive. Like hammer or pliers—but unlike wheel or saw—it cannot do anything man cannot do. But it can do one human job—addition and subtraction—infinitely faster than man can do it. And, being a tool, it does not get bored, does not get tired, does not charge overtime. Like all tools that do better something man can do, the computer multiplies man's capacity (the other tools, such as the wheel, the airplane, or the television set that do something man cannot do at all, add a new dimension to man, i. e., extend his nature). But like all tools the computer can only do one or two things. It has narrow limitations. And it is the limitations of the computer that will force us to do as genuine decision what now is largely done as *ad hoc* adaptation.

The strength of the computer lies in its being a logic machine. It does precisely what it is programed to do. This makes it fast and precise. It also makes it a total moron; for logic is essentially stupid. It is doing the simple and obvious. The human being, by contrast, is not logical; he is perceptual. This means that he is slow and sloppy. But he is also bright and has insight. The human being can adapt; that is, he can infer from scanty information or from no information at all what the total picture might be like. He can remember a great many things nobody has programed.

A simple and a common area where the typical traditional manager acts by way of on-the-spot adaptation is the commonplace inventory and shipping decision. The typical district sales manager knows, albeit most inaccurately, that customer A usually runs his plant on a tight schedule and would be in real trouble if a promised delivery did not arrive on time. He knows also that customer B usually has adequate inventories of materials and supplies and can presumably manage to get by for a few days even if a delivery were late. He knows that customer C is already annoyed at his company and is only waiting for a pretext to shift his purchases to another supplier. He knows that he can get additional supplies of one item by asking for them as a special favor from this or that man in the plant back home, and so on. And on the basis of these experiences, the typical district sales manager adapts and adjusts as he goes along.

The computer knows none of these things. At least it does not know them unless it has been specifically told that these are the facts that determine company policy toward consumer A or in respect to product B. All it can do is react the way it has been instructed and programed. It no more makes "decisions" than the slide rule or the cash register. All it can do is compute.

The moment a company tries to put inventory control on the computer, it realizes that it has to develop rules. It has to develop an inventory *policy*. As soon as it tackles this, it finds that the basic decisions in respect to inventory are not inventory decisions at all. They are highly risky business decisions. Inventory emerges as a means of balancing different risks: the risk of disappointing customer expectations in respect to delivery and service; the risk and cost of turbulence and instability in manufacturing schedules; and the risk and cost of locking up money in merchandise which might spoil, become obsolete, or otherwise deteriorate.

> The traditional clichés do not greatly help. "It is our aim to give 90 per cent of our customers 90 per cent fulfillment of delivery promises" sounds precise. It is actually meaningless, as one finds out when one tries to convert it into the step-by-step moron logic of the computer. Does it mean that all our customers are expected to get nine out of ten orders when we promised them? Does it mean that our really good customers should get fulfillment all the time on all their orders—and how do we define a "really good customer" anyhow? Does it mean that we aim to give fulfillment of these promises on all our products? or only on the major ones which together account for the bulk of our production? And what policy, if any, do we have with respect to the many hundreds of products which are not major for us, though they might well be major for the customer who orders one of them?

Each of these questions requires a risk-taking decision and, above all, a decision on principle. Until all these decisions have been made, the computer cannot control inventory. They are decisions of uncertainty—and what is relevant to them could not even be defined clearly enough to be conveyed to the computer.

To the extent, therefore, to which the computer—or any similar tool—is expected to keep operations on an even keel or to carry out predetermined reactions to expected events (whether the appearance of hostile nuclear missiles on the far horizon or the appearance of a crude oil with an unusual sulfur content in the petroleum refinery) the decision has to be anticipated and thought through. It can no longer be improvised. It can no longer be groped for in a series of small adaptations, each specific, each approximate, each, to use the physicist's terminology, a "virtual" rather than a real decision. It has to be a decision in *principle*.

The computer is not the cause of this. The computer, being a tool, is probably not the cause of anything. It only brings out in sharp relief what has been happening all along. For this shift from the small adaptation to the decision in principle has been going on for a long time. It became particularly apparent during World War II and after, in the military. Precisely because military operations became so large and interdependent, requiring, for instance, logistics systems embracing whole theaters of operations and all branches of the armed services, middle-level commanders increasingly had to know the framework of strategic decisions within which they were operating. They increasingly had to make real decisions, rather than adapt their orders to local events.

The second-level generals who emerged as the great men of World War II —a Rommel, a Bradley, a Zhukov—were all "middle managers" who thought through genuine decisions, rather than the dashing cavalry generals, the *"beaux sabreurs"* of earlier wars.

As a result, decision-making can no longer be confined to the very small group at the top. In one way or another almost every knowledge worker in an organization will either have to become a decision-maker himself or will at least have to be able to play an active, an intelligent, and an autonomous part in the decision-making process. What in the past had been a highly specialized function, discharged by a small and usually clearly defined organ—with the rest adapting within a mold of custom and usage—is rapidly becoming a normal if not an everyday task of every single unit in this new social institution, the large-scale knowledge organization. The ability to make effective decisions increasingly determines the ability of every knowledge worker, at least of those in responsible positions, to be effective altogether.

A good example of the shift to decision which the new techniques impose on us is the much discussed PERT (Program Evaluation and Review Technique) which aims at providing a road map for the critical tasks in a highly complex program such as the development and construction of a new space vehicle. PERT aims at giving control of such a program by advance planning of each part of the work, of its sequence, and of the deadlines each part has to meet for the whole program to be ready on time. This sharply curtails *ad hoc* adaptation. In its place there are high-risk decisions. The first few times operating men have to work out a PERT schedule, they are invariably wrong in almost every one of their judgments. They are still trying to do, through *ad hoc* adaptations, what can only be done through systematic risk-taking decision-making.

The computer has the same impact on strategic decisions. It cannot make them, of course. All it can do—and even that is potential rather than actual so far—is to work through what conclusions follow from certain assumptions made regarding an uncertain future, or conversely, what assumptions underlie certain proposed courses of action. Again, all it can do is compute. For this reason it demands clear analysis, especially of the boundary conditions the decision has to satisfy. And that requires risk-taking judgment of a high order.

There are additional implications of the computer for decision-making. If properly used, for instance, it should free senior executives from much of the preoccupation with events inside the organization to which they are now being condemned by the absence or tardiness of reliable information. It should make it much easier for the executive to go and look for himself on the outside; that is, in the area where alone an organization can have results.

The computer might also change one of the typical mistakes in decision-making. Traditionally we have tended to err toward treating generic situations as a series of unique events. Traditionally we have tended to doctor symptoms. The computer, however, can only handle generic situations—this is all logic is ever concerned with. Hence we may well in the future tend to err by handling the exceptional, the unique, as if it were a symptom of the generic.

This tendency underlies the complaints that we are trying to substitute the computer for the proven and tested judgment of the military man. This should not be lightly dismissed as the grumbling of brass-hats. The most cogent attack on the attempt to standardize military decisions was made by an outstanding civilian "management scientist," Sir Solly Zuckerman, the eminent British biologist, who as scientific adviser to the British Ministry of Defense has played a leading part in the development of computer analysis and operations research.

The greatest impact of the computer lies in its limitations, which will force us increasingly to make decisions, and above all, force middle managers to change from operators into executives and decision-makers.

This should have happened anyhow. One of the great strengths of such organizations as, for instance, General Motors among business firms, or the German General Staff among military groups, was precisely that these organizations long ago organized operating events as true decisions.

The sooner operating managers learn to make decisions as genuine judgments on risk and uncertainty, the sooner we will overcome one of the basic weaknesses of large organization—the absence of any training and testing for the decision-making top positions. As long as we can handle the events on the operating level by adaptation rather than by thinking, by "feel" rather than by knowledge and analysis, operating people—in government, in the military, or in business—will be untrained, untried, and untested when, as top executives, they are first confronted with strategic decisions.

The computer will, of course, no more make decision-makers out of clerks than the slide rule makes a mathematician out of a high school student. But the computer will force us to make an early distinction between the clerk and the potential decision-maker. And it will permit the latter—may indeed force him—

to learn purposeful, effective decision-making. For unless someone does this, and does it well, the computer cannot compute.

There is indeed ample reason why the appearance of the computer has sparked interest in decision-making. But the reason is not that the computer will "take over" the decision. The reason is that with the computer's taking over computation, people all the way down the line in the organization will have to learn to be executives and to make effective decisions.

CHAPTER 8

# Conclusion: Effectiveness Must Be Learned

This book rests on two premises.

- The executive's job is to be effective; and
- Effectiveness can be learned.

The executive is paid for being effective. He owes effectiveness to the organization for which he works. What then does the executive have to learn and have to do to deserve being an executive? In trying to answer this question, this book has, on the whole, taken organizational performance and executive performance to be goals in and by themselves.

Effectiveness can be learned is the second premise. The book has therefore tried to present the various dimensions of executive performance in such sequence as to stimulate readers to learn for themselves how to become effective executives. This is not a textbook, of course—if only because effectiveness, while capable of being learned, surely cannot be taught. Effectiveness is, after all, not a "subject," but a self-discipline. But throughout this book, and implicit in its structure and in the way it treats its subject matter, is always the question: "What makes for effectiveness in an organization and in any of the major areas of an executive's day and work? " Only rarely is the question asked: "Why should there be effectiveness? " The goal of effectiveness is taken for granted.

In looking back on the arguments and flow of these chapters and on their findings, another and quite different aspect of executive effectiveness emerges, however. Effectiveness reveals itself as crucial to a man's self-development; to organization development; and to the fulfillment and viability of modern society.

1. The first step toward effectiveness is a procedure: *recording where the time goes*. This is mechanical if not mechanistic. The executive need not even do this himself; it is better done by a secretary or assistant. Yet if this is all the executive ever does, he will reap a substantial improvement. The results should be fast, if not immediate. If done with any continuity, recording one's time will also prod and nudge a man toward the next steps for greater effectiveness.

*The analysis of the executive's time*, the elimination of the unnecessary time-wasters, already requires some action. It requires some elementary decisions. It requires some changes in a man's behavior, his relationships, and his concerns. It raises searching questions regarding the relative importance of different uses of time, of different activities and of their goals. It should affect the level and the quality of a good deal of work done. Yet this can perhaps still be done by going down a checklist every few months, that is, by following a form. It still concerns itself only with efficiency in the utilization of a scarce resource—namely, time.

2. The next step, however, in which the executive is asked to *focus his vision on contribution* advances from the procedural to the conceptual, from

mechanics to analysis, and from efficiencies to concern with results. In this step the executive disciplines himself to think through the reason why he is on the payroll and the contribution he ought to make. There is nothing very complicated about this. The questions the executive asks himself about his contribution are still straight-forward and more or less schematic. But the answers to these questions should lead to high demands on himself, to thinking about his own goals and those of the organization, and to concern with values. They should lead to demands on himself for high standards. Above all, these questions ask the executive to assume responsibility, rather than to act the subordinate, satisfied if he only "pleases the boss." In focusing himself and his vision on contribution the executive, in other words, has to think through purpose and ends rather than means alone.

3. *Making strengths productive* is fundamentally an attitude expressed in behavior. It is fundamentally respect for the person—one's own as well as others. It is a value system in action. But it is again "learning through doing" and self-development through practice. In making strengths productive, the executive integrates individual purpose and organization needs, individual capacity and organization results, individual achievement and organization opportunity.

4. Chapter 5, "First Things First," serves as antiphon to the earlier chapter, "Know Thy Time." These two chapters might be called the twin pillars between which executive effectiveness is suspended and on which it rests. But the procedure here no longer deals with a resource, time, but with the end product, the performance of organization and executive. What is being recorded and analyzed is no longer what happens to us but what we should try to make happen in the environment around us. And what is being developed here is not information, but character: foresight, self-reliance, courage. What is being

developed here, in other words, is leadership—not the leadership of brilliance and genius, to be sure, but the much more modest yet more enduring leadership of dedication, determination, and serious purpose.

5. The *effective decision*, which the final chapters discuss, is concerned with rational action. There is no longer a broad and clearly marked path which the executive only has to walk down to gain effectiveness. But there are still clear surveyor's benchmarks to give orientation and guidance how to get from one to the next. How the executive, for instance, is to move from identifying a pattern of events as constituting a generic problem to the setting of the boundary conditions which the decision has to satisfy, is not spelled out. This has to be done according to the specific situation encountered. But what needs to be done and in what sequence should be clear enough. In following these benchmarks, the executive, it is expected, will develop and train himself in responsible judgment. Effective decision-making requires both procedure and analysis, but its essence is an ethics of action.

There is much more to the self-development of an executive than his training in effectiveness. He has to acquire knowledges and skills. He has to learn a good many new work habits as he proceeds along his career, and he will occasionally have to unlearn some old work habits. But knowledges, skills, and habits, no matter how accomplished, will avail the executive little unless he first develops himself in effectiveness.

There is nothing exalted about being an effective executive. It is simply doing one's job like thousands of others. There are surely higher goals for a man's life than to become an effective executive. But only because the goal is so modest can we hope at all to achieve it; that is, to have the large number of effective executives modern society and its organizations need. If we required saints, poets, or even first-rate scholars to staff our knowledge positions, the large-scale organization would simply be absurd and impossible. The needs of large-scale organization have to be satisfied by common people achieving uncommon performance. This is what the effective executive has to make himself able to do. Though this goal is a modest one, one that everyone should be able to reach if he works at it, the self-development of an effective executive is true development of the person. It goes from mechanics to attitudes, values and character, from procedure to commitment.

Self-development of the effective executive is central to the development of the organization, whether it be a business, a government agency, a research laboratory, a hospital, or a military service. It is the way toward performance of the organization. As executives work toward becoming effective, they raise the performance level of the whole organization. They raise the sights of people— their own as well as others.

As a result, the organization not only becomes capable of doing better. It becomes capable of doing different things and of aspiring to different goals. Developing executive effectiveness challenges directions, goals, and purposes of the organization. It raises the eyes of its people from preoccupation with problems to a vision of opportunity, from concern with weakness to exploitation of strengths. This, in turn, wherever it happens, makes an organization attractive to people of high ability and aspiration, and motivates people to higher performance and higher dedication. Organizations are not more effective because they have better people. They have better people because they motivate to self-development through their standards, through their habits, through their climate. And these, in turn, result from systematic, focused, purposeful self-training of the individuals in becoming effective executives.

Modern society depends for its functioning, if not for its survival, on the effectiveness of large-scale organizations, on their performance and results, on their values, standards, and self-demands.

Organization performance has become decisive well beyond the economic sphere or even the social sphere, for instance, in education, in health care, and in the advancement of knowledge. Increasingly, the large-scale organization that counts is the knowledge-organization, employing knowledge workers and staffed heavily with men and women who have to perform as executives, men and women who have in their own work to assume responsibility for the results of the whole, and who, by the nature of their knowledge and work, make decisions with impact upon the results and performance of the whole.

Effective organizations are not common. They are even rarer than effective executives. There are shining examples here and there. But on the whole, organization performance is still primitive. Enormous resources are brought together in the modern large business, in the modern large government agency, in the modern large hospital, or in the university; yet far too much of the result is mediocrity, far too much is splintering of efforts, far too much is devoted to yesterday or to avoiding decision and action. Organizations as well as executives need to work systematically on effectiveness and need to acquire the habit of effectiveness. They need to learn to feed their opportunities and to starve their problems. They need to work on making strength productive. They need to concentrate and to set priorities instead of trying to do a little bit of everything.

But executive effectiveness is surely one of the basic requirements of effective organization and in itself a most important contribution toward organization development.

Executive effectiveness is our one best hope to make modern society productive economically and viable socially.

The knowledge worker, as has been said again and again in this book, is rapidly becoming the major resource of the developed countries. He is becoming the major investment; for education is the most expensive investment of them all. He is becoming the major cost center. To make the knowledge worker productive is the specific economic need of an industrially developed society. The tremendous shift of the center of gravity in the work force from manual to knowledge work that has taken place since World War II has not, I submit, shown extraordinary results. By and large, neither the increase in productivity nor the increase in profitability—the two yardsticks that measure economic results—has shown marked acceleration. No matter how well the industrially developed countries have done since World War II —and their record has been impressive—the job of making the knowledge worker productive is still ahead. The key to it is surely the effectiveness of the executive. For the executive is himself the decisive knowledge workers. His level, his standards, his demands on himself determine to a large extent the motivation, the direction, the dedication of the other knowledge workers around him.

Even more important is the social need for executive effectiveness. The cohesion and strength of our society depend increasingly on the integration of the psychological and social needs of the knowledge worker with the goals of organization and of industrial society.

The knowledge worker normally is not an economic problem. He tends to be affluent. He has high job security and his very knowledge gives him freedom to move. But his psychological needs and personal values need to be satisfied in and through his work and position in the organization. He is considered—and considers himself—a professional. Yet he is an employee and under orders.

He is beholden to a knowledge area, yet he has to subordinate the authority of knowledge to organizational objectives and goals. In a knowledge area there are no superiors or subordinates, there are only older and younger men. Yet organization requires a hierarchy. These are not entirely new problems, to be sure. Officer corps and civil service have known them for a long time, and have known how to resolve them. But they are real problems. The knowledge worker is not poverty-prone. He is in danger of alienation, to use the fashionable word for boredom, frustration, and silent despair.

Just as the economic conflict between the needs of the manual worker and the role of an expanding economy was *the* social question of the nineteenth century in the developing countries, so the position, function and fulfillment of the knowledge worker is the social question of the twentieth century in these countries now that they are developed.

It is not a question that will go away if we deny its existence. To assert that only the "objective reality" of economic and social performance exists will not make the problem go away. Nor, however, will the new romanticism of the social psychologists (e. g. , Professor Chris Argyris at Yale) who quite rightly point out that organizational goals are not automatically individual fulfillment and therefrom conclude that we had better sweep them aside. We will have to satisfy *both* the objective needs of society for performance by the organization, and the needs of the person for achievement and fulfillment.

Self-development of the executive toward effectiveness is the only available answer. It is the only way in which organization goals and individual needs can come together. The executive who works at making strengths productive—his own as well as those of others—works at making organizational performance compatible with personal achievement. He works at making his knowledge area become organizational opportunity. And by focusing on contribution, he makes his own values become organization results.

The manual worker, so at least the nineteenth century believed, had only economic goals and was content with economic rewards. That, as the "human relations" school demonstrated, was far from the whole truth. It certainly ceased to be true the moment pay went above the subsistence level. The knowledge worker demands economic rewards too. Their absence is a deterrent. But their presence is not enough. He needs opportunity, he needs achievement, he needs fulfillment, he needs values. Only by making himself an effective executive can the knowledge worker obtain these satisfactions. Only executive effectiveness can enable this society to harmonize its two needs: the needs of organization to obtain from the individual the contribution it needs, and the need of the individual to have organization serve as his tool for the accomplishment of his purposes. Effectiveness *must* be learned.

# 推荐阅读

## 2019年新版 彼得·德鲁克全集

| ISBN | 书名 | 价格 |
| --- | --- | --- |
| 978-7-111-63738-7 | 管理的实践（中英文双语版） | 199 |
| 978-7-111-60402-0 | 卓有成效的管理者 | 69 |
| 978-7-111-60229-3 | 创新与企业家精神 | 89 |
| 978-7-111-62404-2 | 管理：使命、责任、实践（实践篇） | 89 |
| 978-7-111-62405-9 | 管理：使命、责任、实践（使命篇） | 129 |
| 978-7-111-62433-2 | 管理：使命、责任、实践（责任篇） | 89 |
| 978-7-111-60971-1 | 旁观者：管理大师德鲁克回忆录 | 99 |
| 978-7-111-59522-9 | 最后的完美世界 | 69 |
| 978-7-111-59720-9 | 21世纪的管理挑战 | 69 |
| 978-7-111-59777-3 | 德鲁克论管理 | 69 |
| 978-7-111-59780-3 | 已经发生的未来 | 69 |
| 978-7-111-59837-4 | 行善的诱惑 | 59 |
| 978-7-111-59991-3 | 公司的概念 | 79 |
| 978-7-111-60009-1 | 巨变时代的管理 | 79 |
| 978-7-111-60014-5 | 人与绩效 | 89 |
| 978-7-111-60093-0 | 管理未来 | 89 |
| 978-7-111-60097-8 | 非营利组织的管理 | 69 |
| 978-7-111-60101-2 | 新社会 | 99 |
| 978-7-111-60307-8 | 管理的实践 | 99 |
| 978-7-111-60308-5 | 管理前沿 | 89 |
| 978-7-111-60367-2 | 德鲁克管理思想精要 | 89 |
| 978-7-111-60435-8 | 养老金革命 | 69 |
| 978-7-111-60441-9 | 德鲁克看中国与日本：德鲁克对话"日本商业圣手"中内功 | 69 |
| 978-7-111-60511-9 | 下一个社会的管理 | 69 |
| 978-7-111-60611-6 | 工业人的未来 | 59 |
| 978-7-111-60799-1 | 动荡时代的管理 | 69 |
| 978-7-111-61500-2 | 管理新现实 | 69 |

# "日本经营之圣"稻盛和夫经营哲学系列

季羡林、张瑞敏、马云、孙正义、俞敏洪、陈春花、杨国安 联袂推荐

| 书号 | 书名 | 作者 | 定价 |
| --- | --- | --- | --- |
| 9-787-111-49824-7 | 干法 | 【日】稻盛和夫 | 39.00 |
| 9-787-111-59009-5 | 干法（口袋版） | 【日】稻盛和夫 | 35.00 |
| 9-787-111-59953-1 | 干法（图解版） | 【日】稻盛和夫 | 49.00 |
| 9-787-111-47025-0 | 领导者的资质 | 【日】稻盛和夫 | 49.00 |
| 9-787-111-50219-7 | 阿米巴经营[实战篇] | 【日】森田直行 | 39.00 |
| 9-787-111-48914-6 | 调动员工积极性的七个关键 | 【日】稻盛和夫 | 45.00 |
| 9-787-111-54638-2 | 敬天爱人：从零开始的挑战 | 【日】稻盛和夫 | 39.00 |
| 9-787-111-54296-4 | 匠人匠心：愚直的坚持 | 【日】稻盛和夫 山中伸弥 | 39.00 |
| 9-787-111-51021-5 | 拯救人类的哲学 | 【日】稻盛和夫 梅原猛 | 39.00 |
| 9-787-111-57213-8 | 稻盛和夫谈经营：人才培养与企业传承 | 【日】稻盛和夫 | 45.00 |
| 9-787-111-57212-1 | 稻盛和夫谈经营：创造高收益与商业拓展 | 【日】稻盛和夫 | 45.00 |
| 9-787-111-59093-4 | 稻盛和夫经营学 | 【日】稻盛和夫 | 59.00 |
| 9-787-111-59636-3 | 稻盛和夫哲学精要 | 【日】稻盛和夫 | 39.00 |
| 9-787-111-57016-5 | 利他的经营哲学 | 【日】稻盛和夫 | 49.00 |
| 9-787-111-57081-3 | 企业成长战略 | 【日】稻盛和夫 | 49.00 |
| 9-787-111-57079-0 | 赌在技术开发上 | 【日】稻盛和夫 | 59.00 |
| 9-787-111-59184-9 | 企业家精神 | 【日】稻盛和夫 | 59.00 |
| 9-787-111-59238-9 | 企业经营的真谛 | 【日】稻盛和夫 | 59.00 |
| 9-787-111-59325-6 | 卓越企业的经营手法 | 【日】稻盛和夫 | 59.00 |
| 9-787-111-59303-4 | 稻盛哲学为什么激励人 | 【日】岩崎一郎 | 49.00 |